British Parliamentary Parties
1742–1832

To
Richard and Anne

British Parliamentary Parties 1742–1832

From the Fall of Walpole to the First Reform Act

B. W. HILL
University of East Anglia

London
GEORGE ALLEN & UNWIN
Boston   Sydney

George Allen & Unwin (Publishers) Ltd,
40 Museum Street, London WC1A 1LU, UK

George Allen & Unwin (Publishers) Ltd,
Park Lane, Hemel Hempstead, Herts HP2 4TE, UK

Allen & Unwin, Inc.,
Fifty Cross Street, Winchester, Mass. 01890, USA

George Allen & Unwin Australia Pty Ltd,
8 Napier Street, North Sydney, NSW 2060, Australia

First published in 1985

British Library Cataloguing in Publication Data

Hill, B. W.
    British parliamentary parties, 1742–1832:
    from the fall of Walpole to the First Reform Act.
1. Political parties – Great Britain – History – 18th century
2. Political parties – Great Britain – History – 19th century
I. Title
324.241′009   JN1119
ISBN 0–04–942187–5
ISBN 0–04–942188–3 Pbk

Library of Congress Cataloging in Publication Data

Hill, Brian W.
    British parliamentary parties, 1742–1832.
Bibliography: p.
Includes index.
1. Political parties – Great Britain – History.
2. Great Britain – Politics and government – 18th century.
3. Great Britain – Politics and government – 19th century.
I. Title.
JN1119.H535 1985   324.241′02   84–24271
ISBN 0–04–942187–5 (alk. paper)
ISBN 0–04–942188–3 (pbk.: alk. paper)

Set in 10 on 11 point Times by Phoenix Photosetting, Chatham
and printed in Great Britain by
Billing and Sons Ltd, London and Worcester

Contents

Cover Illustration: Sir Charles Barry's New Palace of Westminster,
built after the fire of 1834.

Preface

This volume sees the completion of a project, begun fifteen years ago, of tracing party development from the 'Glorious' Revolution to the first Reform Act. A decade and a half would be a long time to hold unaltered opinions on a wide-ranging subject and I must confess to some changes, one in particular. When writing the previous book, covering the years from 1689 to 1742, I still accepted the view that the Tory and Whig parties virtually lapsed in the mid-eighteenth century and reappeared only towards the end of the century. I now believe that, despite the presence of Whig factions, a basically two-sided alignment existed throughout. Evidence is cited to show, contrary to some received opinion, that the main elements of the Whig party went into opposition from the end of 1762 and that at the same time the Tory party largely went into regular support of successive ministries acceptable to George III. For powerful if transient motives the description Tory was not acceptable to these ministries, and in Chapters 6 to 11 its use has accordingly been avoided as far as possible out of respect for their preference. But to deny the very existence of a stable party of government called Tory by its Whig opponents, containing a great majority of the Old Tories and having a clear place in the longer history of the Tory party would be not simply pedantic but seriously misleading.

As in the first volume, quotations have been modernized as to spelling, capitalization and punctuation whenever this has been possible without loss of the original meaning. Dates before Britain's adoption of the New Style calendar in 1752 are given in the Old Style, but years are assumed to begin on 1 January and not, as in pre-1752 usage, on 25 March (Lady Day).

It is a pleasure to record my sense of gratitude to the owners of all manuscripts used in this work. I am especially indebted to those owners who entertained me, sometimes at considerable inconvenience to themselves, in their homes. But for such kindnesses the profession of historian would be much harder. I have drawn attention in various parts of the text to historians on whose works I have drawn. If, in the process, I have done less than justice to any who have anticipated some of my judgements I apologize: acknowledgement on every agreed point, like amplification of every disputed one, is a luxury not to be indulged in a volume covering ninety years of British political experience. I should not, however, let pass the opportunity of mentioning my admiration for, and indebtedness to, that magnificent instrument for succeeding generations the *History of Parliament*. The many contributors to this work have done an invaluable service to the study of history. I also wish to thank the Leverhulme trustees, who enabled me to take leave for research, and to acknowledge my obligation to conversations over the years with colleagues and with students of my Special Subject on Burke. Especial thanks are due to Madge Robinson who has shouldered the burden of the fair-copy typing. My dependence on my wife and family is acknowledged elsewhere.

University of East Anglia, Norwich
March 1984

Abbreviations

Add. MS(S)	Additional Manuscripts in the British Library
AHR	*American Historical Review*
BIHR	*Bulletin of the Institute of Historical Research*
BL	British Library
CHJ	*Cambridge Historical Journal* (see also *HJ*)
CJ	*Journals of the House of Commons*
Econ. HR	*Economic History Review*
EHR	*English Historical Review*
HJ	*Historical Journal* (continuation of the *CHJ*)
HMC	Historical Manuscripts Commission
HLB	*Huntington Library Bulletin* (see also *HLQ*)
HLQ	*Huntington Library Quarterly* (continues the *HLB*)
JBS	*Journal of British Studies*
JMH	*Journal of Modern History*
LJ	*Journals of the House of Lords*
NS	New Style
PRO	Public Record Office
TRHS	*Transactions of the Royal Historical Society*
WMQ	*William and Mary Quarterly*

Annotation

Two methods of annotation are used in this volume. Notes likely to be immediately useful to readers are placed at the end of each chapter and denoted in the text by superior *letters*. Notes for scholars wishing to refer to source materials are gathered in the Notes section at the end of the book and are signalled in the text by superior *numbers*.

So I have seen the Tory race
Long in the pouts for want of place.

(*The Simile*, 1759)

Naught's permanent among the human race
Except the Whigs *not* getting into place.

(Byron, *Don Juan*, 1824)

PART ONE

Introductory

CHAPTER ONE

History and Historians

Few historians have enjoyed so much influence or subsequently attracted so much criticism as Sir Lewis Namier, whose views long dominated our understanding of eighteenth-century parties. His *The Structure of Politics at the Accession of George III* appeared in 1929 and for a quarter of a century received increasing acclaim, but both his findings and his methodology came progressively under review from 1957 with the publication of Sir Herbert Butterfield's *George III and the Historians*. The work of demolition was perhaps completed twenty years later when Professor Geoffrey Elton, one of the most eminent historians of British political institutions, wrote that he had thought of the *Structure* as one of two possible nominations for a 'most overrated book' by reason of 'deficiencies in historical method aggravating the dominance of pre-conceived ideas'.[a]

First, however, tribute must be paid to what Namier did contribute of permanent value to eighteenth-century studies. It will never again be permissible to think of a two-party 'system' on the Victorian pattern at any time before the first Reform Act. The great nineteenth-century historians who set the tone of the 'Whig interpretation', which both Butterfield and Namier denounced, erred in thinking that the constitutional verities of their day had been an unchanging feature of political history since the Revolution of 1688.[1] It is doubtful, indeed, whether a two-party system has ever existed in a pure form for very long periods. At other times third and even fourth parties have been visible, transitory in themselves but forming a regularly recurring feature of politics. Moreover, the fairly rapid alternation in office of two parties with which British political life has been familiar since 1832 finds little parallel in the earlier period except between 1689 and 1714. With the main Whig party in power from 1714 to 1762 and in opposition, except for four very short spells, from then until 1830, there was hardly a system of alternation in the modern sense.

Unfortunately, Namier's view did not stop short at pointing out that the eighteenth-century party system was in an embryo state but went on to deny the existence of parties at all 'in the modern sense'.[2] It is on this contention that the bulk of the criticism has centred. The reluctance displayed by Namierite historiography to admit the importance of the eighteenth-century parties came about in reaction to the earlier writers; overstatement provoked over-statement, and the structure of post-Revolution and Hanoverian politics went from being assumed to be a Victorian-type constitutionalism to being regarded as a continuance of the seventeenth-century court/country pattern.

The success of Namier's assault was aided, as Butterfield pointed out, by earlier twentieth-century scholarship which had questioned many aspects of the Victorian viewpoint. Much of the Namierite exposition of politics in the 1760s in terms of the breakdown of Tory and Whig parties was anticipated by the work of C. W. Alvord, a pioneer whose work prepared the ground for Namier's much more explicitly revisionist approach. The work of Alvord and other earlier writers was part of a much wider reaction against Victorian historiography, comprehending almost every field of medieval and modern British history, which began with the increasing profes-sionalization of history writing and teaching at the end of the nineteenth century. Thanks to the work of Professor Blaas, we can now see the context of Namier's work.[3] To understand why the 'Whig' ship-of-the-line gave way to the Namieran privateer it is necessary to remember the previous weakening of timbers which rendered the older vessel vulnerable. Like the political Liberalism with which it was so closely associated, Whig historiography was declining in the post-1918 era from long-term causes. Nevertheless, Sir Lewis Namier added to the received picture his own characteris-tic contributions to a new interpretation of the eighteenth century. Freudian psychoanalysis (another product of Europe-wide reaction against the late-nineteenth-century world) was his right arm in his analyses of human motives – analyses which did not bring to light much good in the character of those politicians he examined. A brilliant writing style put his ideas over in an English rarely equalled; his books were, and are, a pleasure to read.

The question has to be asked, however, how far was the 'Whig interpretation', like Victorianism itself, treated with less than justice between the first and sixth decades of the present century. Much of what it had to say about King George III's reign has received subsequent confirmation.[4] Attempts by Professor Walcott to 'Namierize' politics between 1689 and 1714 have been swept away by a deluge of reassertions of the importance of the rival Tory and Whig parties in that period.[5] Other works have reasserted the importance of the Tory opposition from 1714 to 1760, and of the

Whig opposition after 1762, while Professor Cannon's *The Fox–North Coalition* has pointed out that his study of the years 1782–4 'could not have been written except in party terms'.[6] The steady return of most historians to a modified Whig interpretation, that of its last decades rather than its heyday, has been accompanied by a gradual erosion of Namierism's credibility on points of scholarship and detail. Historians have pointed out the bias involved in a pessimistic view of human motivation, in excessive attention to patronage at the expense of issues,[b] in failure to take into account foreign affairs, and in the lack of a longer-term perspective. Butterfield showed that many of Namier's presuppositions concerning George III were in fact a revival of contemporary arguments in that monarch's favour. Sir Lewis's methodology has been criticized above all for its preoccupation with the minutiae of a structural model of political life unsatisfactory because of what one historian has called 'its basic irrelevance to efforts to relate and explain the course (in contrast to the structure) of politics'.[7]

Some of the weaknesses in Namier's basic contention on the unimportance of parties were inherent in his own writing. He conceded Whig and Tory *names and creeds* 'which covered enduring types moulded by deeply ingrained differences in temperament and outlook' and, even more importantly, admitted that 'in a good many constituencies the names of Whig and Tory still corresponded to real divisions'.[8] How names could survive in Parliament, and 'real divisions' continue in those constituencies, without meaning or significance was never fully explained. Despite Namier's remark that 'the political life of the period could be fully described without ever using a party denomination' Professor Brewer points out that 'of course Namier never actually tried to do this. All his writings employ party labels, however modified, and doubtless the remark was something of a *jeu d'esprit* directed against a prevailing whig historiography.'[9] Unfortunately, the *jeu d'esprit* was taken literally and some of those influenced by Namier did indeed come close to writing books covering the whole eighteenth century while managing to ignore the role of Whigs and Tories. Others, however, drew back or even retracted. Romney Sedgwick, whom J. Steven Watson was not alone in regarding as 'that good Namierite', found in the preface to his last work the *History of Parliament, The House of Commons 1715–1754* 'a real difference between the two parties' and discussed both Tory and Whig parties in great detail. John Brooke in his 'Introductory Survey' to the 1754–90 section of the *History* set a terminal date for 'the era of personal parties' preferred by Namierite writers about 1770, leaving room thereafter for the 'Rise of Party' which Namier himself had originally intended to write.[10]

The closer one gets to the heart of Namier's remarkable achievement in revising the views of his predecessors, the more it becomes apparent that it arose less from the method of 'structural analysis', which in his hands became a self-imposed limitation on his breadth of vision, than from the readiness of his generation to receive his message and the scintillating form which he gave to that message. But literary mastery itself has dangers for the historian. One of Sir Lewis's most famous statements was the elegant antithesis: 'In 1761 not one parliamentary election was determined by party, and in 1951 not one constituency returned a non-party member.'[11] But he had himself listed, over twenty years before this was written, no fewer than 113 Tories returned in the 1761 election.[12] To reconcile these statements we must believe that all those Tories elected were returned without reference to their party convictions, a manifestly absurd proposition. The alternative is to relegate this remark to the realm of literary devices. If Macaulay had made it, and he too was fond of 'antithetical judgments', it would be given little credence today, and Namier must be treated with the same scepticism as is meted out to the pioneer of 'Whig' history. Nevertheless, Namier's claims in regard to parties are still being echoed by some historians. Professor I. R. Christie, in a textbook published in 1982, sees little sign of two parties between 1760 and 1815 and remarks that 'Oppositions have been discussed as "Whigs"' in the modern monographs on the Whig party by O'Gorman, L. G. Mitchell, D. E. Ginter and Michael Roberts, works which between them cover all but fifteen years of that period.[c]

Namier's work was a profound but narrow and highly biased body of research. In attempting to exorcise Tory and Whig parties he took little account, in his later work at least, of the great efflorescence of Tories and Whigs in the generation before 1714, and thus he grossly underestimated the lasting influences of the party tradition then set up. Likewise he gave little explanation other than the existence of Whig and Tory 'mentalities', for the appearance of sophisticated parties in the nineteenth century, though these could hardly have emerged without earlier development.

Influenced perhaps by the publications of W. R. Laprade[13] which appeared to show a high degree of patronage control in elections and political affairs generally, Namier set the scene in the first paragraph of his preface to *The Structure of Politics* for his subsequent contentions: 'A re-statement of the arguments or an analysis of what is called "public opinion" would not get us much further; for political problems do not, as a rule, deeply affect the lives and consciousness of ordinary men, and little real thought is given them by these men . . .'. From this basic misconception of the role and importance of public opinion came much of Namier's interpretation of what was going on in political life in the eighteenth century. Professor Browning, whose biography of the Duke of Newcastle deals with Namier's own chronological heartland, has put the opposite point of view, believing that this minister's

> freedom of action was in fact circumscribed by three concentric rings of authority. The innermost ring was the Parliament, especially the House of Commons. To flout its will systematically was to invite a breakdown in orderly government. The second ring was the electorate. Voters' displeasure with a tyrannical ministry or a meek Parliament could find expression at intervals frequent enough to encourage ministerial caution. The outermost ring, generally the most lethargic but also, if aroused, the most invincible, was public opinion.[14]

The influence of Browning's first 'ring', Parliament itself, is the most obvious. No minister could stand without parliamentary support, as Walpole discovered in 1742, Carteret in 1744 and again in 1746, Newcastle in 1756, North in 1782, Addington in 1804 and Wellington in 1830. Ministers who drew back from the brink of defeat by giving way in the Commons included Walpole, over the Excise Bill crisis in 1733, and Pelham over the Jew Act in 1753. Not only Newcastle but any minister who wished to retain his place had to make constant calculations as to his strength in the Commons. In the Lords the situation was different, for in that smaller body patronage and the personal influence of the monarch usually made for safe government majorities. 'We have nothing to do', remarked the veteran fixer George Bubb Dodington in 1741, 'but to confine our considerations to the House of Commons.'[d] A minister who lost control of the Commons could not remain in office.

It has often been argued, however, that the Commons, too, was controllable, in practice, by patronage. As much of the narrative section of the present book is devoted to dealing with this question, directly or indirectly, it may perhaps be enough to say for the moment that the Lower House was never in the hands of a 'court and Treasury' party alone and that this element itself sometimes exhibited an independence which was, to prudent ministers, an alarm bell. Whether the placemen could be relied upon to vote at full strength, and whether the ministry could then obtain the party backing necessary for a government majority, depended upon the state of politics. Walpole and the Pelhams relied for their political longevity on the support of the large independent sector of the Whig party which supported them for party reasons, rather than patronage considerations. Under George III similar conditions prevailed; the court and Treasury element needed to be heavily supplemented by Tories and independent government Whigs. Towards the end of that monarch's active reign, moreover, the placemen declined in numbers, and this threw ministers even more heavily upon the support of the independent element of their party supporters. By the reigns of George IV and William IV party support was all-important, and patronage played only a peripheral role in Commons management.

Turning to Browning's second 'ring' of ministerial circumscription, the electorate, it is of course necessary to remember that this consisted of only a fraction of the adult population, that a considerable degree of governmental or private influence was used to direct voting in the nomination boroughs, and that after 1716 the operation of the Septennial Act made for infrequent elections. That these factors greatly constricted the free play of the eighteenth-century electorate compared with that of the nineteenth and twentieth centuries is beyond question. But Browning's assertion is nevertheless true and important. Even within the confines laid down by eighteenth-century conditions the electors exercised a continuous watching brief on Parliament, between elections as much as at election times. The eighty members of Parliament who represented English county seats, together with those who came from boroughs with large and unmanageable electorates and even those who represented seats where 'influence' played a major part, were all expected by their constituents to reflect a public opinion which, nine times out of ten, was perfectly clear and unequivocal through press, private correspondence and word of mouth. The septennial pre-election increase of nervousness among MPs even in 'closed' boroughs, referred to from time to time in this book and its predecessor, tells its own story. Unless a borough were completely in the grip of a single 'interest', a relatively rare event, the seat of an established member might well be snatched away by a rival. This happened especially at such times of national electoral emotion as 1710, 1715, 1734, 1741, 1754, 1784, 1802, 1820 and 1830, but similar events occurred on a lesser scale in other elections and by-elections. There were no 'pocket' counties in England, and the proportion of boroughs with consistent patron influence was only 34 per cent in general elections from 1734 to 1790. Moreover, in the prevailing system of dual representation this figure did not represent total control of both seats in all the boroughs concerned, for of the sixty-eight boroughs under consistent influence twenty-eight allowed the patron to fill only one seat.[e] In the many boroughs where there was no patron control or where rival patrons alternated in success there was scope for a change of members and political affiliation at election time. Between elections constituency pressure on members was naturally less immediate, but only a very bold or safely seated member could ignore his constituents entirely. Even a septennium comes to an end.

Political issues, then as now, played a crucial part in determining the individual elector's preference. The high degree of free voting permitted even in closed boroughs leaves no doubt that national affairs could, and often did, override mechanical considerations of patronage control. Much depended on the degree of intensity present in national conflicts, which at their sharpest could sweep all lesser considerations into the tail of the party comet. This was certainly the case during the great days of issues over the royal succession and the safety of the Church of England in the early eighteenth century. At that time, and again after the outbreak of war with the American colonies, the parties simply drew the machinery of patronage into a greater struggle. Though this process was less obvious between about 1720 and 1776 it was always liable to flare up. For this reason statistical considerations, such as how many boroughs had electorates of under 100, under 500, or under 1,000, are less important than the presence or absence of overriding national issues which could make a critical difference as to whether a borough of, say, 250 could be controlled by a patron or not. A similar note of caution has to be made in regard to statistics concerning the proportion of elections which actually went to a poll. In general the proportion of polled elections varied throughout the eighteenth century in line with the intensity of two-party politics, being at its highest in the first third, dropping to its lowest in 1761 and picking up again, though not to its original level, in the last third of the century.[15] But polling was relatively low at all periods by modern standards. The impossibility of determining the amount of behind-the-scenes activity which took place before polling in two-member constituencies, often resulting in decisive victories and defeats without the expense of polling, renders questionable detailed conclusions drawn from polling figures. This has been adequately demonstrated by Mrs George for the 1784 election.[16] Party compromises existed, concealed by apparently uncontested elections. Because of the possibilities for such compromises, with Whigs and Tories returning one member each or allocating one constituency to one party and another to the second, polling figures seriously underestimate party activity at all times.*f*

That the influence of electors on their representatives in Parliament was not confined to election times may be seen from the

instructions to members, which were more common than is sometimes supposed. Walpole's fall in 1742 was accompanied by widespread calls for a cleaning of the Augean stables of government and
Parliament. 'The newspapers for these three months', wrote the
fallen minister's youngest son early in April, 'have swarmed with
instructions for these purposes from the constituents of all parts of
Great Britain to their representatives'.[17] In addition to calling for
the removal of the minister himself these instructions demanded
bills for securing the rights of electors, the independence of the
elected, the restoration of triennial Parliaments, the reduction of
the Excise, and the ejection of placemen.[18] A similar outburst
preceded the fall of Newcastle in 1756.[19] Nor did the pressure come
only from the electors. County meetings were attended, and
petitions signed, by a wider body than those who were entitled to
vote, and at times public opinion was of the greatest importance in
parliamentary politics.

Professor Browning's third 'ring' of circumscription of ministerial
power merges imperceptibly with his second. Appeals by parliamentarians to public opinion were not confined to the electorate or
to high politics. Sometimes the appellants misjudged their audience
and failed to get a wide hearing, as when Henry Fox, the strongest
opponent of Hardwicke's Marriage Act, boasted in debate 'that he
knew he should not be heard by above one-third of the House, but
would speak so loud that he would be heard out of the House'.[20]
More often the appeal was heard and had the desired effect. In 1756
the elder Pitt knew that the time had come for him to make his
successful call to the nation. Mounting pressure of the 'popular
dimension' in that and the preceding year can no longer be doubted
as a reason for Pitt's elevation to office after years of exclusion
owing to the hostility of the king.[21] Dr Peters points out in her study
of *Pitt and Popularity* that

> for the generation whose view of politics was dominated by the
> great work of Sir Lewis Namier, such a basis for political strength
> fitted uneasily into their assumptions . . . When they looked at
> parts of his career, they explained his rise to high office in the
> 1750s almost entirely in terms of his securing the support of
> Leicester House and, while sometimes admitting his oratorical
> and popular appeal, regarded it only as window-dressing for the
> realities of power.[22]

Much of Pitt's popular appeal came from a careful cultivation of his
'image' through influence exercised upon newspapers and periodicals on his behalf, but this confirms rather than detracts from the

importance of public opinion and serves also to illustrate the power of the press.

By the middle of the eighteenth century the Fourth Estate was about to break out of the straitjacket in which it had been since Walpole's later years in office. After assuming an outstanding importance from the lapse of censorship in 1695 the political press had reached an early peak in Anne's reign when Defoe, Swift, Addison, Steele and many other literary figures entered the field. The foundation of *The Craftsman* in 1726 to lead the campaign against Walpole initiated a new period of activity during the Grub Street era. This activity was circumscribed by a Commons resolution of 1738, promising condign punishment for newswriters who reported parliamentary proceedings, and by the increasing ministerial practice of proceeding against printers and publishers on the ground of seditious libel. But these limitations could only partly inhibit the newspaper press, which continued to report debates after the close of parliamentary sessions or under thin disguises. The episodes of the Jew Act in 1753 and the rise of Pitt demonstrated the power of both the regular newspapers and the seemingly endless flow of periodicals and pamphlets. By 1760 London's four daily papers, five or six tri-weeklies and four weeklies were buttressed by dozens of local newspapers in other cities and towns. The case of general warrants from 1763 to 1765, involving John Wilkes and the *North Briton*, put paid to this legal device directed at newspaper publications. But the quantum leap in the influence of the political press came with Wilkes's involvement in the Middlesex election case in 1768 which put an end to the Commons' attempts to prevent the reporting of debates. There was a sudden, remarkable increase in political coverage and in the number, frequency of publication and circulation of the newspapers in 1768–9. In the flush of enthusiasm for publishing debates on the Middlesex election, and on every other parliamentary matter, the newspapers could not do enough to satisfy the public's insatiable thirst for political information; during parliamentary session some newspapers devoted practically the whole of their four sides of print to parliamentary reporting, and in so doing provided the basis for the later collected reports of parliamentary debates issued by Debrett, Almon, Cobbett and eventually Hansard. Much of the editorial comment was virulent after years of restraint. The *North Briton* for 27 May 1768 opened with the words 'every King of England ought to keep in mind the memorable year 1648', and when 'Junius' seared monarch and political leaders with his newspaper-long letters in the *Public Advertiser* the demand to read him was such that many other newspapers would reprint the letter in full in the next day or two.[g] Apart from one abortive attempt to punish journalists and their supporters, in the case of Crosby and Oliver in 1771, Parliament submitted to political reporting.

After 1768 no political episode escaped detailed description and commentary for the benefit of the general public, and from the time of the American War this situation was directly reflected in political representation. In the general election of 1780 the 'moral defeat' for the ministry described by John Brooke, with substantial opposition gains in 'open' constituencies, was the first such government setback for nearly four decades. In 1784 the election which resulted in the younger Pitt's victory was conducted amid the blaze of publicity given to recent political events. The lesson which the Whig opposition drew was that they needed to improve their popular appeal in order to better their performance in elections. While their newly acquired party organizer William Adam set up party electoral funds, Charles James Fox and Richard Brinsley Sheridan turned the *Morning Chronicle* and *Morning Post* virtually into party organs. In the 1790s the popular press gave a stimulus to the extra-parliamentary Radicalism which followed the French Revolution and, in turn, inspired a widespread reaction which Dr O'Gorman has described as 'a jingoistic, popular brand of Anglican-Toryism to which many millions of people readily subscribed'.[23] By the early nineteenth century the press was ready to serve the public on the issues of religious and parliamentary reform with the assistance of such new organs as *The Times*, the *Edinburgh Review*, and Cobbett's popular *Political Register*, which between them symbolized the union of the Fourth Estate with all sections of the community, enfranchised or unenfranchised.

In *Monarchy and the Party System* Sir Lewis Namier wrote:

> Parliamentary struggles for office necessarily produce a dichotomy of 'ins' and 'outs'; and two party names were current since the last quarter of the seventeenth century: hence in retrospect the appearances of a two-party system. In reality three broad divisions, based on type and not on party, can be distinguished in the eighteenth-century House of Commons.[24]

The three divisions, according to Namier, were 'the followers of Court and Administration', the 'independent country gentlemen', and 'the political factions contending for power'. However, the heyday of court and country was not the eighteenth century but the seventeenth, before the terms Whig and Tory were introduced to explain a situation no longer understandable in the older terms.

Between 1689 and 1715 the Whig and Tory parties flourished so greatly that by the latter date practically all members of Parliament could be identified, both by contemporaries and by modern analysis, as being of one party or the other.[25] Because of the deep divisions which party conflict made within British society and politics in these years a full return to a court/country situation in the era of Whig hegemony after 1714 was simply not practicable, for it would have involved putting the clock back not only on party development but on the entire post-Revolution enhancement of Parliament's importance relative to the crown, symbolized and confirmed by the sitting of the legislature as a permanent rather than an occasional institution from 1689 onward.

After 1714 any court/country alignment was a bastardized one arising out of successive Whig schisms. 'Country' was a useful term in describing oppositions which consisted permanently of the whole Tory party and temporarily of some changing dissident Whig elements. The main Whig party had a tight monopoly of office but the appellation 'court' acknowledged gracefully that not all of the Whigs were on the government side. More narrowly the terms 'the court', 'the court party', and 'the court and Treasury party' might refer to the placemen or officeholders who formed an element within every ministry's supporters. The slight contemporary confusion in terminology here may have led to a major misunderstanding which has sometimes bedevilled later studies by failing to draw a necessary distinction between the party of government as a whole and its constituent part, the placemen, thereby leaving the impression that Walpole's and the Pelhams' ministries depended solely upon 'corrupt' or at least 'managerial' methods to obtain parliamentary majorities. This view has led, in turn, to the further assumption that a ministry might owe little or nothing to the party, independent of government patronage, which was in fact its usual mainprop in Parliament.

The court and Treasury element was at its highest point of roughly 254 in 1761, though Namier's calculation included army and naval officers and the relatively independent holders of offices for life. Namier cautioned that not all the 254 were 'truly dependent on the Government', and a more realistic figure might have been around 200. By 1780 Professor Christie found about 180 in theory, though he repeated the caution.[26] By 1821 the figure had sunk to below 50.[27] To the effects of the second Rockingham ministry's 'economical reforms' of 1782 were added the much greater cumulative effects of the younger Pitt's administrative reforms, Curwen's Act of 1809 and the outburst of parliamentary commissions and inquiries under Perceval and Liverpool. By the early nineteenth

century, indeed, moral pressure from reformers was too much for
the survival of a court and Treasury party and for most direct forms
of governmental pressure at elections. Lord Hawkesbury (later
Lord Liverpool) confessed in 1807 'it is very material that we should
be able to say in Parliament if necessary that no public money
has been expended . . . in the elections'.[28] Liverpool during his
ministry of 1812–27 willingly led the way in modernizing estab-
lishments, professionalizing appointments and refusing to use
ecclesiastical patronage for political purposes.[29]

At the opposite end of the scale from the placemen, in Namier's
analysis, were the 'independent country gentlemen'. The distinction between the two is less clear than at first sight appears, for there
were few members of Parliament who could not claim to be country
gentlemen in a social sense. As Pares first pointed out 'we cannot
easily distinguish, in their origins and social status, the "independent" members of the House of Commons from the placemen',[30]
and more recently Dr Jarrett has remarked that Namier's published
lecture on *Country Gentlemen in Parliament*, 'though it was in itself
a very cautious piece of work which only mentioned thirty or so
independent country members and made relatively modest claims
for them, has induced among some historians a quite remarkable
eagerness to populate the eighteenth-century political scene with
such men'. Jarrett himself estimates that the true independents
numbered about 80.[31] At all times, in fact, many who considered
themselves independent are to be found in large numbers among
the regular supporters of either government or opposition. Walpole's and the Pelhams' Old Corps of Whigs, Rockingham's Whig
party of the 1760s to 1780s, the Tories before 1762 and the
government supporters called Tory by their opponents after that
date could all provide scores of examples of men who would have
indignantly rejected any imputation that their independence, either
financial or political, was in any way compromised by their volun-
tary espousal of a party. Indeed true political independents, those
whose voting would reveal a wavering pattern over a long period,
were a small fraction of the House of Commons even in the mid-
eighteenth century. Certainly by 1784, Professor Cannon believes,
independence had been scarcely tenable for two years and the
number of independents may have sunk as low as thirty or forty.[32]
By 1830 Professor Beales has found little remaining trace of the
independent member in the sense of men voting consistently outside the party pattern.[h] Even in the eighteenth century independent
gentlemen were as likely to be found in Namier's first and third
broad divisions of 'Court and Administration' and 'political
factions' as in his second of 'independent country gentlemen', and

any attempt to identify them with a particular division of Parliament, however broad, invites failure.

The remaining 'division' which goes to make up Namier's analysis of the eighteenth-century political scene, and the one which has perhaps attracted the most attention, is 'the political factions contending for power'. Alvord and others prepared the ground by pointing out the disintegration of Whig party solidarity in the mid-eighteenth century and the prevalence of rival Whig groups. Here the interesting point is that Namier and his closest associates seem, at least in their earlier claims, to have exerted a reasonable caution. In *England in the Age of the American Revolution* Namier himself took Alvord to task for transposing the 'connections' of about 1767 back to 1761. Namier allowed the Duke of Bedford's connection of MPs only ten members in 1761, found no 'Grenvilles' as yet and did not endorse Alvord's 'adherents of William Pitt' as a separate group, pointing out that 'the politics of 1761 are often discussed in terms of later years, which is wholly inadmissible'. Bute's group, according to Namier, emerged in 1761–3 during that peer's period in office, while George Grenville's group and the enlarged Bedford following of the later 1760s were the product of the Grenville ministry from 1763 to 1765.[33] John Brooke found the factions flourishing in the period covered by *The Chatham Administration, 1766–1768* but, as we have already seen, stated his conviction that the 'personal parties' did not survive the year 1770. Professor Owen, in 1957, not only claimed a conventional Namieran 'complete absence of "party" in any modern sense' but also noted, in an often-overlooked passage that

> even the current conception that, in the politics of the 1740's, the conflict was essentially between collections of family groups is very far from the truth. With the exception of the Walpoles and the Pelhams, most families of any political significance were too divided among themselves to follow any very coherent pattern of behaviour in the House of Commons.[34]

As the Walpoles and the Pelhams worked with each other, and with the major part of the Whig party, there was no political scene of clashing connections in the 1740s; Cobham's Cubs, 'this little body of five' members, Owen refused to enlarge by including in it those who sometimes acted with it, for 'with the possible exception of John Pitt (William's Dorsetshire cousin) it would be unwise to include these people within the group'. The historian of mid-eighteenth-century Grenvilles, Professor Wiggin, pointed out that recent historians except Owen 'attributed to these cliques permanence and stability which patently they lacked'.[35]

One notable exponent of 'personal' parties was Professor Robert Walcott, whose explanation of politics at the beginning of the eighteenth century was both the most extreme and, eventually, the most strongly rejected of all Namierite works.[36] Unfortunately, Walcott's propositions were initially accepted by some writers of general studies including that most respected of British experts on the eighteenth century, Richard Pares, in his influential Ford Lectures published as *George III and the Politicians*. Pares remarked that 'Even in the first classical age of the two-party system, as we know from Mr Walcott's researches, the apparently homogeneous cohorts of whigs and tories were rather aggregations of personal groups, each a few dozen strong at most; and since 1714 the two great parties had dissolved still further, their meaning was still more diluted'.[37] But Pares's adoption of Walcott's analysis as appropriate to the mid-eighteenth century has been shown to be erroneous, by the work of Sedgwick, Owen and Wiggin, and the last-mentioned historian finds Pares's selection of the Grenvilles as 'the best instance of family solidarity' to be an invalid one.[38] Both Namier's and Pares's acceptance of 'personal' parties, rather than Whigs and Tories, as the basic alignment at the beginning of the eighteenth century, was perhaps the crucial step in the emergence of the fully fledged version of the Namierite interpretation as it flourished in the 1950s and the early 1960s. Even when the trickle of criticism of Walcott's ideas became a flood in 1967 only the understanding of Anne's reign was usually amended; accounts of the remainder of the eighteenth century continue to be influenced by his works and constitute the standard textbook version of its politics.

The classic 'personal' parties as described by Namier and Brooke emerged about 1765 and were on the way out by 1770.[i] Two of the group leaders, George Grenville and the fourth Duke of Bedford, died in 1770 and 1771 respectively, after which their followers merged with Lord North's government party. Chatham's death in 1778 largely ended his small following as an independent entity, as it was by then already in alliance with the main Whig party under the Marquis of Rockingham. But even for the 1760s we may question the extent to which the isolated manœuvrings of clientage groups dominated the nature of political life. The pattern of alignment was more purposeful, and more akin to the traditional rivalry of Tories and Whigs, than has always been acknowledged. Three of these groups, the King's Friends, Bedfords and Grenvilles, usually acted together; Namier himself pointed out that in many cases it was difficult to classify men as in one group or the other.[39] In fact of the eight years which passed between the fall of Newcastle's Old Corps of Whigs in 1762 and the beginning of North's ministry Bute's court party (or 'King's Friends' after Bute's withdrawal) is to be found together in office with Grenville and Bedford from 1762 to 1765 and with Bedford from 1767 to 1770. Moreover, both the Grenvilles and the Bedfords found common cause with Bute's followers during Rockingham's ministry of 1765–6 in opposing the repeal of the Stamp Act. The remaining two elements, the Whig party under Newcastle (and later Rockingham) and the handful of Pittites, acted together in opposition for most of the same eight years, namely from 1762 to 1765 and from 1768 to 1770; and Pitt supported Rockingham's Stamp Act repeal in 1766. In short, there existed on one side a working alliance, usually in office, of court party, Grenvilles and Bedfords, and, on the other side, a similar conjunction, usually in opposition, of Newcastle–Rockingham Whigs and Pittites. Chatham's ministry of 1766–8 provided the only complete breakdown of this predominantly two-sided alignment, though Grafton's court–Bedford government of 1768–70 lacked the usual support of Grenville's followers because their leader was in disgrace with George III. The 1760s, too, was a period of mainly consistent and rational two-way politics with the Newcastle–Rockingham Whigs and the 'Buteites' providing its polarity.

From the formation of North's ministry to the first Reform Act most small clientage groups played the role, normal for them since the Tory and Whig conflicts of late seventeenth and early eighteenth centuries, of elements within larger parties. Two possible exceptions sometimes suggested were the second-generation Grenvilles and the Canningites of the early nineteenth century. But the 'Grenvilles', in switching to the Whigs in 1803 and back to the Tories nineteen years later included prominent members such as William Windham unconnected with that family and were actuated mainly by 'Catholic' and anti-parliamentary-reform principles. The group's celebrated gains in patronage when they joined Lord Liverpool's ministry in 1822 were made possible by that minister's willingness to let Catholic emancipation be an open question in his Cabinet and by leading Whigs' espousal of parliamentary reform at that time.[j] The Canningites formed an element within the Pittite or Tory party for nearly three decades and became a separate group in 1828 only as an intermediate stage in a permanent transfer to the Whig party from 1830. This transition formed a precedent for that of the Peelites from Tory to Whig between 1846 and 1852. Both Grenvilles and Canningites were more typical of nineteenth- than of eighteenth-century grouping.

But the poverty of the theory of politically independent clientage groups, even for the eighteenth century, throws doubt on the role once claimed for them. The value of analysing political affiliations according to patronage association is questionable owing to the loose nature of this association itself. That a man would always overthrow political convictions in favour of family or connectional obligations is a large assumption, especially when such obligations were often so tenuous as to defy definition. John Brooke has described the difficulties, experienced not only by himself but by the leaders of the 'parties' about the time of the Chatham administration, of determining group membership: '. . . a party leader could not count on the votes of even his closest followers; while those in the outer circle had to be wooed with affection and persuaded with tact'.[40] Wiggin has noted a similar looseness of ties among the Grenvilles of the 1740s and 1750s, and Professor Sack among MPs and their patrons in the first three decades of the nineteenth century.[41] The mounting evidence that clientage parties did not play the atomistic political role once ascribed to them might suggest that the very nature of the patronage nexus was much less capable of permanent political alignments than has been assumed.

Notes: Chapter 1

a   G. R. Elton, letter to the editor of the *Times Literary Supplement*, 4 March 1977.
b   Thus the author of a book on the Jew Bill of 1753, and its effect in reviving latent Tory and Whig passions, pointed out that 'in Sir Lewis Namier's *Structure of Politics*, which deals extensively with the election of 1754, *the Jew Bill is not so much as mentioned*, even though the public talk of the politicians and publicists at the time was of little else', Perry, *Public Opinion, Propaganda and Politics*, pp. 191–2.
c   I. R. Christie, *Wars and Revolutions, Britain 1760–1815* (1982), p. 330. The principal works referred to are O'Gorman, *Rise of Party*; idem, *The Whig Party and the French Revolution*; Mitchell, *Charles James Fox*; Ginter, *Whig Organization . . . 1790*, and Roberts, *Whig Party*. Professor Christie's views are restated in his review in *History*, vol. 68 (1983) of Frank O'Gorman's recent *Emergence of the British Two-Party System*.
d   William Coxe, *Walpole* (1798), Vol. 3, pp. 566–7. Dodington blamed 'the crimes of this [Walpole's] administration' for the weakness of the House of Lords, though he instanced earlier examples. Compare Wellington's judgement, 'Nobody cares a damn for the House of Lords; the House of Commons is everything in England, and the House of Lords nothing' (*Creevey Papers*, Vol. 1, p. 287). Dr M. W. McCahill writes that 'Governments enjoying royal sanction were unlikely to lose their majority in the upper house', *Order and Equipoise*, p. 1.
e   Electors with two votes, as in the great majority of constituencies, could either cast both for candidates of the same persuasion, or split their votes between contestants of differing views. Voters could also 'plump', that is, use only one vote, for one candidate – see Phillips, *Electoral Behaviour*, pp. 63–4. Professor Phillips finds that 'A considerable, indeed a remarkable, degree of electoral freedom existed in spite of the often successful efforts of patrons . . . Even the burgage boroughs retained a measure of freedom of choice.'
f   For some examples illustrating these types of compromise see Forrester,

Northamptonshire County Elections and Electioneering, p. 43, and *History of Parliament, 1715–1754*, Vol. 1, p. 289 (for Norfolk).

g The government press rallied after 1770 under Lord North's direction and was equally virulent and effective in the writings of such powerful self-avowed Tories as Dr Samuel Johnson, John Fletcher (Wesley's follower), John Lind and John Shebbeare. See: Margaret E. Avery, 'Toryism in the age of the American Revolution', *Historical Studies: Australia and New Zealand*, Vol. 18 (1978–9), pp. 24–36. For Dr Johnson see below, p. 127, n. *c*.

h Beales writes that 'until around 1830 there was a considerable body of "non-political" M.P.s. But almost all those who were politically active were party men', see D. E. D. Beales, 'Parliamentary parties and the "independent" member 1810–1860', in Robert Robson (ed.), *Ideas and Institutions of Victorian Britain, Essays in Honour of George Kitson Clark* (1967), p. 18.

i It is clear, however, that the numbers involved were far fewer than has sometimes been thought. Mr John Brooke found that at about July 1767 the Pittites were 'few, and hardly merit the name of a party' while the Bedfords were about twenty and the Grenvilles twenty-five. By 1770 Rockingham, with about 100 followers, was 'the only party leader in the Opposition with any considerable following'. The remarks and figures on Pittites, Bedfords and Grenvilles are in Brooke's, *Chatham Administration*, pp. 250, 255 and 263. For the Rockinghams his slightly later Introduction to *History of Parliament, 1754–1790*, Vol. 1, p. 198, has been quoted.

j About a dozen MPs were involved in 1822. See below, p. 209.

CHAPTER TWO

Monarchs and Ministers

Contemporary observers were wont to point out that the existence of an active legislature made Britain's form of government distinctly unusual among the European nations. The changes which gave a permanent role to Parliament, after repeated and sometimes prolonged suspensions during the struggles of the seventeenth century, were well known through the works of political theorists and popularizers. European governments recognized that British policy was not simply controlled by normal considerations, the wishes of its monarchs, but was subject to sudden shifts and evasions as the result of struggles having their origin in Parliament. There were classic cases of this, such as the action of a Whig ministry in 1708 reviving a flagging alliance against Louis XIV, to be followed four years later by a Tory abandonment of the Allies. Parliamentary oversight of royal foreign policy, established by impeachment of William III's ministers in 1701, was the culmination of a series of limitations placed upon the monarchy after the Revolution of 1688. The Bill of Rights prevented monarchs from suspending or dispensing with statutes, levying taxes without parliamentary sanction, and raising a standing army in peacetime. Only after accepting these terms were William and Mary adopted as joint monarchs in 1689. The royal power of dissolving the legislature for long periods, or keeping a subservient Parliament for an unduly long time, was blocked by the 1694 Triennial Act. Use of the charge of treason to do away with political enemies was prevented by the Treason Act of 1696. Finally the Act of Settlement safeguarded the judiciary from royal displeasure, excluded the foreign servants of monarchy from office or Parliament and forbade future Hanoverian monarchs from involving Britain in war on behalf of their foreign territories. Above all, parliamentarians made very sure, by their grudging grants of finance from 1689 onwards, that Parliament would need to be kept in session almost continuously. The royal right to veto legislation proved too unpopular under William to be sustained; Queen Anne used it once on a minor matter but thereafter it was tacitly abandoned. The mystery which surrounded a monarch declined, and theories of Divine Right and Passive Obedience went into disfavour.

It was against this background of British restriction on traditional royal authority that the autocratic rulers of the small German provinces of Brunswick and Celle came to the throne in 1714 as the House of Hanover. Some controversy still exists as to the exact measure of authority exercised by George I and George II. They took an active interest in foreign policy and in the military sphere.[a] But George I ceased to evade British ministerial control after he was forced to see his German advisers expelled by a Whig ministry in 1719. The existence of Parliament allowed Walpole to obtain office against George I's wish in 1720 and retain it against George II's initial intention in 1727. Carteret was forced out of the secretaryship of state in 1724 contrary to George I's inclination, and again in 1744 despite George II's stubborn opposition. The second of these monarchs also had to undergo the humiliation of failing to find support for the two-day Bath–Granville ministry in 1746 and of having to accept the hated Pitt as minister from 1756. Although these monarchs' constitutional right to appoint ministers of their choice was legally unchallenged their ability to exercise that choice to the full, or to retain unpopular ministers, was severely circumscribed in practice. Arthur Onslow, the respected Speaker of the Commons from 1728 to 1761, noted the decline of court power from William III's reign to that of George II and commented that 'a court has less power (in fact) than ever it had to pursue measures, or preserve ministers, against the sense and inclination of Parliament, or of the House of Commons alone'.[1] Moreover, there is little doubt that restriction of the royal power of independent action was quietly accepted on most occasions. The Hanoverian monarchs realized their weak position, as only less unpopular than the rival House of Stuart, and left much in the hands of ministers who could be trusted to continue the exclusion of that rival. The failure of George I and George II to sit regularly in the Cabinet, as even Anne had done, demonstrated trust but also delegated authority to the ministers.

The Hanoverian monarchs' need to observe restrictions imposed by Parliament did not take place without occasional displays of their attachment to the older traditions still observed throughout most of Europe. They continued as absolute rulers of their German provinces and controlled these with little or no reference to British ministers or the needs of British policy, creating a frequent source of conflict in Parliament over the interpretation of the Act of Settlement's war clause. As military men, moreover, their Continental assumptions caused trepidation, and the Duke of Cumberland's treatment of Jacobites in the 1745 Rising stirred up much resentment in a nation which had rejected 'standing armies'. George

III's ostentatious disclaimer of Hanoverian interests gained him considerable popularity but he remained a feudal overlord of German states and his government's use of German mercenaries against the British colonists in North America excited much criticism. George's son, another Duke of Cumberland, was to earn a reputation in Britain for his arbitrary rule of Hanover in the age of the Holy Alliance, and the duke's brother, the blunt sailor William, had to caution him in 1829 that 'he had lived so long abroad that he had forgotten there was such a thing as freedom of debate'.[2] Cumberland's subsequent career as King of Hanover, especially his treatment of liberal politicians and academics, was a reminder that the reproach was justified.

In the middle of the eighteenth century most European monarchies were in the ascendant. Despite the reforms of such rulers as Frederick II of Prussia, Catherine II of Russia, Joseph II of Austria, Charles III of Spain and Gustav III of Sweden the absence of legislatures remained endemic in most countries, while in Sweden an experiment in parliamentary rule which had begun with the constitution of 1720 came to an abrupt end with the royalist *coup d'état* of 1772. The general framework of European monarchy, despotic though sometimes genuinely enlightened, explains the determination of British politicians to retain against the Hanoverian dynasty those gains which had been made against the Stuarts. It also does much to explain the widespread alarm built up by King George III's actions when he came to the throne maintaining that his predecessor had been in 'a state of bondage' and determined 'to put an end to those unhappy distinctions of party called Whigs and Tories'.[3]

George III, whose active rule of fifty-one years covers considerably more than half the period dealt with in this book, set himself throughout in virulent opposition to party government. His tutor, the Earl of Bute, encouraged him as a boy to have a low view of parties as detrimental to the constitution. The young prince's good intentions when he inveighed against 'party' as the supposed fount of corruption need not be questioned, though the element of self-interest involved in the alternative of resurgent royal authority should not be overlooked. Though few historians now deny either George III's basic probity or the affection which this inspired, especially during the latter part of his reign, it would be unwise to ignore other aspects of his outlook including a view of kingship received, via his close family connections, from the common European practices of his time. His often cavalier treatment of his ministers appeared mild indeed in courts from Stockholm to Madrid but were resented in Britain and boded ill for flexibility of

government in a nation which was becoming increasingly sophisticated as it passed through imperial expansion, industrial revolution
and the unprecedented pressures of increasing population.

Much of George III's self-assurance in dealing with politicians
continued to come from a certainty of his own good intentions, and
consequent determination to put his will into action as the best
course for Britain. A letter which he wrote to Lord North in 1775 is
revealing in its tone of moral certitude:

> If the Opposition is powerful next session it will much surprise me
> for I am fighting the battle of the legislature, therefore have a
> right to expect an almost unanimous support; if there should arise
> difficulties they will not dismay me for I know the uprightness of
> my intentions and therefore am ready to stand every attack of
> ever so dangerous a kind, with the firmness that honesty and
> attachment to the constitution will support.[4]

The unyielding nature of his attitude which comes out in this passage was a natural development from unselfcritical confidence. The
result is seen in what Pares noted of George III's attitude to politics:
'His idea of firmness was extremely simple: flat refusal to make any
political concessions to anybody.'[5] Such a stance did not make for
success in the parliamentary political system which he inherited.

Modern scholarship has endorsed Namier's exoneration of
George III from the accusation of would-be tyranny, though stopping short at believing that his activities were in accord with his youthful intentions. For the king was perhaps more ambivalent about the
constitution than his frequent protests would suggest. During his
physical and mental breakdown for about three months in the
autumn and winter of 1788–9, when a number of his true feelings
came to light, he confessed to one of his doctors that, though he
thought the constitution 'the finest thing in the world; if it had a fault
it was that of its not being fit for a king: he was the only slave',
though he added characteristically, 'yet he admired it, and thought
it worthy of having been framed by Heaven'.[6] George did not wish
to overthrow the constitution, but he believed that others had done
so before his time, and was less than happy with the state of politics
as he found it. So far as the king's dislike of parties was concerned
there is no need to postulate a 'Stuart' or Jacobite education, as did
hostile contemporaries and some later 'Whig' historians, for his
father Prince Frederick was the only necessary source. The latter's
surviving papers show amply his undertaking to do away with party
distinctions by admitting Tories to office on equal terms when he

came to the throne, a promise which his own death prevented him from carrying out but which his son honoured.[7] To his late father's political obligations, however, George III added the alchemy of his own personality. The abolition of parties became, in the younger man's hands, a crusade. When he was in a position to appoint the nation's administrators he not only avoided party men, when he could, but chose those of whose moral and political purity he felt assured. Bute until he proved a broken reed, North until he rebelled, Addington and perhaps Perceval measured up to this standard. Grenville, Rockingham and Fox did not, and were dismissed. Such arbitrary treatment raised not simply opposition but resentment. Namier's contention that 'the practice of George III's earlier years was no real innovation; the difference was merely in emphasis and degree' has been rejected by Pares, Professor Fryer and others.[8] Though not illegal the king's view of his role in government went in the face of eighteenth-century convention and at times of common sense, as when he made his inexperienced tutor Prime Minister and dispensed with Bute's two immediate successors over the control of appointments.[b]

George III's conception of the integrity of monarchy and empire was more rigid than those of either the earlier Hanoverians or their ministers and played an important role in Britain's conflict with the American colonists. The historian of the war for America, Piers Mackesy, writes that 'the King was determined to play for the whole stakes, believing that the only alternative was ruin. He was sustained by the stubborn strength which he had drawn all through his life from the faith that God was with him . . .'.[9] When North told the king that the Commons had withdrawn their support for the war and that George must 'yield at length', Professor Foord comments that 'practically everyone but George III had come to share this view'.[10] The king, however, continued for years to lament the betrayal, as he saw it, that had lost an empire.[11]

King George III dealt dextrously and vigorously with unwanted ministries at all stages of his career. Professor Cannon writes that when the king was forced to accept the Whig second Rockingham administration in March 1782 'his objective from the beginning was to drive a wedge into the opposition, and he was not unduly squeamish in his methods'.[12] He destroyed this ministry after three months, seizing the chance of its leader's death, and though unable to prevent the setting up of the Fox–North ministry in 1783 also brought this down after a further eight months over its India Bill. His tactics on the second occasion were equally determined and questionable, and as John Brooke has written, 'whether unconstitutional or not, the King's conduct was certainly unscrupulous. The ministers were entitled to complain that he had given no hint of his opposition to the bill until it reached the House of Lords'.[13] George's descent from his own moral ideals in politics is plain.

The issues of Catholic emancipation and parliamentary reform hastened the decline of 'personal' monarchy. In 1801 George III's declaration on emancipation that he would consider any man who voted for it 'as personally indisposed towards him' (echoing a similarly worded message to the House of Lords in 1783 over Fox's India Bill)[c] led to the resignation of the ablest members of the younger Pitt's ministry, including Pitt himself.[14] Addington's administration, which followed this débâcle, brought royal intervention into retrospective disrepute. A further, and almost the last assertion of monarchic independence came on basically the same issue in 1807, when the king brought down the 'Talents' ministry over a minor aspect of Catholic relief. His determination to have his way in politics was not without its dignity, for he spared himself as little as he spared others, working long hours over public affairs and keeping a close oversight on even the minutiae of government. But his actions resulted in some of the weakest administrations on record, Bute's, Chatham's, North's and Addington's. As a result there was political dislocation leading to extra-parliamentary agitation in the 1760s, an end George did not wish for, while in the 1770s his opposition to coming to terms with the American colonists prolonged the war to beyond the point where it could be ended without long-lasting scars. His interventions in the early 1780s were of dubious constitutional propriety, stimulating rather than suppressing the Whig opposition, and in the first decade of the nineteenth century he prevented measures which might have reduced Irish Catholic discontent at the beginning of the Anglo-Irish parliamentary union.

George III's sons, less morally determined and in George IV's case less popular, were unable to stand up to the more modern form of party politics which their father's activities had unwittingly fostered. The middle class despised the prince regent for his tastes at the expense of the nation, for the extramarital adventurism which contrasted so strongly with the old king's strait-laced rectitude, and for his abandonment of the Whigs after three decades of political and social alliance. The break with his old friends in 1812 put the regent into the hands of their opponents. Canning reminded him in that year, not without a touch of malice, 'worse as his condition might be in the hands of the Whigs, he was equally under control with his present government'.[15] George IV was dependent on the Tories for the rest of his life and was obliged to give up many of his father's functions, a process encouraged by his aversion to the everyday duties of government. By 1827 so staunch a Tory as the Duke of Wellington could advise the king that the choice of a Prime Minister 'was the only personal act the King of England had to perform. When he had appointed his First Minister, all the rest devolved upon the person appointed, who became responsible for the King's acts.'[16] But against George IV's weaknesses must be set his improved grasp of political realities, a strength which his successor shared. George felt as strongly as his father about Catholic emancipation but gave way to it in the end. William IV shared George III's repugnance for reform but made its passage possible. Had they not done so they might have precipitated a crisis in the continuance of monarchy itself. The restored French royal family proved too rigid to survive, as did many other European monarchies at later dates. Britain's way with kingship was milder, assisted by a good sense in George IV and William IV which was conspicuously lacking in George III.

By 1742 there was already a formidable body of precedent for the appointment of ministers, and for ministerial policy-making, which sidestepped or overrode the wishes of post-Revolution monarchs. The Treaty of Ryswick in 1697 was followed by a massive parliamentary reaction against King William's arbitrary mode of government, reducing his army and forcing his Whig ministers out of office. In 1700 that king accepted Rochester's Tory government, together with terms which included the restrictions upon a future Hanoverian monarchy subsequently included in the Act of Settlement.[17] Queen Anne allowed policy-making to be carried out by her ministers, who developed a suitable instrument in a Cabinet with stable membership, regular meetings and recorded decisions.[18] In 1708 the Whig Junto stormed their way into office against her strongest wishes, aided by a change in the party balance of the Commons. Within three years of George I's accession a formidable body of Whigs led by Walpole rebelled against the Stanhope ministry's alleged subservience to royal foreign policy and went into opposition, thereby enabling Stanhope to rid himself in 1719 of the worst aspects of royal intransigence. Walpole's subsequent rise to power, his retention of his office under a new monarch, and the manner of his eventual fall established several further precedents for defeating the intentions of George I and George II on the highest appointments.[19]

The Pelhams who succeeded Walpole as leaders of the Old Corps of Whigs were well aware of these and other precedents. Charles Yorke, son of their associate Lord Chancellor Hardwicke, wrote in 1742 to his brother that 'in 1708 Lord S[underland] drew up a very remarkable and severe paper to be communicated to Lord Godolphin concerning the terms on which the Whigs entered into administration'.[20] Yorke had been reading the papers of Lord Somers, leader of the Junto, and living memory doubtless supplied material on later incidents. In addition to being prepared on occasion to 'force' George II over appointments, Newcastle and Henry Pelham were ready to override him on policies. In one key vote in the Cabinet they defeated by a large majority a proposal by the monarch's preferred minister, Lord Carteret, for concluding a treaty which, they considered, 'engaged the King too closely' in expensive Continental commitments.[21] Their campaign against the royal subsidy policy ended in the threat of resignation in 1744 which brought their rival down. George had to defer to the Whig party which had brought his father to the throne; and the main body of that party, the Old Corps, backed leaders who reflected their own presuppositions. The king's clashes with the Pelhams usually arose from his use of British resources apparently in the interest of Hanover; but underlying Whig criticism derived from the assumption, essentially unchanged since the days of the Junto, that the inclination of the monarchy should in the last count be subordinated to the wishes of the party. This attitude was well represented by Newcastle when he wrote to his brother, concerning the quashing of George II's proposal for a subsidy to Saxony: 'His difficulties with regard to the engaging the elector of Saxony are in some measure got over, and he knows what his servants will, and what they cannot do, so that he has nothing further to expect from them.' George II might show his resentment 'by manner, by looks, by harsh expressions' but his need to obtain the support of the 'servants', who alone could carry monetary supplies in the Commons, was the ultimate determinant of all policy.[22]

The most prominent example of Pelhamite views triumphing over those of the monarch came with the mass resignation of dozens of ministers and other officeholders in February 1746, and their reinstatement on their own terms. For some Whigs, it is true, so drastic an action may have caused misgivings; Hardwicke and Chesterfield are known to have had retrospective qualms.[23] But Pelham and Newcastle do not appear to have regretted their action, and Pelham is found writing to Henry Fox on a clash of opinion in 1751 that he had talked 'without reserve' to the king, who 'now knows upon what terms I can be his servant and of *use* to him'.[24] Pelham stayed on at the Treasury until his death in 1754. George II made no demur in accepting the ministers' recommendation of Newcastle as Pelham's successor, only specifying that the Duke of Devonshire should be added to the Cabinet for its deliberations on this matter.[25] Newcastle was at least as willing as his brother to carry out Whig policies where these conflicted with the king's views, but was far less frank about it. He felt a constant need to placate the more conservative and timorous Hardwicke, whose reservations continued at the thought of a repetition of 1746. Newcastle's constant need to quieten Hardwicke's misgivings, while at the same time taking action which the latter deplored in theory, has provided material from the two friends' correspondence in which the duke appears to abhor 'forcing' the king. Namier used the Newcastle–Hardwicke letters on the ministerial crisis of 1757 to illustrate his thesis that these men had no conception of a party government unconnected with the king, or of a constitutional parliamentary opposition. This was far from being the case.[d] Newcastle had personal memories of Whig tradition in dealing with monarchs going back to Queen Anne's reign, and he was nothing if not a party traditionalist.

To support them in their stand against monarchical pressure the ministers of George II and George III resorted to a concept of responsibility which was rarely legalistically defined but certainly excluded remaining in office to carry out policies inimical to them. This attitude was not confined to the Old Corps. The elder Pitt, who held the Pelhams in little esteem, had a view of ministerial responsibility which differed little from theirs. When he was forced to resign over war policy in 1761 by the activities of George III and Bute he put on record 'that in his station and situation he was responsible and would not continue without having the direction; that this being his case, nobody could be surprised that he could go on no longer, and he would repeat it again, that he would be responsible for nothing but what he directed'.[26] When the Old Corps leaders threatened or carried out resignation in 1744 and 1746 they put their case in hardly less explicit and forceful terms.[e]

The objections of such diverse ministers of George III as Pitt, George Grenville, Bedford and Rockingham to what they believed were incorrect royal policies and unwise or unconstitutional resort to irresponsible advisers are well known. Less often stressed, because less openly expressed at the time, is the mounting resentment of Lord North in the later 1770s to the activities of the King's Friends, though at a time of war emergency he hesitated to carry out his frequent offers of resignation. His principal tactic, other than these threats, was to drag his heels in government business, a reaction which the king chose to interpret as arising from lethargy. George wrote to North in 1778 complaining of sluggish attendance by ministerial supporters in the Commons and giving 'directions' for him to produce an improvement.[f] After receiving this thinly veiled recrimination the minister offered to resign his second post of Chancellor of the Exchequer immediately to Charles Jenkinson, the king's unpopular confidant, as a step towards resignation as First Lord at the end of the parliamentary session.[27] By such responses North kept some measure of control over the situation, since George III was not unaware of the likely consequences of exposing Bute's former associates to the Commons as senior ministers. North's methods were unheroic, but his position was unenviable; both personal loyalty and a concept of national unity held him to office to provide a figurehead for a policy about which he had increasingly serious doubts. When he had finally been relieved of his burden and was first discussing with the opposition Whig leadership the new alliance which he kept up thereafter he spoke in heartfelt terms what must have been his true thoughts: 'There should be one man, or a Cabinet, to govern the whole, and direct every measure. Government by departments was not brought in by me. I found it so, and had not vigour and resolution to put an end to it. The King ought to be treated with all sort of respect and attention, but the appearance of power is all that a king of this country can have.'[28]

The agreement of the Foxite Whigs with such sentiments may be taken for granted. Much more interesting is the attitude of the younger Pitt, who played a leading part in the re-establishment of ministerial authority, *vis-à-vis* the crown, a part which was largely overlooked in Namierian historiography. The traditional Whig interpretation had recognized Pitt's importance in this respect, though seeing his activities as little more than a pale imitation of Whig ideas. It was in reaction to this view that the American historian D. G. Barnes offered in 1939 an interpretation of George III's relationship with this minister which generally appeared to conform with Namier's conclusion of monarchy's continuing political predominance. But Barnes also pointed out that: 'Once a chief minister was appointed, however, Pitt held that he must have the predominant voice in the councils of the King and be free to place before his royal master any proposals upon which the Cabinet had reached an agreement. The King then had the choice of accepting or rejecting such measures and of retaining or ousting his ministers.' And the same author went on to state that Pitt's attitude towards George III had much in common with that of the Tories of Charles II's and James II's reigns, for 'these Tories stressed the doctrine of passive obedience, but only so long as the kings issued the kind of orders which they wished to obey'.[29] The case for Pitt's supposed weakness against George III was thus never pressed to the conclusion of ministerial subservience except in respect of the early years of Pitt's first ministry. Professor Foord has depicted Pitt even in those years as making considerable strides in diminishing the 'influence of the crown' by reducing royal and governmental patronage in the Commons, while Dr Ehrman points out that Pitt's early setbacks and consequent caution 'can scarcely be explained simply by an implicit surrender to the King'.[8]

The younger Pitt's position relative to George III depended upon the amount of support the minister could draw from other sources. Although his initial appointment was solely the work of the king alternative sources of power quickly became available. Even before the general election of 1784 independent opinion in the Commons was swinging towards him.[30] That election, far from being the triumph of 'management' it has sometimes been portrayed as, exhibited a marked degree of popular support for Pitt as a reformer, as an alternative to the infamous coalition of Fox and North, and not least as his father's son.[31] A document of 1788 shows the government party composed of a large court element and a small following of Pittites, but power in the Commons was neither so bifurcated nor so unequally distributed as this suggests.[32] The long ministries of Walpole, Pelham and North and shown that a minister seated in the Commons could build up a loyal personal following from among the placemen. That George III tried to influence policy during his young minister's first five years of office is not to be doubted, but of the misfortunes which beset Pitt's planned legislation in the mid-1780s only one, the failure of his Reform Bill in 1785, is directly attributable to the king. On this occasion George III ostentatiously insisted upon a free vote for government supporters; but it was the aversion of the Whig opposition from parliamentary reform, as much as George's action, which ensured the destruction of Pitt's hopes.

The effect of parliamentary setbacks upon Pitt's relationship with the king was not to render the minister more dependent upon the monarch but to make him more careful in obtaining his ends. Although Pitt dropped reform of Parliament as hopeless his reforming spirit continued in the professionalization of civil and military appointments, government contracting, and lease of crown lands which continued throughout his career. By as early as 1786, Dr Langford has maintained, Pitt had succeeded in taking control of most aspects of foreign policy, overriding both Foreign Secretary and king.[33] In 1788–9, during George III's months of mental breakdown, the minister earned the monarch's gratitude by effective tactics which prevented a regency of the Prince of Wales and a Foxite Whig ministry. Thus during most of the 1790s the king was content to leave policy and the oversight of government business to the Prime Minister. At the outset of the decade Pitt insisted upon the removal of

remaining court-oriented ministers from the Cabinet. By this means
the early stages of the negotiation which brought Portland and a
large section of the opposition into the government in 1794 were
conducted without reference to the king; and on one occasion
thereafter George wrote to Portland, without hint of censure, that
he had learned of transactions in a Cabinet meeting by reading of
them in the newspapers.[34] It was only in the later 1790s that
differences over the conduct of an increasingly unsuccessful war
brought the king to a stage of considerable dissatisfaction with a
ministry which by this time was taking little notice of him.[h]

The Cabinet's growing habit of excluding the king from most of
its calculations, though encouraged by his own decreased activity,
led to its downfall in 1801, though the long-term result of the
episode was to discredit the king's intervention in matters of policy.
In the parliamentary union of Britain and Ireland discussions of the
crucial Catholic emancipation question were not revealed to
George III until a late stage, probably in the hope that his known
reluctance to countenance such a measure would be overtaken by
events. His intervention when it came was explosive and decisive,
but the ministerial reaction was equally strong. What is sometimes
referred to as Pitt's resignation in February was in fact the withdrawal of the major part of the wartime ministry including Foreign
Secretary, Secretary at War, Secretary of War and First Lord of the
Admiralty. Outside the Cabinet a long list of resignations was
headed by the able Secretary of the Treasury, George Rose, and
also included the rising junior ministers, Canning and Castlereagh.
The self-removal of such a range of experience of talent automati-
cally condemned any succeeding ministry, in default of a recourse to
the Whigs, to be a scratch team. The outgoing men, despite the
seriousness of their move in time of war, had no reservations about
their action, which they saw in terms of constitutional necessity. For
William Wyndham Grenville 'there was no alternative except that
of taking this step or of agreeing to the disguise or dereliction of
one's opinion on one of the most important questions in the whole
range of our domestic policy'.[35] Pitt's young admirer Canning had
no doubt of the propriety and indeed necessity of his resignation.
Canning believed that, after the Whigs' secession from Parliament
in 1797 reduced their credibility as a possible alternative
government, Pitt's authority had been eroded by a gradual revival
of royal interference on bad advice. 'Government had been
weakened exceedingly' in the last three years, he complained, 'and
if on this particular occasion a stand was not made, Pitt would retain
only a nominal power, while the real one would pass into the hands
of those who influenced the King's mind and opinion out of sight'.[36]

Camden, a Pittite who had occasion to know Pitt's mind, recorded in a detailed account of the whole affair that the intervention of the king on the Catholic question 'induced Mr Pitt to lay a great stress on the King's ceasing to interfere, if he remained in office'.[37] In effect, the Pittite resignations were a reassertion that Cabinet policy-making must take precedence over the wishes of the monarch, a view long expressed by the opposition Whig party.

The Pittites' stand in the crisis of 1801, together with the weakness of the ensuing Addington administration, confirmed future Cabinets in their hardwon sense of independent authority. Grenville, Windham and other resigners eventually joined the Whigs and strengthened that party's beliefs. Canning and Castlereagh were at the centre of the younger generation of Pittites who formed the Tory party after their leader's death. Pitt himself retained his independence of action and asserted it again after a period of self-imposed restraint from opposition. George III's short mental breakdown a few weeks after the minister's departure in February 1801 occasioned Pitt's celebrated promise never to reintroduce the emancipation issue in the king's lifetime, but a promise tardily given out of concern for the monarch's sanity can hardly be construed as a major victory for royal authority. After nominally supporting Addington's government for over two years Pitt resorted to opposition in 1803 in order to force his way back into office and restore effective government, establishing that the king could no more keep a congenial but weak ministry than he could afford to alienate an uncongenial but powerful one. Pitt's terms for taking up office again in the negotiation with Addington demanded, in words reminiscent of Portland's on the appointment of the Coalition ministry in 1783, that in any 'plan of arrangement'

> the *whole and every part* of such Plan when submitted to His Majesty must of course depend on his approbation or rejection . . . but that in case of any such objection, it must be open to me to judge whether it did not in my opinion render it impossible for me to engage in His Majesty's service.[38]

In short, Pitt would only serve on his own terms. The negotiation failed but was successfully renewed in the next year. By this time Pitt had reached a point in his dealings with George III not far removed from that which would have been adopted by Fox in like circumstances. For in Pitt's reappointment, as Professor Barnes remarked, the king had 'Hobson's choice.'[39] His continued refusal in that year to take Fox, even in a non-party government, acted decisively in favour of Pitt's stand. In telling Pitt that 'he should consider it as a personal insult if Mr Fox was pressed upon him' the king effectively put himself into Pitt's hands.[40]

Pitt's second ministry was weakened by Addington's capricious behaviour, as was the succeeding Talents ministry, but the lesson that exclusion of the Whigs could only result in more independence for Tory ministries was underlined by the fall of the Talents in 1807 and a return of the Pittites under Portland. Portland's successors as leaders of the Tory party received fresh strengthening against monarchical authority from the prince regent's quarrel with the Whigs. Ever-increasing pressure from Parliament, in which 'the influence of the crown' was now barely visible, ensured that the ministers and their followers had fresh incentive to keep commitments to the throne to a minimum. Lord Liverpool took a further step towards a modern type of prime ministerial authority by keeping aloof from the various departmental duties assumed by so many of his predecessors. He thereby freed himself for the important task of ministerial co-ordination essential for government and useful for obtaining a Cabinet solidarity which could parry the regent's numerous pretensions. Though willing on occasion to threaten resignation, as when he was barely dissuaded from giving George IV twenty-four hours' notice in 1822 if Canning were not taken into the ministry, Liverpool could usually rely on less abrasive pressure.[41] When the powerful Wellington was tempted by dislike of Canning's liberal foreign policies to closet with the king, Liverpool was able to isolate the rebel in the Cabinet.[42] Wellington himself, as we have seen, later lectured the king on the omnipresence of ministerial authority. Even elevations to the peerage, perquisite of the crown from time immemorial, were now too important as the main source of patronage remaining to the Prime Minister to be left to the whim of a monarch. It was Lord Liverpool the Tory, not Lord Grey the Whig, who informed the new king in 1820 that he might commit himself to bestow peerages only 'through one of the regular and official responsible channels', not on his own authority.[43]

Notes: Chapter 2

a   Namier's case against the 'King in Toils' theory was dismissed by Richard Pares in its essential feature, control of ministers (*King George III*, p. 183), but received some support from J. B. Owen, 'George II Reconsidered', in A. Whiteman, J. Bromley and P. G. M. Dickson (eds), *Statesmen, Scholars and Merchants* (Oxford, 1973), pp. 113–34. The latest assessment concludes reasonably that 'neither Crown nor ministers enjoyed an easy or automatic pre-eminence' in George II's reign: Clark, *Dynamics of Change*, p. 448.

b   For George III's quarrels with George Grenville and the Marquis of Rockingham, see below, pp. 104, 106–7 and 115–16.

c   See below, pp. 149–50 and 175–6.

d   Namier quoted in *England* (2nd edn, p. 50), a lengthy passage from Hardwicke's letter of 9 April 1757 concerning his objections to going into 'formed opposition' but does not appear to have noticed Newcastle's triumphant description on the 15th of Mansfield's advice to the king that if Newcastle went into opposition the Whigs in the Commons would follow, an assertion which Newcastle rightly concluded must have an effect (see below, pp. 85–6). Namier also noted (*England*, p. 51) a paper in which Newcastle wrote of his intention not 'in any degree to force the King, contrary to his inclination, to admit any persons into his Administration' (*nota bene* 'in any degree'); but Professor Reed Browning quotes the duke as writing 'what the King will do I know not, but I believe he will be forced to yield, what I own I am very long for' (*sic*). Browning comments: 'Thus, with Newcastle's approval, though perhaps not at his explicit command, Lord Holderness gave up the seals he had held during six tumultuous years. Other officials promptly declared their readiness to follow him. The meaning of these shenanigans was not lost on the spectators of this drama: Newcastle apparently had the power to topple any government he disliked. Lord Mansfield quickly convinced George II that a Waldegrave–Fox ministry could not succeed, and a chastened king finally submitted to what Waldegrave called "the necessity of the times"' (Browning, *Newcastle*, p. 260).

e   See below, pp. 62–3 and 66–7.

f   The king enclosed a copy this letter with a covering letter to John Robinson, North's subordinate at the Treasury, adding that North 'though perhaps hurt at being obliged to enter on a plan, will I am confident find the utility of it' (Add. MS 37,834, f. 31).

g   Ehrman, *Younger Pitt*, pp. 633–43; A. F. Foord, 'The waning of the "influence of the crown"', *EHR*, vol. 62 (1947), pp. 584–607.

h   See below, pp. 174–6.

CHAPTER THREE
Tories and Whigs

One of the themes of my preceding book^a was the continuance of two-party strife after the climax reached in 1714, a strife now complicated by the presence of often transient groups of Whig dissidents who could not co-operate for long with either government Whigs or Tories. That this situation extended beyond the fall of Walpole has been confirmed both by Dr Colley's study of the early Georgian Tory party and by Dr Clark's judgement of 'what to contemporaries was obvious: that the old parties survived into the 1750's'. From 1756, however, a suspension of customary conflict between Tory party and Old Corps Whigs took place when the Tories followed Prince George in supporting William Pitt on his accession to office, leaving no regular opposition in Parliament during most of the Seven Years' War.[1]

That the two-party tradition survived the dual effects of this truce and of George III's determination to rid himself after 1760 of Whig dominance has often been questioned since Sir Lewis Namier first wrote on the subject. Certainly the 1760s saw the end of a phase of party history which had remained relatively stable for nearly half a century. For several years politics bears a strong resemblance to the 1690s when the first Tory and Whig parties were re-forming and adjusting themselves to the reversal of governmental and opposition roles demanded of them under the new monarchy of William and Mary. Later in this chapter, and in those which follow, it is argued that the element of party continuity was in fact present in the 1760s, with a transfer of allegiance to government by the main body of Old Tories and with the excluded Whigs' decision to take up active opposition. Such a reversal of roles was as difficult to stabilize after the long period of Whig domination as had been the similarly unstable situation in the decade after 1688 brought about by the ending of Tory domination under James II. Nevertheless, the period of transition under George III was largely complete by the first year of Lord North's ministry in 1770.

Much of the difficulty in conceding the renewal of the two-party tradition under George III arises from the reluctance of most ministers to accept the label of Tory. The reason for their objection is understandable. Until recently most of these men had been classed as Whigs and they had no wish to be burdened with the newly revived connotation of subservience to monarchy implied by the Tory title. Nevertheless, what Namier once called the inconvenience of playing a 'two-party game' under a 'one-name system' could not continue indefinitely.[2] The first relaxation came with the French Revolution, making monarchy more popular in Britain and rendering 'Toryism' innocuous. Pressure mounted for the general acceptance of a useful traditional name. Dr Harvey believes that the election of 1807 was the occasion of the return of the term Tory to common, as distinct from abusive use.[3] The habit quickly spread from constituents to ministerial backbenchers. In the new era after 1815, writes Professor Foord,[4] 'out of consideration for the self-styled Tories who voted with them, the ministers' fierce renunciation of the title came to an end'.[b]

Despite terminological difficulties, however, the party of government from North to the younger Pitt disputed on more than equal terms with the opposition Whigs under Rockingham and Fox. By the 1790s the parties began to exhibit a major characteristic of the nineteenth century; the organizational developments pioneered by the Whig manager, William Adam, and others resulted in a formal concerting of debates between Adam and his ministerial opposite number, Rose. Both parties could now muster formidable and centrally organized resources at election times, and both had the continuous services of paid or subsidized sections of the news-paper press. By the early nineteenth century the Whig opposition began to make good their claim to be 'His Majesty's Opposition', and were accepted thereafter as a recognized part of the consti-tution.[5] Even more significantly the last decades of the eighteenth century saw a more definite pattern of two-party politics emerging in many constituencies. Professor Phillips writes that 'it seems highly probable that by the late 1780's, party politics generally and partisan considerations specifically had become crucial in structur-ing the behaviour of a substantial proportion of the English borough electorate'.[6] And for the early nineteenth century Dr O'Gorman notes that: 'At four-cornered contests, over 80 per cent of electors voted a clear party ticket, at three-cornered contests about 65 per cent. What is even more spectacular is the loyalty of the voters to their parties. Where there were contests at successive elections, only around 10 per cent would completely switch their votes from one party to the other.'[7]

The stability of three decades of Whig–'Tory' strife suffered a setback in 1801 when Pitt's fall shattered his party into 'Pittite',

'Addingtonian', and 'Grenvillite' elements, but a further eleven years saw the reunion under Lord Liverpool of all but the small group of Grenvillites, whose readmittance was delayed almost a further decade. Dr Austin Mitchell's study of 1815–30, based upon analysis of divisions, shows 'a two-party system modified by the existence of unreliable groups on the fringes of both sides'.[8] A contemporary assessment confirms that by 1821–2 these fringes could be very small and that the great majority of MPs were voting highly consistently with either Tory or Whig parties.[c]

The history of the Tories from Walpole's fall until the death of George II was long misunderstood because of Namier's identification of them with his third 'broad division', the 'independent country gentlemen'.[9] It is now clear, however, that the Tories were related to the class of country gentlemen only as a part to a whole; they were typical of that class in their general economic standing but cut off from their Whig opposite numbers by debarment from officeholding and by their own obstinate refusal to sink their political identity. Namier poured scorn on the idea that 'anyone could have controlled the votes of a hundred independent country gentlemen' around 1755, but Dr Colley has succeeded in identifying an effective party organization which did just that.[10] The Tories were accustomed to acting as a parliamentary party, with well-known policies, active leaders and regular meetings. Their party affiliation made them a breed apart, sometimes persecuted but proud of their stance. They were upheld by loyal constituents like those of Northamptonshire who for over a century 'never returned a Whig as Knight of the Shire'.[11] Tories sat typically for the counties and greater urban constituencies, both of which boasted large electorates and furnished the Tory voters, possibly sometimes a majority in the nation, whose numbers were (as in the case of the Liberals today) by no means commensurately represented in Parliament.

A second source of the Tory party's strength and independence was its traditional support from the Church of England's lower clergy, an attachment which was little weakened by the Whigs' control of the bench of bishops. At times when defence of the Established Church against Dissent or other possible rivals seemed called for, as in 1753, Tory warmth could become a formidable political blaze. Other major subjects for opposition were such matters as the 'standing' or regular army, the Septennial Act which favoured Whig patronage management in the Commons, 'Hanoverian' foreign policies, landed qualification for MPs and naturalization of resident foreign Protestants. On these topics, as well as on country issues such as taxation and 'places', the Tories could base a regular opposition. Tory attendance at divisions was good – an average of 76 per cent is recorded in the known division lists from 1729 to 1755 – and generally much better than that of Whig opposition members. Despite a notorious inability, not confined to Tory members, to keep up full attendance at the conclusion of parliamentary sessions the party managers were able, through an organization based on London clubs and circular letters, to obtain exceptionally high turnouts for key divisions.[12] Individual defections from the party were negligible after an early exodus of weaker brethren in George I's reign. Two occasions when sizeable groups of Tories are claimed to have transferred their allegiance to government can be shown in one case to have involved only five members, Gower's friends in 1744–5, and in the other to have been non-existent (because based on the misunderstanding of a document) as with the seventeen Tories who were supposed to have usually supported the ministry after the 1754 election.[13]

The problem of whether Jacobitism was an important element of Tory thought, at least down to the defeat of the Young Pretender in 1745–6, need not detain us long. Contemporaries and most modern historians are agreed that there was a small band of Tory MPs whose preference for the exiled House of Stuart was the chief reason for their presence in Parliament; such men as William Shippen in an earlier generation and Sir John Hynde Cotton made little secret of their beliefs and were even admired as men of honest if misguided opinions. The suspicion that most other Tories were clandestine Jacobites or sympathizers was sedulously fostered by Whig politicians and press from Walpole onwards; but the failure of the main body of English Tories to support the Old Cause at any of the major crises of its fortunes in 1688, 1714, or 1745 must throw serious doubt upon any claim that Toryism and Jacobitism were synonymous.[d] Mere suspicion sufficed to keep the Tories out of office from 1714 to 1760. But the actual views of the average Tory were of a need to preserve order in church and state, and Catholic Stuart monarchy spelt state disruption with danger to the Anglican Church. For monarchy itself Tories had a lingering reverence, but this sentiment contained a steadily increasing element of belief that the monarch was part of the post-Revolution constitution; the political theories of John Locke affected them hardly less than the Whigs. By the later 1740s the active support of all but a small Jacobite minority was ripe for transfer to the *de facto* monarchy from Hanover. The Tories' alliance with the heir apparent, Prince Frederick, in 1747 was a major step in the revival of their long-suspended monarchism. The accession of his son as George III completed that process.

While the Tories still remained a politically and socially ostracized body they developed a feature that should surprise no student of parties in opposition. A form of Tory radicalism which had never been entirely absent from their dealings with government since 1689 blossomed in the fifth and sixth decades of the eighteenth century among many members, especially those with urban constituencies. This aspect of the Tories' thought was to survive into the new reign and condition their voting on certain popular issues long after the great majority of their party had undertaken general support of George III's chosen ministries. From 1742 to 1760 some Tories were foremost in supporting such causes as a redistribution of parliamentary seats in favour of large-franchise boroughs and counties, enfranchisement of the rising industrial cities of Birmingham, Manchester, Leeds, Halifax and Sheffield, and even the repeal of the Black and Riot Acts. As often, the opposition experience brought an excluded and socially conservative party to a consciousness of a need to reform the system which was used to keep them from power.[14]

At the outset of George III's reign the Old Tories were welcomed at court. As ministerial material, however, they were of little immediate value, for they lacked experience and few of them were of the administrative calibre needed. Despite these drawbacks to Tory usefulness, it is no longer possible to accept the view which sees the Old Tories as 'disintegrating' after 1760 or 1761 to join a number of Whig groups. Of the 113 Tories Namier listed as returned in the election of 1761 he wrote that 'during the next few years disintegration set in among them: a few turned courtiers under Bute, some joined the Rockinghams, another batch joined Chatham in 1766'. But his early writing did not extend much after 1762 and he never corrected his account from the biographies of careers of the Tories of 1761 by the various contributors to the volumes of the *History of Parliament* issued under the editorship of Romney Sedgwick and of Namier and Brooke. These biographies yield a very different account from that found in standard 'Namierite' texts. Of the Old Tories only twelve allied themselves to the opposition which arose from the end of 1762, sometimes in association with Newcastle and Pitt, to which number may be added a further four who settled down later with the opposition. Against these sixteen must be set the 'few' turning 'courtiers', who prove to be forty-four Tories who became supporters of government and a further eight who preserved their independence at first but eventually became supporters of North. Two Tories followed Bedford and two adhered to George Grenville, while eight pursued erratic courses and the remainder died or left Parliament too soon for classification. If the unclassified thirty-three, the erratic eight and the four Bedfordite and Grenvillite members are left out of account, the sixty-eight remaining Tories elected in 1761 may be divided into fifty-two who moved to the 'court' side under George III against sixteen who gravitated to opposition except, when associated with Rockingham or Chatham, during these leaders' ministries of 1765–6 or 1766–8.[e]

Over three-quarters of the Tories whose activities we can follow in their biographies thus accepted the amnesty offered by George III because their party's ancient preference for monarchy could now be indulged alongside an equally deep-rooted and continuing antipathy for the fallen Whigs. The respected Tory member for Oxford University, Sir Roger Newdigate, wrote at about the time of the king's accession: 'I like the King and shall be with his ministers as long as I think an honest man ought.' But Newdigate could never love 'tyrant Whigs'; nor could that other crusty Tory, Sir Armine Wodehouse, of a Norfolk family who proudly retained their Toryism throughout the eighteenth century: 'Those of the complexion I have been trained in [he wrote on 19 July 1767], must always honour Lord Bute for many reasons, but particularly for taking from 'em that brand which has been upon 'em the last two reigns, of excluding 'em from being concerned in Government, and their families from the minutest degree of attention . . .'. Most Tories, whether they sought the fruits of office or, like Wodehouse's Suffolk counterpart Rowland Holt, 'accepted of no place, or applied for any', continued after 1760, as before, to hold themselves aloof from the Old Whigs.[15]

A notable exception to the Tories' general support for the court from 1762 onwards arose out of their recent record of reformist endeavour. This concerns those occasions, few but spectacular, when Tories could be found voting against the court on what one politician of an earlier age had described, in connection with the Tories in George I's reign, as 'topics of liberty'. The career of John Wilkes from 1763 found many Tory government supporters voting for 'Liberty' in the general warrants and Middlesex election cases despite their customary adherence to the ministry. Also under the heading of libertarian causes comes Grenville's Election Act, 1770, and its renewal in 1774. But the Tories were at pains to demonstrate that there was a difference in quality between their abhorrence of the Whig opposition and their occasional objection to court dictation on taxation or other (as they saw it) matters concerning the liberty of the subject. Such was the case in 1770 when Sir William Bagot stated their reasons for supporting Grenville's bill against the court. Bagot took occasion to distinguish, by very strong marking of party, his and their friends opposition in this case from that systematical opposition of gentlemen of a quite contrary description, he declared that he and his friends kept their attention solely to measures, and not to men; that they desired to support the constitution only as settled at the Revolution in church and state – while they saw others aiming to wound the constitution through the sides of the ministry.[16]

A more succinct, if hostile, account of this speech stated that: 'Sir W. Bagot in a set speech supported the Bill, and answered for the Tories . . . and characterized the Tories as a body who disinterestedly supported Government, &c. &c. &c. &c. who were friends to the Monarchy as limited by law, to the Church as it was established by law.'[17] The libertarian issues which arose during the earlier part of George III's reign should not be allowed to obscure the reality, revealed in lists drawn up by party managers and used by the *History of Parliament*, that the great majority of the Tories elected in 1761 voted steadily for the court, year in and year out, in the dozens of divisions each session to which the government Whips invited them.[f]

The Old Tories who supported George III's ministries were too few to form a government party by themselves. For the leadership and most of the placemen element a different type of material had to be found. This was available in those Whigs who were willing to work with the king on his own terms. That these men came to be called 'Tories' by their recent friends, the Old Whigs, is a misnomer, though one which in many cases had some basis in political logic. In its original connotation 'Tory' had meant supporter of monarchy and the title now proved a useful pejorative in this sense. Moreover, many of George's ministers and other officeholders came from what have sometimes been called 'service families', those with a tendency over several generations to gravitate to government positions. As such, they tended to be the descendants of Tories who had changed party under George I and now ranked as Whigs of a sort, though regarded with suspicion even before 1760 by those of their fellows who could boast purer descent from the Whigs of the Revolution era.[18] Bute himself was the son of a known Jacobite.[19] In the course of George III's reign many Whigs with (in the eyes of the Old Whigs) tainted origins came to the fore – Egremont and Grenville, North and Shelburne to name but a few of the more eminent representatives of sometime Tory families. Men whose forebears had only with difficulty acquired a claim to be considered Whig could not abandon the name lightly, but they provided an important element of a new governmental party which the Whig opposition called Tory.

Underpinning the new generation of top ministerial talent after

1760 there emerged the rank and file of a new court party, castigated in contemporary literature as the 'King's Friends'. This group was built up under Bute and survived into Grenville's ministry, though Grenville regarded it as a rival not amenable to his own influence; after a struggle he succeeded in getting rid of one of the most important members, Bute's brother James Stuart Mackenzie whom the king had insisted on placing in control of Scottish patronage, but in doing so Grenville brought about his own early dismissal. During the royal negotiation in 1765 for the support of the Old Corps under Rockingham, writes Professor Brewer, 'The King's Friends . . . were determined on the substance of power as well as its shadow, and would treat only as a party'.[20] Nevertheless, some of them, including Stuart Mackenzie, were excluded by Rockingham, and neither they nor the king forgave this action. From the first, George III would have preferred Pitt to Rockingham and, though Pitt had demurred, the King's Friends were careful to keep him informed of their master's discontent at his 'absolute submission' to Rockingham and continued desire for a Pitt ministry.[21] Under Rockingham the King's Friends who remained in office formed an autonomous group who voted against the ministry in divisions on the Stamp Act Repeal and other issues. The repeal débâcle and fall of Rockingham gave the King's Friends a new fillip of confidence, and Dr Langford points out that by the end of 1766, in the ministry of Pitt as Earl of Chatham, 'almost all those numbered among the King's Friends had been taken in'.[22] Chatham's ministry soon followed Grenville's and Rockingham's into oblivion but the former 'Buteites' were now established as an élite body until the second Rockingham ministry was formed in 1782; Stuart Mackenzie regained his office from Chatham's ministry onwards, and although Bute himself ceased to play a part after 1766 his protégé Charles Jenkinson, of Tory family, emerged by the 1770s as a leading figure.[g] Together the King's Friends and Old Tories helped to form the ministerial party which emerged as the alternative to the Whigs of Newcastle and Rockingham.

Despite the Old Tories' support for any government which enjoyed George III's favour most ministers, as we have seen, eschewed the title 'Tory' when applied to themselves. When Lord North took office in 1770 he continued this practice. Sir Lewis Namier and those who followed his lead went further than a denial of North's 'Toryism' by claiming that it was this minister, rather than Rockingham, who was the true inheritor of the Whig tradition of Newcastle's Old Corps. 'Newcastle, Hardwicke, etc.', wrote Namier, 'so far from being the spiritual ancestors of the Whig opposition of, say, 1780, were the direct forerunners of Lord North, who served his apprenticeship as the trusted young friend of New-castle'.[23] This unlikely paradox bears little examination. Namier offered no evidence for his assertion other than the statement that Hardwicke's and Newcastle's families joined Lord North. Inter-esting though this fact is, it is atypical. Hardwicke had risen by ability rather than inherited wealth, and his sons needed incomes from officeholding. Newcastle's political heirs consisted of his first cousin once removed, Thomas Pelham, together with Pelham's two sons in Parliament. Pelham could not, as he pointed out, drown his seven children, and he continued to hold household and other posts after the fall of the Rockingham ministry in 1766, though his family returned to the Whig party soon after the fall of North in 1782.[24] To consider the Yorkes and Pelhams as transmitters of Whig tradition, rather than the many Revolution Whig families who remained with Rockingham in the 1770s, just will not do.[h] Nor is it possible to consider these two families as typical of most of North's colleagues and supporters in the 1770s. Those who surrounded this minister were of the type which had been favoured since the accession of George III, men from families with a strong service tradition and often also of pre-1714 Tory descent like North himself. In 1771 the office of Lord Chancellor was filled by Henry Bathurst, son of Bolingbroke's old crony, the first Earl Bathurst. Gower, a Whig only since the 1740s, became Lord President while Weymouth, the grandson and namesake of a Tory of Anne's reign, served North in various capacities. Jenkinson, with strong Tory connections, con-tinued to hold a succession of posts culminating with the secre-taryship at war in 1778. With such men as John Robinson and Grey Cooper as Joint Secretaries of the Treasury and William Eden, of an old Tory family, in a series of appointments the second rank, too, was well stocked with men who did not accept the title Tory but were hardly to be considered as mainstream Whigs. In matters of patronage management North may have learned in youth from Newcastle the techniques which were the common stock of any eighteenth-century government. That Newcastle's Old Corps Whigs were the 'direct forerunners' of North's ministry in any other sense would have been as unwelcome a concept to those ministerialists who denigrated party government as to those opposition Whigs who upheld it.

The Whigs and Old Tories in support of North's ministry drew closer together during the American Revolutionary War. But the final stage of the unsuccessful British campaigns saw a withdrawal of support by some Old Tories and others elected since 1761. Noel Hill, member for Shrewsbury or Shropshire since 1768, explained that though 'educated in Tory principles' he could no longer continue to prop up the government.[25] The leader of the group was Thomas Grosvenor, a wealthy Old Tory hitherto in independent support of North's ministry. The group as a whole, led by Grosvenor and Hill, swung decisively to support of the younger Pitt when his first administration was formed in December 1783.[26] Pitt's two ministries, detailed in chapters below, mark the gradual transformation of the Pittites into the Tory party of the early nineteenth century, a process which was not completed and fully admitted by its members until some years after Pitt's death. The accession of the more conservative Whigs under Portland to the ministerial ranks in 1794 was an important landmark in the process by providing politics with a single party of conservatives. Historians have seen the drawing together of the Pittites under Portland's leadership from 1806 as healing internal wounds and demonstrating that Pitt's and Portland's former followers were a party in their own right, out of office as well as in.[27] Returning to power in 1807 they united, by the beginning of Liverpool's ministry in 1812, nearly all the elements which had served under Pitt. By 1819 Croker could recount with pride the principles for which he conceived they stood, 'principles of morality, loyalty, respect for constituted authorities etc., – in short, *Toryism*'.[28]

In the development of Whig party and ideology from George II to George IV there was no hiatus, even partial, in use of the party name. On the contrary, the term 'Whig' was the boast of the main opposition party under George III and was also claimed by many other politicians until the popularity of the rival title 'Tory' was re-established in the early nineteenth century. The essential link between Walpole's and the Pelhams' Old Corps of Whigs and the party of Fox and Grey was the Rockingham Whig party of the 1760s and 1770s. Though dismissed by Namier as a mere 'connection' differing little from other such connections, the Rockinghams included among their leadership not only Newcastle himself until his death in 1768 but the majority of the great Revolution Whig families. Consisting at core of a closely associated web of aristocratic dynasties the party increasingly differed in size and importance from connections such as those of Bedford, Grenville and Chatham, and succeeded in attracting the all-important support of a large number of independent Whigs. The Rockinghams made good their claim to be *the* Whig party by surviving as such after the disappearance of other groups as separate entities.

Newcastle's Old Corps Whigs, by the time of their fall from office in 1762, were accustomed by almost half a century of officeholding to think of themselves as a governmental party. Nevertheless,

neither Newcastle and his elderly associates nor others too young to
remember the struggle against Queen Anne's Tory governments
were unaware of the basic principles of parliamentary opposition
pioneered by the first Whigs and the Junto. Newcastle, as we have
seen, had been ready to go into opposition in 1757 (not for the first
time) and would almost certainly have done so if he had not
succeeded in forcing George II to accede to pressure. Far less was
the duke deterred five years later when his resignation was followed
in due course by the dismissal of other Whig leaders, and a purge of
'Pelhamite innocents' at lower levels, on the instructions of Bute.[i]
Namier's belief that Newcastle and other senior Whigs disapproved
in December 1762 of their younger colleagues' desire to go into
immediate opposition has been dismissed by Dr O'Gorman:

> Kinnoul, for example, quoted by Namier, may well have disliked
> the blundering initiatives of the young men and feared a chal-
> lenge to the aristocratic leadership of Newcastle's connection but
> had Sir Lewis's quotation of the letter in question been somewhat
> more extensive it would have appeared that Kinnoul did *not*
> oppose the principle of opposition at all.

O'Gorman points out that 'the old Whigs, as well as the "Young
Friends", accepted the principle of opposition', and that even the
conservative Hardwicke differed from the younger men on the
timing rather than the legitimacy of setting up in opposition.[29]

Nor can it any longer be maintained that there was any change in
the nature of Old Corps Whiggism due to an infusion of Tory
personnel and ideas in the ranks of the Rockingham Whigs. The
twelve or so Tories who transferred were hardly a significant proportion either of the Old Tories or of the Rockinghams. Neither of
the Rockinghamites cited by Namier as Tory converts, Sir William
Meredith and William Dowdeswell, is a convincing example.[30] The
History of Parliament shows Meredith as a fringe Rockinghamite
who began to drift away from the party in 1770 and took household
office for four years from 1774, while Dowdeswell and his father are
shown as having sat in Parliament as Whigs before 1760, though the
younger was sometimes classified as Tory and was clearly highly
independent.[31] Even less convincing than alleged discontinuity
by reason of the presence of Tories in the party is the supposed
inheritance of Tory ideas making the Rockinghams, according
to Brooke, 'the true spiritual heirs of the Tories'.[32] It is certainly the
case that after 1762 the Newcastle–Rockingham Whigs supported
many country demands put forward by the Tories in the foregoing
period; not to have done so would have been highly unusual and

indeed unique in the conditions available to an opposition party in the eighteenth century. But to regard the Rockinghams as spiritual heirs of the Old Tories on the ground that along with more important policies they exhibited a stock 'country' programme, one adopted by every Whig or Tory opposition since Shaftesbury and the first Whigs in the 1680s, is to exaggerate the extent of the Rockingham party's country commitment and to ignore the distinctive nature of their avowedly Whig inheritance.

The Whigs led in opposition by Newcastle after 1762 and by Rockingham, with much advice from the older statesman, from 1765 regarded themselves as exponents of the true Whig tradition even though many of the pre-1762 party chose to stay in office or follow other leaders. Those thus excluded from the Whig paradise were understandably resentful and could point to the relatively exiguous survival of Old Corps men among the Rockinghamite ranks in the Commons by late in the 1760s. However, lack of continuity of personnel in the Commons was not restricted to the Rockingham Whigs, for MPs of all types returned before George III's accession formed only two-fifths of the membership of the House by 1768.[33] The real continuity of the Whigs lay not in the changing Commons but in the group of peers around Newcastle and Rockingham who, together with their personal adherents in the Lower House, provided a permanent core of the party. If the Russells, among the great Whig families, still ploughed their own furrow, the Rockingham Whigs could boast the adherence of the whole Cavendish clan, led in the Commons by three brothers of the late Duke of Devonshire. Valuable and active members of the party were the Bentinck and Keppel descendants of William III's Dutch favourites, carrying the titles of Portland and Albemarle. Along with allied peers, such as Rockingham's friends Scarborough and Monson and the Cavendishes' brother-in-law Bessborough, these families formed a closely knit cousinhood of shared interests and views with a formidable claim between them to speak for Revolution Whiggery. Family or other close relationships centring upon the aristocratic leaders made the fifty or sixty most committed members of the party in the Commons after 1768 a powerful and united body, flanked by about double that number of other opposition voters of varying degrees of party commitment.[34] Great Whig gentry like the Yorkshire magnate, Sir George Savile, could be almost as closely involved in Rockinghamite policy-making as the inner circle of peers, and dozens of his type voted regularly for the Rockinghams, as their fathers had done for the Old Corps. It was this acquisition of the all-important independent Whig voters in large numbers, as much as the 'Revolution' descent of aristocratic

leaders, which in the eyes of contemporaries marked out the
Rockingham party from other Whig groups and ensured its gradual
enlargement while the others disappeared as independent entities.

If the future lay with the Rockinghams this was not always
obvious in the 1760s, when several other splinter groups from the
old Whig party also existed. But though the 'personal parties' of
Chatham, George Grenville and the fourth Duke of Bedford
bulked large at times only the first still survived by 1771; both
Grenville and Bedford were dead and their followings joined
North's government. The Grenvilles formed an independent group
from 1765 to 1770. Despite the clash of wills with the king over
control of government which characterized their leader's ministry
of 1763–5 they were natural government men. As one percipient observer remarked, just after Grenville's death in 1770, the majority
of his friends had 'never embarked with great cordiality' upon
opposition, and within weeks of that event they were swept up by
North.[35] The 'Bedford gang', usually closely associated with the
Grenvilles in the 1760s, were often described as the political mercenaries of the day, willing to sell themselves to government to satisfy
their considerable appetite for office. The family under the fifth
duke did not join Rockingham permanently until the latter stages of
the American War. Until then the Grenvilles and Bedfords were
often closely associated with each other and isolated from Chatham
and Rockingham on a number of points concerning American
policy and the career of John Wilkes. Chatham's following of a
dozen or so members made up in oratory and extra-parliamentary
appeal what they lacked in numbers. In the House of Lords their
principal leaders were Chatham himself, by now a legendary figure,
and his principal aide and successor the Earl of Shelburne. Most
prominent of Chatham's friends in the Commons was Colonel Isaac
Barré, whose 'savage glare to one eye' and harsh speech affrighted
timid listeners. All Chatham's associates had to subscribe to their
leader's anti-party sentiments, born of the days when the young Pitt
had so frequently run foul of the Old Corps. Shelburne explained
that Chatham 'did not cultivate men because he felt it an incumbrance, and thought that he could act to more advantage without
the incumbrance of party'.[36] Such views put the Chathamites
ideologically very close to the opinions of George III himself,
though differences of personality and policy kept them apart for
most of the time. In his sympathy with the American colonials
Chatham found some common ground with Rockingham, especially after the latter's more wholehearted espousal of the American
cause around 1776.

But differences between Whig groups in the 1760s do not tell the whole story. References by men of all political shades illustrate that contemporaries saw the era in terms not so much of isolated groups as of fragmented parts of the Whig party seeking reunion amid the welter of new issues raised since George III's accession. The assumption that there was one Whig party, temporarily disunited but capable of reconstitution, was a natural one in the light of party tradition. The logical step was, in the Duke of Richmond's words, 'to reunite in party, to hold steadily together, and by acting upon true Whig principles, to recover the weight and party of the Whigs'.[37] The ideal did not come about. Though all opposition Whigs united in blaming the king for the breakup of the party by a policy of divide and rule, their divisions were partly of their own making. Such incidents as Grenville's and Newcastle's failure to support Pitt in 1761, Pitt's refusal to join Rockingham in forming a ministry in 1765, and Rockingham's attempt to prevent his friends from propping up Pitt's administration after 1766 were signs of the impracticality of reunion. Negotiations to find common ground finally failed in 1767–8, and the transitional ideal of reunion cleared a way for the revival of a Whig party centred not upon all surviving Old Whigs, but on the gravitational pull of the Rockingham party.

It was the ideal of reunion of all the Whigs which encouraged Newcastle and Rockingham to take office in the ministry of 1765, hoping that Pitt would join them later and hoping, too, that George III after the failure of the Bute and Grenville ministries would bow to the necessity of reinstating the status quo of about 1760. The Rockinghams' first impulse towards a new policy of narrowing the party base and cutting down royal influence came after the 1765–6 administration as a result of the desertion, as the Rockinghams saw it, of the King's Friends during the passage of the Repeal of the Stamp Act. George III's refusal to countenance dismissal of the culprits convinced the ministry of the king's personal complicity in the affair, and his encouragement of Bute and the Friends before they took their celebrated action is now clear from his correspondence with Bute, 'as to my friends differing from Ministers where they think their honour and conscience requires it, that I not only think right, but am of opinion it is their duty to act so; nay I think it is also incumbent on my Dear Friend to act entirely so also'.[j] Bute himself led the dissident King's Friends in the House of Lords against the ministers' stated policy. The Rockinghams' belief that they must control the monarch grew from about this time. Their new outlook took form in a memorandum drawn up by Dowdeswell in 1768. In any further negotiation for office, he wrote, conditions should be demanded of the king, who must deal with Rockingham in person. George III should be told bluntly that public misfortune 'must be imputed not to the influence of particular persons but to the prevalence of a political principle which says that the power of the Crown arises out of the weakness of the Administration'. If a ministry were formed by the Whigs they should not – as in 1766 – 'maintain the pageantry of an Administration an hour after it is divested of its necessary weight in the Closet and its necessary power in other places'.[38] Such ideas, broadcast increasingly in the Rockingham Whigs' polemics, hardened the party line. From 1769 the leaders' efforts were largely directed towards securing the support of independent Whigs and winning opinion outside Parliament. The greatest of several pamphlets commissioned to lay the case before the public was Burke's *Thoughts on the Cause of the Present Discontents* in 1770, pronounced by Rockingham to be 'a fair state of our principles'.[39] The pamphlet did much to formalize the somewhat inchoate ideas developed by the party. Burke predictably belaboured 'the court system', and his playing down of Bute's personal role served to focus blame on the king himself. Many of Burke's phrases, including his concluding vision of a coming 'dead repose of despotism', left no room for misunderstanding. Nor did he spare the rival Whigs who, he claimed, either sought places rather than pursuing principles or, in the case of Chatham, decried the value of party unity altogether. Some of Burke's most famous invective was reserved for the section of the pamphlet where he described Chatham's ministry of 1766–8. If the pamphlet was a considered step away from the concept of re-union of the Whigs, and toward a revived ideology of party opposition, Rockingham believed that these developments were implicit in the party's experiences since 1765.

Following Burke's assertion that the crown's influence, dead as prerogative, now resided in patronage the Rockingham Whigs focused their attacks in the 1770s increasingly on 'the influence of the crown'. Particularly open to attack were the Civil List, popularly supposed to be the source of more secret bribery than it actually was, and the placemen. The king's own role in politics was not spared. Charles James Fox, when he joined the party, did not shrink from reminding the Commons that in 1688 'ministers were forgotten, and the prince alone was punished' – words for which George III never forgave him.[40] But if the party was consciously reviving the aristocratic Whig tradition of criticism of monarchy it also contained a genuine element of respect for liberty. Whiggism for Savile was to support 'the noblest half of liberty and power, that of doing good' and to restrain them from doing ill.[41] Charles Turner, another independent supporter of the party, even extended this concept by calling for an amelioration of the game laws, stating flatly that 'as being a Whig he could not but reprobate them'.[42] The cause of America called for the Rockingham Whigs' sympathy, like that of the Chathamites, not simply because the colonists were at odds with George III but because their political ideas seemed to be those of the Whigs' own revolution a century earlier. What Professor Brewer has seen as 'a determined unwillingness to use force to keep the North Americans within the empire' which characterized the Rockingham Whigs' thought as early as the 1760s was indeed an enduring trait in party thought, responsible for the light hand with which the Americans had been handled for several decades before 1760.[43] After several years of war with the Americans most Englishmen, however originally chauvinist, had come round to this same point of view. Towards the end of the war the Whigs in opposition were popular in the country and made marked advances in the open constituencies during the 1780 election.

The alliance of Rockingham's large and Chatham's tiny followings did not outlast the American War. The Rockingham Whigs were increasingly dominated by the ideas of party unity based on historical precedents to which Burke and other writers constantly pointed, ideas which Chatham and the younger Pitt always found distasteful. Chatham, a Whig himself, had often courted Tory support. Pitt, though an 'independent Whig' by his own description, could hardly be expected to stomach the attitude of such hardcore Foxites as Thomas William Coke, who claimed to have entered Parliament when he was told that a Tory might otherwise represent Norfolk, and that 'at the mention of a Tory . . . my blood chilled all over me from head to foot, and I came forward'.[44] The Whigs, for their part, could not accept the ideas for parliamentary reform with which the Pittites began to toy from the later 1760s. Chatham himself cautiously accepted the need for more county members to increase the 'honest and independent' element in the Commons. His son adopted some aspects of the extreme proposals drawn up by reformers, including the removal of some closed boroughs, a programme unwelcome to the great borough owners surrounding Rockingham. The followers of Rockingham and Chatham parted company permanently within three months of the fall of Lord North's ministry of 1782. The Rockingham–Foxite Whigs, in their two short periods of office in 1782–3, carried out their intention of forcing their chosen ministers upon the king and carrying through most of their programme of 'economical reform' directed at reducing crown patronage. Pitt not only became further involved in the cause of parliamentary reform but also, by taking office from December 1783, helped George III to rid himself of the Whigs.

The party was thereby condemned to nearly half a century of

further opposition, except during the ill-starred Talents ministry of 1806. The insuperable obstacle to the Whigs' return to power was the dual unpopularity brought about by their antipathy to monarchy, acceptable to the nation only during the last stage of the American War, and their resistance to borough reform. Despite their genuine attachment to liberty and support for many reformist causes other than a sweeping reform of the parliamentary system, they lost the sympathy of the electorate in 1784 and failed to regain it in subsequent general elections. None were more aware of this loss of appeal to the public than the Whig leaders themselves. Among several attempts to remedy this situation, including the great improvements in party organization, Fox's political instinct led him to call for removal of the Protestant Dissenters' remaining disabilities while younger members of the party led by the young Charles Grey began in the 1790s to press for borough reform. The conservative British reaction to the French Revolution put an end to these and other reform campaigns during most of the war with France, but from 1807 the demands of an increasingly vociferous band of Radical Whigs revived reformist pressure. For a time Fox's successors in the party leadership, even Grey, avoided further commitment to the reform of Parliament in the conditions of the Napoleonic War and postwar depression. But Grey's reluctance in the middle decades of his career to undertake this task until the party arrived at a consensus should not obscure the fact that Parliament's system of representation was only one aspect of a whole range of reforms pressed by the party, including amendment of the penal laws and trade legislation, abolition of the slave trade and the raising of the political disabilities on Protestant Non-conformists and Roman Catholics. Parliamentary reform itself was not forgotten, and the measure which finally carried it in 1832 has been shown to exhibit the same philosophical basis as Grey's abortive proposals of the 1790s.[k]

Notes: Chapter 3

a   Hill, *Growth of Parliamentary Parties*.
b   The often-quoted protest by the ministry to the prince regent in 1812 that 'the present administration is, as every administration in this country must necessarily be, a Whig administration' sounds a little shrill and should be considered in context. The memorandum in which the protest occurred was concerned to bolster the regent's wavering political allegiance to the drafters shortly after he had continued his father's appointments and broken his Whig affiliations of thirty years' standing. There had been recent taunts of desertion in the opposition press, and the ministers were concerned at the possibility of a new veer on the prince's part towards his old friends, or at least towards a coalition; hence the attempt to provide him with the argument that in continuing his father's ministers he was

supporting a Whig administration (A. Aspinall, *Letters of King George IV*, Vol. 1, p. 143).

c   Hansard's analysis of 1821–2 shows that of 658 members 320 voted regularly for the Tory ministry, 226 for the opposition, 89 did not vote at all and only 23 cast votes on both sides (*English Historical Documents*, Vol. 11, p. 254).

d   The principal exponent of the view that English Toryism was more Jacobite than has been supposed is Eveline Cruickshanks, *Political Untouchables*.

e   See Appendix. The above calculation receives interesting confirmation from Dr O'Gorman: 'in the various "States of the House" drawn up in the 1760's and on the critical issues separating out supporters from opponents of the court three or even four times as many old Tories supported the court as opposed it', *Emergence of the British Two-Party System*, p. 45.

f   The Tories' adherence to the court party extended to those occasions during voting on the repeal of the Stamp Act when the Rockingham ministry was deserted by many placemen who took their cue from the king. On the Old Tory voting Dr Langford writes: 'The turnout of the Tory party against the repeal of the stamp tax was a marked feature of the divisions of February 1766. The names as they appear in the lists appear like a roll call of the Tory families' and 'Namier's suggestion that 34 Tories voted in favour of repeal is speculation "on a *pro rata* basis"; it is also quite out of line with the comments of contemporaries' (Paul Langford, 'Old Whigs, Old Tories, and the American Revolution', in Peter Marshall and Glyn Williams, eds, *The Atlantic Empire before the American Revolution* (1980), p. 123 and n. 68).

g   Jenkinson entered Bute's service in 1761 as under secretary of state and was shortly afterwards elected for Cockermouth in the interest of Bute's prospective son-in-law, Sir James Lowther. Jenkinson's family had represented Oxfordshire as Tory members for the last three generations, and he was Bute's principal successor as parliamentary butt for the Whig opposition. Jenkinson held a variety of offices of the second rank until the early nineteenth century. He was father of Robert Banks Jenkinson, who, as second Earl of Liverpool, became from 1812 to 1827 the first admittedly Tory Prime Minister since Anne's reign.

h   For some of the leading Whigs who remained with Rockingham after Newcastle gave up leadership of the Old Whigs see p. 46.

i   See below, pp. 98–9.

j   Sedgwick, *Letters*, p. 242. See also below, pp. 114–5.

k   Professor Ellis has stressed the continuance of an underlying Whig tradition of parliamentary reform from Grey's bill of 1792 to the first Reform Act in terms of an attempt to clear away corrupt practices and thereby strengthen aristocratic influence and leadership: Harold A. Ellis, 'Aristocratic influence and electoral independence: the Whig model of parliamentary reform, 1792–1832', *JMH*, vol. 51, on-demand supplement (1979). Similar conclusions about Whig political philosophy are reached by Abraham D. Kriegel, 'Liberty and Whiggery in early nineteenth-century England', *JMH*, vol. 52 (1980), pp. 253–78.

PART TWO

The Early Parties in Decline

CHAPTER FOUR

A 'Broad Bottom' without Tories
1742–47

When the Tories agreed with the opposition Whigs in December 1741 to combine in bringing down Walpole's ministry they did so for a variety of motives. The Jacobites among them were acting upon the latest instruction from their absent and erratic master 'James III'. The non-Jacobites who probably formed a large majority acted from more complicated reasoning. Like many Whigs they were dissatisfied with the ministry's drift towards hostilities with France and with the neutralization of the electorate of Hanover. Further, the recent death of Sir William Wyndham and the elevation of Edward Harley to the Lords as third Earl of Oxford deprived the Tory party in the Commons of its pro-Hanoverian leaders, making its members more inclined to listen to Jacobite spokesmen. But most of all the main body believed, on the authority of such Broad-Bottom Whig spokesmen as Argyll, Chesterfield and Dodington, that there was a genuine opportunity of attaining office in a non-party coalition. On Walpole's resignation such an arrangement appeared to be on the point of achievement. At a meeting which took place on 12 February 1742 in the Fountain Tavern, a Tory social and political centre in the Strand, well over 250 parliamentary Tories and opposition Whigs, including 35 peers, assembled to hear the Duke of Argyll deliver what Oxford described as a 'declaration for a coalition of parties for altering measures for bringing in the Tories as well as Patriots into place without distinction of party, called the Broad Bottom'.

Only a few of the Whigs at this assembly were aware that the case for a true 'Broad Bottom' was already lost, and that Walpole's henchmen had already come to terms with William Pulteney's set of opposition Whigs for the formation of a ministry in which the Tories would play little or no part. This clandestine arrangement became manifest within a month of the Fountain meeting, however, when the king refused Argyll's recommendation that Sir John Hynde Cotton should be given a place on the Admiralty Board. George II correctly suspected this rising leader of the Tories to be a concealed Jacobite. Cotton, for his part, was reported to be unwilling to join the government unless more Tories were appointed. Almost overnight new lines formed in Parliament. Argyll resigned his new posts and, together with the Broad-Bottom Whigs still out of office, drew even closer for the moment to the Tories. Pulteney's friends joined the surviving Walpolites in an ostentatiously Whig ministry.[1] Although future years were to see further movements in the stately minuet of Whig cliques in and out of office, the continued exclusion of the Tories ensured their survival both as a party and as a rallying point for opposition.

The ministry was broadened only sufficiently to include the Pulteneyites. Walpole's place as First Lord of the Treasury went to Spencer Compton, Earl of Wilmington, a relatively recent adherent to the former opposition. Pulteney's associate Lord Carteret took one secretaryship of state and Newcastle retained the other. Newcastle's able brother, Henry Pelham, remained Paymaster but Samuel Sandys became Chancellor of the Exchequer with two of Pulteney's other followers, Sir John Rushout and Phillips Gybbon, also on the Treasury Board. Pulteney himself took a seat in the Cabinet but chose to remain without office, underlining his claim to have been disinterested in his late opposition. Walpole's friends thus had a minority of the 'efficient' offices, but this disadvantage was more than offset by their preponderance in the Cabinet as a whole where thirteen members surviving from the old ministry, including the increasingly formidable Lord Chancellor Hardwicke, confronted five Pulteneyites. The two elements which formed the new ministry were to differ increasingly, but they shared a strong antipathy for the Tories. Pulteney openly thanked God that he was no longer in alliance with them and in their power. Carteret 'now affected a zeal for the party's exclusion from public employments'. Sandys spoke for all the New Whigs, as the Pulteneyites came to be called after their admittance to office, when he said: 'As to the Tories he had always an ill opinion of them and knew them well. He hated them, and they hated him, and always opposed him when he acted with them.' The Walpolites were no less emphatic. Professor Owen writes that Walpole himself, Newcastle and Hardwicke, 'all urged the necessity of maintaining government on a strictly Whig basis'.[2]

In Parliament a closing of ranks was visible immediately after the ministerial changes. Some 40 New Whigs joined the government contingent in the Commons alongside more than 250 of Walpole's Old Corps supporters. Observers who had long witnessed the Pulteneyites' onslaughts on the fallen minister noted grimly that these men were now ready to block the appointment of a committee of inquiry into his former conduct. The committee had to be conceded, but its reports were largely ignored by the ministry. By the end of the session punitive action against Walpole was stifled in the interest of ministerial unity and stability, though at the cost to the New Whigs of further loss of the popularity they had enjoyed in opposition.[3]

The opposition's attempts to pursue their old bête noire were thus frustrated, but they were still formidable with a strength of some 150 Tories and 80 dissident Whigs.[a] Their best strategy lay in enhancing their numbers on particular issues by attracting support from among the government's usual independent Whig supporters. Such issues arose when the perennial 'country' matters of place and pension bills were considered. Old Egmont, a veteran spokesman of country Whiggery, had warned Sandys when the New Whigs came to office that 'the nation would expect some popular bills'. Both place and pension bills were accordingly allowed by the ministry to pass in the Commons, as they could be comfortably defeated in the Lords where Carteret now led the government peers. But the resort to the government's safe majority in the Upper House did not allay the anger of the Tories and opposition Whigs against their former comrades. Oxford wrote that Carteret 'voted against the bill though he had always spoke for it when he was out of office'. When the New Whigs attempted to silence criticism by introducing a new and attenuated place bill for excluding certain commissioners and other governmental officials from the Commons after the end of the existing Parliament they obtained little credit for it. 'A sham bill and of no use', noted the same observer tersely. But, as had been the case for many years, Tories and opposition Whigs could have little hope of effective action when they could not agree among themselves except on a narrow range of 'country' activity. A new attempt by the Tories to obtain the repeal of the Septennial Act could not attract sufficient support from among the dissident Whigs to ensure its success even in the Commons.[4]

Though the new ministry survived its first session some strengthening was clearly desirable. Pulteney, regarded by the Walpolites as an unreliable ally and by the opposition Whigs as a traitor, was persuaded under pressure from the king to accept the Earldom of Bath, thus leaving Sandys as leader of his group in the Commons. But the removal of Bath left the government in greater need of a spokesman to face the rising orators of the opposition, and attempts were made to secure Cobham, whose followers in the Commons included William Pitt, George Lyttelton and the brothers Richard and George Grenville. Cobham accepted military advancement for himself, and Lord Gower accepted a Cabinet place, the first overt Tory to do so for many years. By his action Gower enabled his associates Bathurst, the latter's son Henry, and Sir Charles Wyndham, son of the late Tory leader William Wyndham, to take their first steps towards Whiggery.[5]

For the moment, however, the loyalty of both Cobham and Gower to the government remained problematic. During the summer of 1742 the ministry's conduct of affairs decisively pushed its new supporters back into the arms of the opposition, especially when 16,000 Hanoverian troops were taken into British pay in flagrant disregard of British public opinion. Cobham, simmering uneasily at the thought of good British money being spent on Hanover, moved towards laying down his recently acquired military posts. Tories drew closer to Whig dissidents in preparation for renewed parliamentary attacks. In the western shires a political tour was made by Cotton, the Tories' undisputed leader in the Commons since Shippen had largely retired from activity after the fall of Walpole.[6] Cotton visited not only Tory MPs but also such dissident Whig stalwarts as Dodington.[6] Prospects for opposition appeared good, in regard to both its own unity and the hope of driving a wedge between the old and new sections of the ministry.

But when Parliament reassembled in November the expected onslaught proved insufficient, even though opposition speakers were early joined in debates on the Hanoverian troops issue by Pitt and Lyttelton, or 'Brutus' and 'Cassius' in current court parlance. Pitt delighted his audience and enlarged his reputation as well as greatly enraging George II by reflections on the inconsistencies of the dual role of king and elector. The Tories joined zestfully in the baiting, with forceful backing for Cotton from Sir Watkin Williams Wynn and one of their younger leaders, the recently elected Sir John Philipps. However, government speakers rallied their waverers even on the employment of the Hanoverian troops, defending the measure as necessary to prevent partial demobilization. A series of opposition attempts to revive the committee of inquiry and to bring a new place bill met similar ill success. Only in widening the rift in the ministry did the opposition campaign show signs of success. For though the New Whigs voted steadily alongside the Old Corps their activity served only to strengthen their ministerial rivals. Without Pulteney in the Commons it was Pelham who clearly emerged as the government's principal speaker. Sandys shared Pelham's labours but, subjected to virulent attacks from his erstwhile companions in arms, was left battered and discredited.[7] The apparent solidarity of the government forces in fact barely survived the second session of Parliament after Walpole's fall. Even before Sandys's humiliation in December 1742 Pelham was being ceaselessly encouraged by his old mentor to take the lead in the Commons. Pelham, urged Walpole, should take the opportunity of the usual eve-of-session meeting of government supporters at the Cockpit to assert himself:

> Under you [he wrote] all the independent Whigs will list and unite; no man can answer for or secure a zealous and cordial union of the Whig party, if anybody takes upon them the lead that they know have been instruments, and active, in destroying the Whig party for twenty years together and have brought it into such danger that the Tories think they have now an opportunity of making a push for the whole.[8]

Such encouragement found a willing response. That the Pulteneyites should presume to give orders to those whom they had so long and so bitterly opposed was more than Walpole's Old Corps of Whigs could stomach. And Walpole knew, none better, that this solid body was a force in its own right, willing to hear good advice, eager for good leadership, but stubborn and recalcitrant when its leaders adopted courses which appeared inimical to traditional Whig causes. The Pulteneyites' recent defence of Walpole himself would never be enough to convince the Old Corps of their reliability or integrity.

Of the 'court patriots' (to use Walpole's contemptuous description of those who had abandoned the Patriot cause for that of the court) the most important, now that Bath's self-denying gesture had kept him from office, was undoubtedly John, Baron Carteret. Having entered the House of Lords as a Hanoverian Tory in 1711 and become a devotee of Whiggery only after the accession of the House of Hanover, this politician was an easy target. The favour he had found with George I did not endear him to his Whig rivals. Throughout his active political life Carteret was regarded as a concealed Tory, and he had never been admitted into the closed circle of the Old Whig believers. Typical of contemporary comments was that of the Rev. H. Etough, who noted soon after Carteret's appointment in 1742 that[9] 'proofs of the adherence of his original Tory principles and inclinations had been numerous, but he now affected a zeal for the party's exclusion from public employments'.[c] Nevertheless, Carteret's outstanding abilities now made him a formidable challenger to the Walpolites in the closet. Further, his willingness to carry out a system of war alliances among the German princes, whose language he spoke fluently, made him within a few months of his appointment a close confidant of George II.

More exposed were Pulteney's old associates of the former Patriot opposition in the Commons, Sandys, Rushout and Gybbon. These three often outvoted and overruled the physically ailing Wilmington at the Treasury. But with their parliamentary position weakened after their unpopular defence of the ministry against their former comrades, the initiative had passed from them even before unmistakable signs of Wilmington's illness became visible in the spring of 1743. Their future in the office could only be secured by a court stroke, that of securing Bath's appointment as Wilmington's successor. Before the First Lord's death in July both Bath and Pelham staked their claims for his office with the king, who was resting after his victory at Dettingen. George wavered under strong pressure from Carteret on Bath's behalf, but eventually accepted the truth that the Old Corps would not follow Bath.[d] By August, Pelham was installed as the new First Lord. For the moment he was not also given the post of Chancellor of the Exchequer as Walpole had been, and Sandys, Rushout and Gybbon remained at the Treasury. But Pelham's fear that he might be challenged at his own board ensured that there could be no more future for Bath's men than for Bath himself.

Before the support of the Pulteneyite Whigs in the Commons could be dispensed with some substitute votes had to be provided. Thus the autumn was occupied by a negotiation between the Pelham brothers and the Broad Bottom. Walpole's advice in this endeavour, however, was against the admission of Tories or the withdrawal of Old Corps' support for George II's electoral mercenaries to suit the Broad Bottom. The veteran statesman dismissed as a chimera Newcastle's fears of a rival juncture of Pulteneyites with the Tories; he had too often exploited their mutual dislike to be unsure on this point. Even Bath, wrote Walpole, could not reconcile the unreconcilable: 'it will be utterly impossible for him to show the king any method of bringing the Tories into that system that must be the foundation of all his interest. The distinction of Hanover and England is too much relished by them to imagine that any consideration will bring them into the support of Hanoverian measures.' Giving in to George's wishes concerning the Hanoverian troops would not, Walpole further counselled the alarmed Pelhams, alienate the Old Corps, since Tory attacks on Hanover 'will provoke the Whigs and engage them to go further than they would naturally be inclined to'. But the king himself must be made well aware of the Whigs' service: 'shew him the unavoidable necessity there will be of dissolving this parliament if he departs from the main body of the Whigs; and let him see the consequences of going to a new election in the height of the war, which will certainly end in a rank Tory parliament'.[10]

Despite Newcastle's qualms Pelham took Walpole's advice. After long years of subordination to his elder brother the First Lord was now ready to assume leadership. He saw the Broad-Bottom Whigs' representative Chesterfield and delivered an unacceptable ultimatum. The Hanoverian troops must remain in British pay until the war ended. Moreover, the Pulteneyites could not be removed for the moment unless they opposed their colleagues. Finally, Pelham stated that though opposition Whig leaders might have some posts vacant at the moment he would 'not take in the few Tories proposed, upon the coalition, but only upon a personal foot, and that even he would rather have 'em without their followers than with, for fear of offending the old Whig corps'. Chesterfield concluded that a 'treaty' could only be obtained 'sword in hand'. Gower and Cobham resigned their political offices and the Tories and Broad-Bottom Whigs prepared for Parliament determined to 'blow the Hanover flame to the height'.[11]

Although the Pulteneyites were spared for the moment, their position was now sufficiently weak for Pelham to feel he could afford to strengthen his control of the Treasury and lead in the Commons at their expense. Sandys had to relinquish the chancellorship to his rival in December 1743 accepting instead a peerage and post in the royal household. Rushout was likewise replaced in a new Treasury commission. The new commissioners included Henry Fox, whose abilities made it impossible to overlook him any longer, and by securing control of this body Pelham greatly strengthened his hold on government patronage.

For the moment, however, the king's favour continued to protect Carteret in the office of northern Secretary and to retain the other New Whigs in their new places. A further year was needed before their position could be finally eroded, thus making possible the juncture of the Pelhams and the Broad-Bottom leaders. In the Commons the opposition began their campaign, directed by an *ad hoc* joint committee consisting of three Tories and three Whigs. One member of this body, Pitt, excelled all other opposition orators in the bitterness of his attacks in the Commons on Carteret as 'a Hanover troop master', but he was careful to refer to the Pelhams as 'the amiable part of the Administration' for their known reservations about the policies of the king and his Secretary of State. In January 1744 the government majority in favour of retaining the Hanoverian troops was reduced by 22 votes compared with the previous year, with no fewer than 138 Tories (of a possible 147) voting alongside 88 opposition Whigs, against the ministry's 271. Throughout the session the paucity of the New Whigs' voting strength became even more apparent as the ferocity of the Broad-Bottom attack and the popularity of its causes grew. The Pelhams' awareness of the unpopularity of Carteret's policies gave them confidence to use their majority in the Cabinet to defeat him and to fire a warning shot for the king's attention. When Carteret concluded a convention committing British resources to Queen Maria Theresa his rivals greatly outnumbered the Secretary's four votes. As the centre of activity shifted to private negotiations in the summer the Pelhams renewed their approach to the opposition spokesmen, including some of the Commons joint committee together with Bedford, Chesterfield, Cobham and Gower.[12]

Before the commencement of the 1744 session the Pelhams' planning was complete, with Carteret's maxim that 'give any man the crown on his side and he can defy everything' due to be exposed as a hollow boast. In November the Pelham brothers and two-thirds of the Cabinet combined in support of a memorial, drawn up by Hardwicke, demanding that the king should dismiss the Secretary. Several of their number visited the Closet to argue a jointly prepared case stating the ministry's inability to carry unpopular Hanoverian policies in the Commons for a further year. The king's protests, even when joined with those of the heir to the throne, proved unavailing. Overtures from monarch and prince to the opposition in an attempt to save Carteret were instantly rejected, and the ministers hung grimly together while their weaker members were summoned and unsuccessfully browbeaten by royal father and son. Carteret had to go, along with other New Whigs, pitied by few. Arthur Onslow, a popular and already long-standing Speaker of the Commons, recorded approvingly that 'this Parliament has torn two favourite ministers from the throne'. The parallel between Carteret's case and Walpole's nearly three years earlier was clear. Carteret, though not defeated in the Commons, would have seen his policies rejected if he had remained for a further session.[13]

There was, in truth, a consensus of public opinion against the fallen Secretary. Pitt had refused his offers 'for fear of losing the people', while Pelham dreaded loss of control of a Commons which ultimately responded to national pressure.[14] It was left to Newcastle to elaborate their fears in a statement of constitutional practicality which was, in its cloudy way, a forerunner of doctrines of ministerial responsibility. The threat of resignation was the Pelhams' only alternative to sharing the blame for policies of which they did not approve:

My opinion [he wrote to Hardwicke] is always the same, that the only means to act effectually for the public and honourably for ourselves is to remove the cause and author of all these misfortunes, or to continue no longer ourselves, since we should in some measure be answerable for all the general conduct of the ministry though we should not be in a condition to direct affairs according to our own opinion and judgment.[e]

The king was forced not only to give up his preferred minister, but also to accede to an undignified stratagem concerning the employment of the Hanoverian troops, whereby they were no longer kept on the British pay-roll but were paid indirectly by the Treasury.

The reconstruction of the ministry in late 1744 was intended by the Pelhamites to put an end to the existing opposition, but this aim reckoned without the Tories. Despite the considerable preponderance of Tories over Broad-Bottom Whigs most of the more important offices vacated by the removal of Pulteneyites went to the Whigs. Chesterfield became Lord-Lieutenant of Ireland, Dodington took the post of Treasurer of the Navy, and Bedford headed a new Board of Admiralty with his friend Sandwich and the rising young Cobhamite, George Grenville, among his colleagues. Only Pitt was too obnoxious to the king to be considered. From among the Tories, Gower received back the Privy Seal, Cotton was given the post of Treasurer of the Chamber, and Philipps joined the Board of Trade. Most Tories, however, remained suspicious of any pact with the Pelhams. Horace Walpole noted that

several Tories have refused to accept the proffered posts: some from an impossibility of being re-chosen for their Jacobite counties. But upon the whole, it appears that their leaders have had very little influence with them; not above four or five are come into place. The rest will stick to Opposition.

Even those Tories who took office gave the ministry only limited support; they waited to see how many of their known desires would be granted.

The limited measure of co-ordination with the Broad-Bottom Whigs which had taken place over the last year had been unpopular with backbench Tories, who regarded the arrangement as an infringement upon the more democratic methods of arriving at Tory policy favoured by the more usual method of mass meetings at the Fountain. The negotiation with the Pelhams by a predominantly Whig Broad-Bottom leadership left an even sourer taste. In the long run only Gower himself and his few followers in the Commons^f were to remain loyal to the ministry, and they rapidly ceased to be regarded by their former friends as Tories. Cotton and Philipps, as Professor Owen notes, 'were more likely to follow the main body of the Tories than the main body follow them'. They joined Gower tentatively in expectation of further concessions from the ministry, which soon proved to be insufficient. The main difficulty was noted by Hardwicke in a paper for the Cabinet as early as December 1744 as arising from the Old Corps: 'By taking in the Tories the Old Corps of Whigs, who adhere to the present ministers, will think their party ruined or greatly endangered, be frightened and discontented and at last alienated from the Ministers.' The principal answer to this objection, he suggested, was that 'if this scheme be set about with discretion and the Old Corps of the Whigs see that no material Court power or Country influence is put into the hands of the Tories, their jealousies will be quieted and the alarm subside'. Little time elapsed before the Tories became aware of this attitude. One of their number was allowed to bring in a bill to make effectual an Act of 1732 which had been intended to provide that justices of the peace be qualified by the possession of land worth £100 a year in their county, but amendments had to be conceded in face of Old Corps backbench protests. The bill, wrote Yorke,

> was by no means agreeable to the Whigs, not only as it seemed to cast a general reproach on those of that party, with whom most of the Commissions were filled up, but as they apprehended it would be followed by a further concession in admitting the Tories into a larger share of that power, which would increase their influence in elections.

A bill for annual parliaments received no government support, and with its failure trouble mounted rapidly. While the Tories became disillusioned, the Whigs saw with alarm that the new Tory placemen continued to vote with their friends. 'On the first tinkling of the brass', noted Horace Walpole sourly in February 1745, 'all the new bees swarm back to the Tory side of the House.'[15]

The Tories' position hardened, probably early in January 1745, when Wynn and the Duke of Beaufort handed Gower a list of demands to be put before the government. These included the issue of new commissions of the peace in all counties to which 'all gentlemen of fortune be admitted without distinction' of party, the disenfranchisement of customs and excise officers, a place act, an inquiry into naval management, a reduction in the army when circumstances should permit, a 'spirit of economy', and measures 'consistent with the interest of Great Britain'. But many Tories doubted Gower's willingness or ability to act for them in obtaining concessions, and on 20 March Beaufort by-passed him by handing to Hardwicke an ultimatum demanding alterations in the commissions of the peace in six counties, as earnest of good intention. Beaufort added ominously that the Tories were 'desirous that the coalition should take effect and continue, but now very apprehensive that it could not, or words to that effect'. To give further emphasis to their point, the majority of the Tories voted the next day against a vote of credit for £500,000 required by the government. Philipps resigned and Cotton was reported wavering; in the event, the latter waited to be dismissed the following year, but he was henceforth reckoned as once more an opposition leader, along with Wynn, Philipps, Beaufort and Oxford. The ministry took hasty action, in conjunction with Gower, to issue new commissions of the peace in a number of counties, but though this appears to have been sufficient to prevent further overt demonstrations from the Tories for the remainder of the parliamentary session the rift continued to widen between Gower and the party.[16]

That Tory discontent did not manifest itself in complete repudiation of Gower before the opening of the next session was due to the Young Pretender's landing in Scotland. English Tories had no desire to be branded as disloyal to Hanover at this point. With some exceptions in the north-west they rallied to King George II; even the Jacobites among them refused to support Charles Edward when they learned that he had failed to bring with him the expected French army without which his attempt had little chance of success.

Another event which was delayed by the rebellion was a Pelhamite constitutional coup against George. The Pelham brothers and Hardwicke, together with most of their ministerial associates, were increasingly incensed during the early months of 1745 because George II continued to give every mark of confidence to the dismissed Carteret rather than to themselves. In May they warned the king of 'the impossibility of *our* opening another session of parliament' unless he conceived 'a more favourable opinion' of them. But the Pretender's presence in the British Isles put aside, for the moment, all lesser quarrels. The ministry remained in office to meet Parliament in October despite increasing evidence of George's clandestine attempts to replace them, and found very little resistance from the opposition benches. The most important criticisms of the government came from Pitt and the Grenvilles who, having given their support during the previous session on the understanding that Pitt and other 'cousins' would soon be allowed to share the fruits of office which some of the group already enjoyed, now calculated that the time had come to press their claim.[17]

But by the end of 1745 the Highlanders' foray into the English Midlands was past and the Pretender's cause was on the decline even in Scotland. Pitt's pressure in the Commons and behind the scenes provided the Pelhams with an occasion for the course of action they had already long contemplated. Coming to terms with Cobham by January 1746, on the basis of removing Carteret's remaining friends to make way for Pitt and other Grenvilles, they also agreed to accept Pitt's call for a reduction of British troops on the continent of Europe while the Pretender remained on British soil. They had for some months been collecting assurances of support from other ministers in case of their resignation. On 6 February Pelham saw the king 'to insist upon making Pitt Secretary at War', and on George's indignant refusal Newcastle and his fellow Secretary, Harrington, led the way of resignation, to be followed by Pelham, Bedford and Gower for the New Allies, Hardwicke, Fox, Devonshire and several other ducal ministers. Almost all members of the Boards of the Treasury, Admiralty and Trade declared their intention of following suit. Their total number was probably in the region of forty-five, and their next threat was not far from that of their leader Pelham, who told the king that he would avoid going into opposition 'as long as possible'.[18] The king shut himself in his closet and refused to see anymore would-be resigners who, in the words of one wag, 'were pouring in upon him with white sticks, and golden keys, and commissions etc'. He authorized Bath and Granville to form a government, but their efforts to obtain support in the Commons, even from the Tories, were without success. For forty-eight hours, another joker remarked 'that it was not safe to walk the streets at night, for fear of being pressed for a cabinet councillor'. The king, convinced at last of his chosen ministers' inability to govern, ignominiously called upon the Pelhams and other resigners to resume their offices. Cobham's requested appointments were made though, in deference to the king's wishes, Pitt became Paymaster-General, after a short interval, rather than Secretary at War.

In this new confirmation and extension of the 1744 ministerial reshuffle the Tories played no part. Apart from feeble protests from Chesterfield, no Whig attempted to revive the original concept of a cross-party Broad Bottom. Since November, Gower had virtually severed contact with the Tory leaders, and with the dismissal of Cotton in May 1746 they ceased to have any representative in office. Cobham now willingly agreed to the Pelhams' requirement that he drop his advocacy of places for Tories, for as Newcastle wrote in epitaph to the whole Broad-Bottom endeavour which now lay derelict: 'it was the dread and apprehension of taking in Tories that hurt us with our great friends in the House of Lords and the bulk of the party in the House of Commons. And it is those we must stick by; and it is those that have stuck by us'.[19] The Tories, disappointed of all hope of office, could undertake full opposition. Likewise now fully estranged from the ministry was the Prince of Wales, who with his household 'family' and the Pulteneyites had been in intermittent opposition since Granville's fall in 1744. The annihilation of the Young Pretender's cause removed a last barrier between the prince and patently harmless Tories who had refrained from supporting the Rebellion. The Pelhams appeared to have a stranglehold on the king. If the prince wished to avoid a like restraint when he came to the throne he might do well to look to that party which had traditionally been the support of monarchy and could now have no future monarch in view but himself.

In agreeing to return to office after Bath and Granville had admitted defeat in February 1746, the Old Corps and its leaders did not omit to present clear conditions in a minute for the king's acceptance. They could not serve, the minute stated, 'without being honoured with that degree of authority, confidence and credit from His Majesty which the ministers of the Crown have usually enjoyed in this country'. George must 'be pleased entirely to withdraw his confidence' from advisers 'behind the curtain' who made difficulties for 'his servants, who are responsible for everything, whilst those persons are responsible for nothing'. Surviving Pulteneyites, specified by name, were to be dismissed and replaced by Pitt and his friends. Garters were to be distributed by the king to 'give a public mark of his satisfaction' with the ministry. These conditions were carried out to the letter, save that two of Granville's friends were suffered to retain their household posts in return for his undertaking to remain neutral rather than join his friends in opposition.[20]

Although there were some later changes of personnel, the ministry was now settled on the basis of an alliance between Old Corps and New Allies, and within a year or so the king was largely reconciled with it. The process was eased when it became clear that the ministry had no intention of tampering with the king's personal fount of household patronage, that they would not unnecessarily humiliate him when he took his periodic stands on the disposal of governmental patronage, and that they would not trespass on his purely military appointments unless opinion in Parliament was likely to be aroused by his decisions. This *modus vivendi* was to last until Pelham's death in 1754, and in many ways until the end of the reign, though George II would have to be reminded once more in 1756/7 that when national considerations overrode his dislikes, as in the case of the emergence of Pitt as national leader and military arbiter, he must give way.

The ministry's strength was indicated in the first major vote in the Commons after its reappointment in February 1746. Pelham's scheme for a war loan was carried by over a hundred votes despite the opposition of most of the New Whigs along with the Tories. One month later, on 11 April, a government proposal to meet the cost of re-engaging Hanoverian troops was passed by an even larger majority of 133, with the prince's followers and many of the Pulteneyites this time supporting the court and leaving only 28 Whigs to vote with 94 Tories against the motion. Thereafter, however, the prince moved steadily towards an arrangement with the Tories, so that by January 1747 it was reported 'understood that the Tories were not to oppose foreign measures and the Prince to join them in opposing domestic ones'. The *rapprochement* between the heir to the throne and the Tory party was furthered by a general election. The prince had begun to make preparations for the support of 'popular bills' and secure seats for his supporters as early as October 1746, though he was taken by surprise when the government decided to dissolve Parliament in the summer of 1747 one year before this became necessary. The Pelhams' reasons for the move were summed up by Newcastle: the new opposition, though not yet formidable, might become so in certain circumstances; the none-too-successful peace with France which was now in prospect, or any 'reverse of fortune' would 'undoubtedly give strength to Opposition, raise some flame in the nation, and render the choice of a parliament more difficult'. The obvious course was to dissolve while circumstances were still favourable.[21]

The results of the election justified the ministers' decision. Neither the Tories nor the prince were popular. Vaguely worded government appeals to Tory supporters of the House of Hanover to desert their Jacobite friends and join with the Whigs could have no meaning in terms of sharing power or office but sounded moderate and served to remind electors of the recent rebellion.[g] The prince shared the unpopularity of the Pulteneyites, whose desertion of the Patriot cause in 1742 was widely remembered. Moreover, the early dissolution came before any understanding between Tories and prince could come to fruition in a definite understanding so that there was little co-operation in elections; many constituencies saw the Tories withholding support from the New Whigs and the prince's candidates. At the same time the support of the Broad-Bottom

Whigs, which many Tories had enjoyed in the last election before Walpole's fall, was now denied to them. At Bedford, where two Tories had been returned in 1741, the joint efforts of its duke and Gower now ensured that the Tories were defeated. In Cornwall the Tories and the prince's supporters were disunited and faced the influence of Lord Falmouth, who had recently joined the government, with the result that the opposition returned only nineteen members, or ten fewer than in 1741. Walpole's friend Islay, now Duke of Argyll, ensured that in Scotland the opposition share of the seats fell from twenty-six to ten. All the constituencies of the London area saw government advances. Middlesex, with its county franchise and urban electorate, rejected the influential sitting Tory member, Sir Roger Newdigate, who had neglected to join the loyal county association during the '45, thus forcing him to wait several years before he could resume his long and distinguished career as member for the more cloistered constituency of Oxford University. Philipps, as a known Jacobite, did not offer himself for re-election. 'The eyes of the people are much opened by rebellion' commented a government diarist with satisfaction. Pelham wrote to his Treasury colleague Lyttelton that 'our elections have gone beyond expectation; and I will venture to say that Parliament has been chosen with less public expense on one side than any former one has been since the Revolution'. There were seen to be 351 government supporters returned, including the tiny handful of recent Tory defectors, against 92 opposition Whigs and 115 Tories.[22] The Rebellion and the snap election had reduced the Tory party to its lowest number ever, but its members were returned as usual for most of the English county seats and showed little sign either in the elections or subsequently in the Commons of diminishing their usual vigorous opposition.[h]

But a principal result of the election was that of providing the Tories and the prince with the final incentive to come to an understanding. During the first session of the new Parliament negotiation probably took place, while a working relationship in both Houses was resumed. On 4 June 1747 the prince made his first formal approach, though it was not until the following 6 February that the Tory leaders felt able to make an undertaking of support for him. The prince's promises, read aloud and then given in writing to a group of Tories for transmission to the party, were preambled by his statement of intention 'totally to abolish for the future all distinction of party' and remove all proscription when this should lie in his power. He further engaged his support for an effective militia to supplement the Tories' bugbear, the regular army, together with a place bill to exclude from the Commons all officers below the ranks of colonel and rear-admiral. There would be inquiries into the abuse of government offices, and justices of the peace would be appointed from among all those whose landed income qualified them for the position, regardless of party. Finally, the prince undertook to join no administration without previously obtaining these points, and to limit his own patronage and expenditure as future king by accepting no more than the present Civil List of £800,000. There was no reference to the Tories' desire to minimize Britain's use of German mercenaries, but they had already virtually given up this point for the time being in the tentative co-operation of the past session. Nor did the prince promise shorter Parliaments; but if he came to the throne determined to admit Tories to office on equal terms with Whigs this long-standing desideratum might, in any case, be a questionable blessing.[23] Frederick's undertakings were workmanlike and acceptable, and they provided a basis for closer co-operation between two elements of the opposition who had everything to gain from each other's help. Above all, they were the first definite move ever made by a member of the House of Hanover towards a reconciliation with the original party of the crown. Although Prince Frederick's early death frustrated his intention of personally raising the proscription on Tories and attempting to abolish the distinction of parties, his son George, 10 years old in 1748, was to honour the first and attempt the second when he came to the throne twelve years later.

Notes: Chapter 4

a   As there is, as always, some disparity between different contemporary estimates and between these and the best modern analyses the party strengths are given here in approximate round numbers. Some modern figures are given in *History of Parliament, 1715–1754*, Vol. 1, pp. 53–5, and in Owen, *Rise of the Pelhams*, pp. 113, n.1, 144 and *passim*. Because of low attendance the theoretical strengths of both government and opposition were rarely reached in divisions.

b   Sandys referred to Cotton as 'leader of the Tories' in September, 1742 (Add. MS 47,089, p. 2).

c   On the other hand, Henry Fox recorded in August 1743: 'Some think he must intend to turn Tory and have a new Parliament', Ilchester, *Fox*, Vol. 1, p. 99.

d   Even if the Pelhams had been willing to accept Bath, pressure from the Old Corps would have made them unable to guarantee support if, as one supporter put it, they were to 'disoblige two hundred and odd of your old Whig friends by putting the man in the world they dislike the most at the head of the Treasury' (Add. MS 32,700, f. 335).

e   The text quoted is from Newcastle's letter (Add. MS 35,408, f. 54) as received by Hardwicke, and differs somewhat from the form quoted in Coxe, *Pelham*, Vol. 1, p. 175, particularly in including the words 'according to our own opinion and judgment'. Coxe's version is from Newcastle's draft or copy, and Newcastle's addition to the letter as sent makes more explicit the tenor of his statement.

f   These were his son Lord Trentham, his brothers the Hon. Baptist Leveson Gower and the Hon. William Leveson Gower, Charles Gore and Thomas Gore.

g   The Cobhamite George Lyttelton's *A Letter to the Tories* (1747) called for 'all the Tories who wish well to this establishment and all the Whigs who love the constitution, united in the administration and defence of the government' (p. 17). Similar appeals had been made in 1745–6 – see *A Letter to a Tory Friend* (1746), by Samuel Squire, Bishop of St Davids.

h   Professor Owen correctly comments that '. . . Tory opposition in the 1747 elections was as widespread and as resolute as it had been in the past. The "breaking of the old Tory party" by the formation of the Broad-Bottom, earnestly desired by Newcastle and confidently prophesied by Chesterfield, had come to nought' (*Rise of the Pelhams*, p. 309).

CHAPTER FIVE

Court Whigs, Tories and 'Leicester House' 1747–60

The Pelhams' emergence as unchallenged leaders of the government Whig party by 1746 meant an end to experiments which involved the appointment of individual Tories. The term Broad Bottom, when still used, now denoted only the presence of some non-Old Corps Whigs in the government. Though the Tory party supported Pitt after he took high office in 1756, none even then achieved a significant place in administration. Until George III's accession in 1760 the Old Corps led by the Pelhams remained the only permanent element in office. They differed from Walpole in their style, recognizing as he had never done the need to buy off some Whig dissidents from time to time. But former New Allies who were allowed to take office rarely did so for an extended period. By conniving in keeping Tories from the table they were able to enjoy its crumbs; the jealousy and calculation of the Pelhams kept them from the main repast.

Down to the death of Henry Pelham in 1754 the leading element in the administration was a triumvirate of Pelham himself, Newcastle and their confidant and mediator, Hardwicke. The latter described their relationship to his son, who recorded the following account:

> The elder of the brothers is quickest in his temper, but the other retains longer, frequent uneasiness in the Cabinet, disagreeable to their friends and everybody else. [Hardwicke] had carried the bucket between them for many years, almost at the end of his line. Sir R[obert] W[alpole] had the art early to detach Mr. P[elham] from his brother, told the former he should be his successor.

Much of Newcastle's discontent during the years of their ministry must have arisen from the promotion of his younger brother over his head. There is little doubt that Pelham as First Lord expected and obtained the dominant position to which his office entitled him and was not averse from checking Newcastle even in the latter's own domain of foreign affairs. Newcastle possessed, however, a shrewd intelligence and long experience at his task, and Pelham was not always right in judgements outside his immediate competence. Newcastle's quarrels with a series of fellow Secretaries have often been remarked to his detriment, but it is noticeable that these differences arose from Pelham's successful determination to avoid sharing the lead in the Commons with a Secretary of State, so that Newcastle was always challenged by fellow Secretaries in his own House. Hardwicke's mediacy between the brothers often took the form of protecting the volatile Newcastle, whom he preferred, from the more restrained but more powerful and effective brother.[1]

Internal differences among the leading ministers did not affect their solidarity in facing the new opposition. All were conscious that, again in Hardwicke's words, 'Tories and P[rince] of Wales party lie by and wait for opportunities to blame'. Despite growing war-weariness the ministry's large majority in the Commons continued to carry government business until the conclusion of the indecisive Treaty of Aix-la-Chapelle in 1748. Thereafter, peacetime economies in the army and navy together with Pelham's scheme for consolidating and lowering the rate of interest on public debts led to the satisfaction of the backbench Whigs. Frugality and financial integrity, practised by Pitt at the Paymaster's office as well as by Pelham himself, were appreciated by country members and the nation alike. So, too, were measures to make rebellion impossible for the future, including the disarming of Scotland, an extension of the system of military roads and fortifications begun after the '15, and a social reorganization of the Highlands to reduce the powers of the clan chieftains.

After the Pelhams' defeat of Bath and Granville Whiggery was doing what it was first designed to do: destroy the Stuart cause and reduce the power of monarchy itself. And this was being done, *mirabile dictu*, with the compliance and even, as the years passed, the approval of the Hanoverian monarch himself. The landed class was tolerably satisfied, and the Established Church was co-operative. Looking at the scene in historical perspective a Whig clergyman set out in a pamphlet his paean of praise for his ideal Whig, who bore a close resemblance to a Pelhamite: 'A true and consistent Whig is a balancer, a mediator; always against violence, and against encroachment from whatever quarter it is derived – under a Henry VIIIth, a Charles or a James he is a Countryman; under a William or a George he is a courtier.'[2]

If the government Whigs had the comfort, despite their frequent internal quarrels, of a sense of homogeneity and a shared tradition, their opponents had no such advantage. The Whig element among them centred upon the members of Prince Frederick's following, numbering eighteen in the Commons after the general election and rising to twenty-eight by the time of his death in 1751. To these were added the remnants of the Pulteneyites led by Rushout and Gybbon, and other dissident Whigs who were recruited from time to time. The prince did not always find the task of co-ordination easy.[3] The remaining Jacobites, a small and ever-diminishing band, refused to follow Cotton and Wynn into any working alliance with Frederick's Whigs, while at the other extreme Dodington, whose judgement of his best future prospects led him and his small group of adherents into the prince's camp in 1749, made no secret of his dislike of co-operation with Tories. Nevertheless, some measure of amity was gradually obtained so that the historian of the Leicester House opposition, Dr Aubrey Newman, considers that 'by the end of 1750 most of the Tory members had in practice allied themselves to the prince, and in his manœuvres in the Commons the prince could usually rely on their support'.[4]

In the first session after the election of 1747 the Tories were still debating their response to the prince's overtures of June. Their eventual reply, in February 1748, undertook that 'they will constantly and steadily use their utmost endeavours to support his wise and salutary purposes, that the Throne may be strengthened, religion and morality encouraged, faction and corruption destroyed, the purity and essence of Parliament restored, and the happiness and welfare of our constitution preserved'. But co-operation, even on the level of the last session of the former Parliament, was still slow to come, and Horace Walpole's assertion in December 1748 that 'to the great surprise of the ministry, the Tories appear in intimate league with the Prince party' somewhat anticipated intimacy. As Walpole himself was soon to point out, the Tories had not forgiven Egmont, the rising leader of the prince's party, for abandoning them on Walpole's fall in 1742. Nor, doubtless, had they forgotten the prince's similar action. But at an ostentatious joint rally at the St Alban's Tavern in May 1748 the Leicester House men – Egmont, Thomas Pitt, Sir Francis Dashwood and Henry Bathurst – declaimed alongside Wynn and the Tory peers Oxford and Beaufort, when the last-named lauded 'the stand that had been made this winter against so corrupt an administration, and hoped it would continue, and desired harmony'. The opening of the next session duly saw Cotton and Egmont speaking together against the Address, though the paucity of issues reduced them, in the opinion of their new ally Dodington, to minor cavils.[5]

A new stimulus was given to growing opposition harmony early in 1750 by the return in a by-election of Sir Roger Newdigate, who had defeated an opponent supported by the Jacobites at Oxford University. The mounting evidence of the waning of the Pretender's cause, even in the home of lost causes, was not lost upon Frederick's Whig followers. Egmont recorded his conviction in reference to one reputed Jacobite that 'if it were not for proscription there would not be a Jacobite in England'. Among the voluminous plans drawn up by Egmont for the first days of Frederick's expected accession to the throne exist lists of appointments and honours. These include most of the leading Tories: Oxford to have the Privy Seal, Cotton to be again Treasurer of the Chamber, Beaufort to receive the Garter, and the recent Whig convert, Bathurst, to be rewarded with the secretaryship at war. Lichfield, William Northey, the rising Commons spokesman Thomas Prowse and a number of other Tories were booked for future promotion. But the Tories had present as well as future needs, and Frederick confessed to Dodington on one occasion that 'the Tories wanted something to be done, and if he did not do something they immediately thought he was negotiating'. The Tories had had so many experiences of being first befriended and then deserted by Whig allies that they had little confidence in his sincerity. They might have had more confidence had they seen Egmont's papers, with drafts of Frederick's proposed first speeches as king expressing his determination 'to countenance and employ (without any distinction but that of merit) those who shall approve themselves most able' and 'to abolish those unhappy distinctions which have so long subsisted, and are productive of every mischief that can attend a divided state'.[6]

Well in line with his plans for the ending of proscription was the prince's firm intention, when it should be in his power, of cutting the royal link with Hanover, a measure most welcome to all Tories and many Whigs. To this end he proposed to make Prince Edward, his second son, Elector of Hanover when the boy grew up. Another move which would please the Tories would be the removal of the army command from Cumberland, much hated for the savagery with which he had put down the last remnants of the Rebellion. The decision to do this, the prince admitted, was taken on the advice of Bolingbroke. The old politician was enjoying an Indian summer of princely favour and had recently published *The Idea of a Patriot King*, first circulated in manuscript during Frederick's opposition to Walpole, as an encomium of the virtue of princes who ruled states undivided by parties or proscription. Altogether the Leicester House plans, including the prince's promises of 1747 to the Tories, were underpinned by his hope of removing the 'distinction of party' which he believed had been used by the Whigs to tame monarchy under George I and George II. As he wrote in his instructions for his eldest son Prince George, concerning his project for the separation of Hanover, the outcome would be that 'Jacobitism will in a manner be rooted out, and you will not be forced then to court your ministers for one job or another: as unfortunately your predecessors have been forced to do'.[7]

Prince Frederick's plans were far from being as futile as his early death has sometimes made them appear. By the autumn of 1750 his immediate prospects in opposition were improving by a negotiation with Pitt and the Grenvilles, whose detachment from the ministry would greatly weaken its debating strength. Pitt's genius had been restrained in 1746 by his appointment to a lesser office and the hope of more to come, but he could not afford to wait for ever; moreover, he was no party bigot and had imbibed from his Broad-Bottom experience an attitude to government not far removed from that of Bolingbroke or Frederick himself. Pitt's great clashes with Rockingham and Burke, the exponents of party, lay in the future, but his political vocabulary already contained the seeds of the dogma of 'measures not men' and he signalled his dissension from Pelham, by voting against the further reduction of seamen. If he had moved into opposition with the Prince of Wales the combination would have been formidable. But the scheme fell when Frederick died unexpectedly on 22 March 1751.

The official chief mourner at Frederick's funeral was the Duke of Somerset, formerly the Tory MP Sir Edward Seymour, grandson of his namesake the great Tory leader spokesman from Charles II's reign to that of Anne. A greater mourner was old Bolingbroke who, it was reported, 'acted weakly by showing a great deal of despair at the Prince's death'. But if the immediate expansion of Prince Frederick's party was thus frustrated, with his Whig supporters scattered and Tories left to their own devices for the moment, the value of his aspirations was not to be wasted upon Prince George or his future preceptor, Lord Bute, another of Frederick's supporters. By the time the younger prince attained his majority the *sine qua non* of his and Bute's intentions for the reign to come, like that of Frederick and Egmont, was to be the removal of proscription from the Tories with a view to the releasing monarchy from what they saw as a bondage to the Old Corps of Whigs.[8]

The immediate effect of Frederick's death was to strengthen the Pelhams and leave the opposition in disarray. His widow Princess Augusta withdrew from politics and saw her son's best interest as being reconciliation with the king. She was rewarded by being nominated regent in case George II should die during his grandson's minority. So strong did the ministry now feel that they allowed Newcastle to accelerate a long-standing quarrel with his current fellow Secretary. Bedford was attacked by the dismissal of his friend Sandwich from the Admiralty. Bedford immediately resigned, as expected, and was replaced by the more tractable Earl of Holderness while the loss of Sandwich was made good by Hardwicke's son-in-law, Lord Anson. At the same time the king was gratified by Granville's appointment to the dignified office of Lord President. Thus rewarded for not following his friends into opposition under Frederick, Granville proved to be a wise choice, adding knowledge and weight to the Cabinet's deliberations without again attempting to dominate. Granville was followed into the government's service by Gybbon and other old Pulteneyites. Bedford was accompanied into opposition not only by his own friends and followers but also by most of Gower's other than Gower himself, who chose to remain. The departure of the Gower clique gave more reason than usual to justify the ministry's resolution in the spring of 1751 'to have an entire Whig administration'.[9]

If the ministry was strengthened, the opposition was weak and divided. Although most of the Leicester House men chose to follow Augusta's lead and join the government, Egmont and a few followers continued to carry out what they saw as the late prince's work of opposition in conjunction with the Tories. But these, too, were affected by the new situation. Jacobitism as a focus for opposition was almost vanished since the failure of the '45 rising, with Philipps out of Parliament and Cotton nearing the end of his career. The principal Tory spokesmen were now Thomas Prowse and William Northey. But Prowse was on good personal terms with the Pelhams and Northey with Leicester House. The centre of what remained of a discontented 'reversionary interest' was now Cumberland, disappointed of his desire to control any future regency. But Cumberland was hated by the Tories and provided no possible focus of any opposition in which they could take a concerted part. Bedford moved close to the royal duke and lost no opportunity to attack government, but the Tories' dilemma was reflected in an increasing absence from Parliament over the next three years.

Opposition quiescence, however, could not entirely be taken for granted. When Parliament assembled in 1751 Cotton spoke against the Address and moved unsuccessfully, a few days later, to reduce the army estimates. Bedford signalled his move into opposition by opposing in the Lords a subsidy which Newcastle proposed to pay Saxony, to keep that electorate from alliance with the French. The Tories in the Lower House followed up with a motion against subsidy treaties in time of peace, but succeeded in rallying only 52 votes against the court's 182. Moreover, the Tories were deprived of Cotton's leadership by his death in February 1752. With him died the unaccommodating toughness which had characterized Toryism in the days when future Hanoverian court favour had seemed an impossibility.[10]

The death of a true Jacobite was followed by farce, a *cause célèbre* which was to have considerable repercussions. This affair began as a quarrel among those who had been entrusted with the education of the late Prince Frederick's sons. Lord Harcourt, the princes' governor, and their preceptor Thomas Hayter, Bishop of Norwich, accused sub-governor Andrew Stone of 'Jacobite connections, instilling Tory principles'. Others implicated included the brilliant Solicitor-General, William Murray, the only Commons orator who could be compared with Pitt and Fox. The charges were fanned secretly by the younger Horace Walpole to embarrass the Pelhams, against whom he held a personal grudge, and he later perpetuated the story of Prince George's alleged education in Jacobite principles. There was enough smoke to indicate possible fire. Murray had the disadvantage of a brother in the service of the court-in-exile, and a witness was produced to testify that some of the accused men had drunk toasts to the Pretender many years earlier. The fact that both Stone and Murray were numbered among Newcastle's closest associates added piquancy to the situation at a time when real political issues were in short supply. Richard Rigby, one of Bedford's men in the Commons, wrote to encourage the duke to take the matter up against the Pelhams 'if these zealous Whig brothers have been no worse [sic] than the dupes of three or four artful Jacobites'. Bedford duly made the best use he could of the matter, though all official investigations completely rejected the charges. The accused men retained their offices but they suffered, and were to continue to suffer, the sting of irrational prejudices. In Chesterfield's words: 'No reasonable man, I believe, thinks them Jacobites now, whatever they may have been formerly. But parties do not reason, and every Whig party man, which is nine in ten of the Whig party, is fully convinced that they are at this time determined and dangerous Jacobites.' Stone never again took government office, though he remained in the service of Leicester House, and Murray's career in politics proved subsequently to be a dead end from which he escaped only by becoming a celebrated lord chief justice.[11]

The session of 1752/3 saw little other political excitement. Lord Hardwicke's Marriage Bill, aimed at preventing clandestine marriages, aroused fierce opposition from Fox, who had made such a marriage, but did not divide Parliament on party lines. There also passed quietly into law a bill sponsored by Pelham to permit a very limited measure of naturalization to Jews, a concession to the Jewish financial community which was important in government credit operations. It was this measure, however, which provided an occasion for the fresh display of a traditional Tory stance.

Throughout the summer of 1753 Tory and opposition Whig politicians, with an eye to the general election due in 1754, publicized the Jew Act through the length and breadth of the country, fanning xenophobia to fever pitch. Fears of the 'monied interest', never absent from Tory mythology since the Revolution of 1688, and of incursions by the *nouveaux riches* into landed society combined with the party's resentment against residents of foreign origin who had been favoured by a succession of Whig governments.[a] Like opposition to the Act naturalizing Palatines in 1709, the campaign against the Jew Act was irrational but deep-rooted. Pelham repealed his measure in the autumn of 1753, and even so he did not entirely succeed in averting the wrath of the electorate. But he did not see this outcome. He died on 24 March 1754 and his death, like that of Prince Frederick three years before, brought about a new phase in politics.

Hardwicke explained to Archbishop Herring of Canterbury the problem of obtaining a suitable successor for Pelham at the Treasury: 'The opinion therefore which I, with my friends in the Cabinet, have formed, is that there is at present no person in the House of Commons fit to place entirely in Mr. Pelham's situation, with safety to this administration and the Whig party.' The king left the choice to the Cabinet, indicating a personal preference for Sir Robert Walpole's old friend, the Duke of Devonshire. But Devonshire did not see himself as a successor to Walpole and Pelham in the Whig leadership, and the Cabinet named Newcastle as the man to whom the party would rally. Pelham's death in the midst of his strenuous exertions for a general election made his brother's appointment a good one for immediate needs but exacerbated the equally important problem of finding a successor for Pelham as leader in the Commons. The obvious candidates were Fox, Murray and Pitt but all had drawbacks. Fox possessed, as the younger Horace Walpole believed, 'his parts and the Whigs and the seeming right of succession' but was not disposed to play second fiddle. He was offered a secretaryship but, on finding that Newcastle proposed to control patronage management in the Commons himself, refused it precipitously. Murray was suitable in many ways but, after his rough handling in the affair of the royal tutors, preferred not to invite criticism by taking a prominent position; as Newcastle pointed out to Hardwicke, the opposition 'conclude (and with reason) that if they can blacken him with the Whigs, we shall neither be able to employ him with success, nor *he* be willing to be employed, and in this they are in the right'. Pitt, though in some ways the best qualified of the three, was barred by the king for his hostility to Hanover and regarded with suspicion by the Old Corps for his former Broad-Bottom activities. After his eight years in minor office, acquiescent in the Pelhams' regime, Pitt's overwhelming potential for opposition oratory was overlooked for the moment. Having thus made the mistake of offending, in Fox and Pitt, the two most dangerous men in politics, Newcastle compounded his error by appointing to the vacant secretaryship his follower, Sir Thomas Robinson, an able and experienced diplomat but no performer in the Commons. When Devonshire pressed Hardwicke for at least Cabinet rank for Fox, to avert his wrath, even this was withheld.[12]

The ineptitude of these arrangements was masked for the moment by successful election results as Newcastle took over smoothly from his late brother. Government propaganda branded the Tories, exultant from their victory over the Jew Act, as 'Papists, Jacobites and bigotted Churchmen'. The Tories and Whig dissidents traded on the remaining ground swell of opinion against the Jew Bill but failed, by their quarrels, to emulate the advance of the Broad Bottom in the 1734 election following the withdrawal of Walpole's Excise Bill. The lack of co-operation between the Tories and dissident Whigs is exemplified in the débâcle at Reading where the Bedfordite, Richard Aldworth, was forced to withdraw in face of better-supported government Whig and Tory candidates.[13] In a straight party contest for Oxfordshire, where the Treasury and the Duke of Marlborough spent thousands of pounds on behalf of the Whigs while the Tories raised similar sums, the latter managed to achieve a double return of two Tory candidates against two Whigs. But, with petitions from the Whig candidates left to the partisan judgement of the House when assembled, few doubted the outcome. Newcastle's chief election manager, Dupplin, found only 106 Tories altogether among members returned, and classified only 42 of the Whigs as currently in opposition. Newcastle exulted that 'there are more Whigs in it, and generally well-disposed Whigs, than in any Parliament since the Revolution'.[14]

Optimism about the good disposition of the government Whigs proved misconceived in some cases. When the new Parliament assembled in November both Pitt and Fox chose the opportunity offered by election petitions to harass Newcastle and joined in overwhelming the unhappy Robinson. Pitt sounded a clarion call to resist 'the arbitrary edicts of one too powerful a subject'. The First Lord capitulated abruptly to the lesser opponent, and on 12 December Fox was bought off pro tem with a Cabinet place.[15] This brought some respite, especially when the Tories, defeated over the Oxfordshire election petition, momentarily showed some signs of following Prowse and Northey in adhering to the Princess Augusta's line in conciliating government. On 24 March 1755, after much confusion and hesitation, it was reported that 'the whole party' except for five or six Tories supported Newcastle's candidates against Bedford's over the disputed election at St Michael's in Cornwall.[16] But if Newcastle obtained temporary Tory support he gave little or nothing in return; and the shifting sands of the scene since Pelham's death were soon to move again. Secretary Holderness was occupied in directing a foreign policy in which the defence of Hanover in the renewed war which loomed over Europe had become almost as important to British diplomacy as it had been when Granville had held the seals. To this end two crucial subsidy treaties, with Hesse-Kassel and Russia, would have to be ushered through Parliament. The summer was therefore taken up with a variety of political negotiations to avert as much as possible of the wrath which such a policy would, as usual, arouse. By July, Newcastle and Hardwicke were dangling hopes of office before Pitt's eyes. Pitt, however, sensed a popular cause which he could use to force more concessions than were offered. He was already in the process of coming to an understanding with Leicester House where Princess Augusta, fearing that Cumberland's power was growing with the rising star of Fox, was now willing to join forces with the rival interest. And a junction of Leicester House with Pitt, in opposition to the Old Corps, offered far more to the Tories than Newcastle could ever promise.[17]

Soon after the meeting of Parliament in the autumn of 1755 the beginning of new lines on the political map was thus visible. The wavering Fox was steadied; he replaced Robinson as southern Secretary and Leader of the Commons. Pitt and the Grenvilles were dismissed, and Lyttelton was detached from them to take the office of Chancellor of the Exchequer. Dodington's five votes were bought by the office of Treasurer of the Navy, and Bedford's support was obtained for the ministry by places for Sandwich, Rigby and the younger Gower, who had recently succeeded his father as second earl. The Address to the throne revealed a new miscellaneous Commons opposition composed of Pitt, most Leicester House MPs, and most of the Tories. Pitt delighted the House by his scornful comparison of Newcastle and Fox with the Rhône and the Saône, one 'gentle, feeble, languid', the other 'a boisterous and overbearing torrent', together 'the comfort of each other'. The combined opposition, however, raised only 105 votes of whom, by the computation of a ministerial supporter, there were 76 Tories. And the handful of dissident Whigs rallying to Pitt proved to be not fully reconciled with the Tories, who were willing enough to vote against the Address on a Hanoverian issue but whose affinities were with the Prince George rather than with Pitt. 'The Tories hate both [Fox] and Pitt so much, that they sit still to see them worry one another' wrote Walpole.[18]

Reconciliation was essential, and the first step was taken by Pitt in December, when he gave his support to one of the Tories' favourite causes. This was the establishment of an effective militia, such as the late Prince Frederick had promised them, to reduce the expense of the professional army and to restrain the influence of its head, the Duke of Cumberland. In March 1756, however, the Tories again showed that their true predilection lay with Bute and the princess. When Pitt unwisely assumed that the Tories would follow him if he opposed a proposal for bringing Hanoverian troops to England as a precaution against invasion, even though it was made by Lord George Sackville who was *persona grata* at Leicester House, it was the young court which obtained Tory support. But for the time being the militia proposal had served its purpose of beginning an understanding between Pitt and the Tories. Henceforth they could see him as a practical means, providing that he worked in conjunction with the Prince of Wales, of breaking the hold of the Old Corps of Whigs upon politics. Thus Holderness could write after the end of session that 'the Opposition consisted of the Leicester House people; [*sc.*] the remains of the Old Opposition, and the Tories'.[19]

European events in 1756 drew the prince, Pitt and the Tories closer yet. Prince George reached his majority at 18 and was given a separate establishment in which Bute's leading role was formalized by the office of Groom of the Stole. The ministry's stock fell steadily as war broke out with France, and British diplomacy and arms met defeat; Austria came to terms with France, leaving Britain with Prussia as a less powerful and untried ally, while the French advanced in America. Admiral Byng failed to relieve the beleaguered garrison of Minorca, and the island was lost. In newspapers, petitions and addresses abuse was deluged upon the ministry, encouraged by Pitt and the Tories.[b] In October, Fox resigned, fearful of meeting the Commons and blaming Newcastle's interference there. Murray decided not to take the vacated post, preferring to go to the Lords as Lord Mansfield. Their desertion was followed precipitately by Newcastle's own resignation. These events, taking place while the ministry's enormous majorities in both Houses were as yet unshaken, were the outcome not only of the situation abroad but even more of Newcastle's failure since his brother's death to provide or allow firm leadership in the Commons.

Lack of any alternative now made inevitable a ministry headed by Pitt, increasingly the nation's choice and the only major politician unsmirched by recent military failures. But Pitt's solid refusal to share power with either Newcastle or Fox rendered his administration weak from the start. Taking one secretaryship for himself, he consented to retain in the other the incumbent Holderness, who regarded his task as now being 'to keep the door open for the [Whig] Party to have access to the closet, and to check the new people, in case they should mean to push their popularity and lower the crown beyond the bounds of decency'. The king made desperate attempts to avoid taking Pitt but bowed to the inevitable, comforted somewhat by the appointment to the Treasury of the fourth Duke of Devonshire, who had recently succeeded his father in the title. Devonshire was closest of the Whig grandees to Pitt, but remained equally acceptable to the Old Corps. Moreover, Pitt was circumscribed by sheer numerical shortage of acceptable supporters to fill offices; a commission replaced Hardwicke at the Chancery, Pitt's ally Henry Legge became Chancellor of the Exchequer and the Grenvilles took Admiralty posts, with Temple the eldest as First Lord, but otherwise most of the former ministers were retained, including Bedford, who had recently been appointed Lord-Lieutenant of Ireland, Gower and old Granville.[20]

Equally weak was Pitt's position in the Commons, where he could survive only by the Old Corps' unwillingness to incur the public odium of opposing him. But from the opening of Parliament in December it became clear that he was receiving in both Houses the support not only of Leicester House but of the whole Tory party. Fox wrote that Pitt 'has engaged the Tories . . . has Lord Bute and Leicester House absolutely'. And one of Pitt's supporters, Richard Lyttelton, boasted that 'the Tories are determined to attend one and all and support Mr. Pitt and his friends'. Nor, he added, had they 'hinted at any terms for themselves'; however, the whiff of a promise, if not of 'terms', emerges from Lyttelton's subsequent assertion of the Tories' confidence that public money, 'tho' some of it should go into Germany, will even there be employed to British purposes only'. Even without a provable commitment on Pitt's part, the late ministers' correspondence became full of speculation about the Tories' action. Lyttelton's brother and political opponent Lord Lyttelton wrote that 'the alarm has been taken so strong by the Whigs that if the Duke of Newcastle and my Lord Hardwicke would have joined with Mr. Fox to turn him out, it is certain they might have done it by this time, and may do it tomorrow'. Pitt himself, however, assured Hardwicke that he had made no promises to the Tories, and in the absence of appointments from among their ranks the Old Corps remained quiescent.[21]

The Tories themselves were in no doubt as to the wisdom of adherence to the Pitt–Leicester House alliance. At the opening of the session their leaders, assembling at their usual organizational centre the meeting room of the Cocoa Tree, sent out circular letters to demand their friends' 'early and steady attendance' in support of Pitt. Up and down the country they had already been highly active in addresses which were coming in, calling for parliamentary reforms, governmental purity and inquiry into mismanagement under Newcastle. Polemics suitable for the consumption of the populace were not, however, necessarily suitable material for practical politics. Pitt's intermediary with the Tories, Thomas Potter, made clear to them that a witch hunt was not possible. The majority of the party were willing to be reasonable though Potter expected that Sir John Philipps, now back in the Commons with his Jacobitism behind him, or 'any Tory friend of Fox's' might stir up trouble to embarrass Newcastle. The proposed inquiries were deferred in January 1757, as Rigby reported to Bedford: The language of the Tories is to drop all thoughts of it, lest it should hamper their new friends the new administration, in difficulties that might force them to quit. This is being steady to them indeed; but what is to become of their addresses and instructions, and above all their popularity under this acquiescence I cannot guess.'[22] But if the Tories thus compromised something of their popular stance, they derived solid advantages. In January 1757 a Militia Bill was again introduced and, with some modification from the Whigs, allowed to pass. The Act represented a considerable benefit to the Tories, who were enabled to participate on equal terms in the new militia.[c] They also had the considerable satisfaction of hearing Pitt speak of pursuing a strategy which Cumberland angrily denounced as the 'Tory doctrine of a sea war', putting Britain's major military effort into colonial enterprises. But Pitt could not entirely satisfy the Tories. Some refused their support when he also asked the Commons for subsidies for the German allies, and with the assistance of Leicester House they obtained an inquiry into the loss of Minorca: 'The Tories are to affirm that the ministers were very negligent; the Whigs, that they were wonderfully informed, discreet, provident, and active; and Mr. Pitt and his friends are to affect great zeal for justice, are to avoid provoking the Duke of Newcastle . . .', summed up the cynical Walpole. With Pitt backing furiously, as previously he had promised to Hardwicke, the attack foundered.[23]

At the beginning of 1757 Pitt was unready to risk his popularity by alliance with the Old Corps, but he recognized the weakness of his position if they should choose to go into opposition. By early April both he and Newcastle realized that events were throwing them together at an accelerated rate when the king, urged on by Cumberland and Fox, dismissed first Temple and then Pitt. Dismissal proved easier than replacement, as a succession of lesser politicians was approached and demurred. Clearly any ministry acceptable to the public must include Pitt. Outside Westminster, public opinion continued to run strongly in his favour, with a newspaper campaign and the 'rain of gold boxes' on him from London and many other areas orchestrated by his supporters and by the Tories.[24] The king at first reacted angrily when the Old Corps leaders, sensitive to public opinion, did not respond to his suggestion of their forming a government without Pitt. Newcastle agonized to his friends on the likely loss of their following, some to Fox and some to Pitt, unless he went into opposition to the king's intended patchwork administration. Hardwicke objected on 9 April to a 'formed general opposition' and advised following the middle way, 'to oppose wrong measures, and concur in right ones'. But even Hardwicke saw that 'this is not the political way to keep a party together' and that it could be continued only, at longest, 'to the end of the present session', and Newcastle made clear to the king, through Mansfield, that the Old Corps were likely to go into opposition. On 15 April Newcastle related Mansfield's report of his audience to Hardwicke, not without relish:

> The King then said, 'But why then will not the Duke of Newcastle promise me his support . . . Will he go into opposition?' – 'He will never do anything contrary to his duty and zeal for your Majesty's service' – 'But tell me your opinion, if the Duke of Newcastle should go into *opposition, would the Whigs of the House of Commons follow him*' – 'Since your Majesty commands me to tell you my opinion, I think they would.'

'That', continued Newcastle triumphantly, 'was a strong answer indeed and must have an effect. H.M. made no reply . . .'. The king was being 'forced' again, as in 1746, and he knew it. From this point events began to take a turn distinctly reminiscent of his attempt then to turn to Granville and Bath in order to avoid the appointment of Pitt, though this time the only political figures he could turn to were

Fox and no more distinguished a person than Waldegrave to head the Treasury. Waldegrave's account makes it clear that George expected the Old Whigs to go into opposition not later than the next session, routing any ministry which could be brought together.[25] To add to the similarity with events in 1746, Newcastle encouraged Holderness to resign on 9 June, with Rutland, Leeds, other old Pelhamites and Newcastle's young Yorkshire supporter, Rockingham, threatening to follow suit immediately.[d] The threat proved decisive, as on the earlier occasion, and the king capitulated. Within a few days a Pitt–Newcastle ministry was effected. Devonshire gave way gracefully to Newcastle at the Treasury, and Pitt and Holderness were reinstated as Secretaries. Fox acquiesced in the arrangements and accepted the lucrative post of Paymaster-General. Temple received the Privy Seal, making way for Anson at the Admiralty, while George Grenville and Legge regained their former places as Treasurer of the Navy and Chancellor of the Exchequer. Bedford took up Ireland again, and even Waldegrave was made happy with a Garter. Hardwicke declined to serve as Chancellor but took a seat in the Cabinet. After months of uncertainty a government was now formed which could pursue vigorous and, as it proved, highly successful war with France over the next few years.[26]

The first two years of the Pitt–Newcastle ministry saw little party controversy. Soon after the first meeting of Parliament, Chesterfield heard 'the Tories have declared that they will give Mr Pitt unlimited credit for this session'. Though given no share of office the Tory party displayed, while Leicester House continued apparently on good terms with the ministry, little overt sign of discontent. Pitt appears to have believed the substance of Hardwicke's later assertion that 'Pitt made the Tories his party'. In furtherance of this belief Newcastle was forced to make some unpalatable concessions, notably the inclusion of the Tories along with the Whigs in Treasury circulars calling members for attendance in Parliament. In return the Tories showed their often remarkable discipline by refraining from opposition to such unpalatable but necessary measures as subsidies to Britain's main German ally the King of Prussia. But even before the commencement of the coalition ministry the Tories' disappointment was visible to discerning eyes.[27] By 1758 Pitt's decision to send British troops as well as subsidies to Germany was bringing out some active discontent. This became more marked when the Whigs found their own sticking point over a revival of the Tories' desire to repeal the Septennial Act. This Tory attempt achieved little debate and secured only seventy-four votes, for the Whigs as a body could also cling to their traditional prejudices. By 1759 there were clear signs of strain between the ministry and a Tory party which was increasingly enjoying the open favour of the heir to the throne even if its support was not absolutely necessary to the coalition.[28]

Growing tension among his Tory allies in the spring of 1760 made Pitt force Newcastle to make one last concession, by withholding the Whigs from opposing Philipps' bill for strengthening the Property Qualification Act passed in 1711 by the last Tory ministry. But when Pitt and the Tories together supported a bill to extend the militia principle by promoting the militia in Scotland, Newcastle had seen enough. His manager Kinnoul (formerly Dupplin) wrote to him of spirited objections to both these measures from 'a noble band' and, in the Commons, from a 'flying squadron' of younger Whigs. Kinnoul complained of these elements that their 'refined speculations, and an excess of righteousness which measures every proposition abstractedly . . . will render any Government impracticable'. Newcastle, however, was sufficiently impressed by the party considerations put forward by this new generation of younger men to take credit for the rejection of the Scottish Militia Bill and, moreover, to state his intention of opposing in the next session the continuance of the English militia; he and 'the general sense of our Friends' were both opposed to it, he told Hardwicke, and it should be 'rejected by as great a majority as we did the Scotch militia'.[29] Newcastle's long-standing sensitivity to opinion in the Whig party, especially when this found expression not only in the Commons but also in his own House among such rising young men as Rockingham, drew him away from Kinnoul's more managerial viewpoint.[e]

As the Tories drew ever closer to the prince's court while at the same time strengthening their demands on Pitt as the price of their support, Newcastle and Hardwicke had an eye to the general election due in 1761, the first since Pitt had been in high office. Among other possible desires, Pitt might well want Treasury support for Tories in many constituencies. This being the case, Hardwicke advised his friend, the Secretary should not be given a share of government election management, though his friends should be cared for.[30] Because the death of George II took place in the autumn of 1760 the expected election was to take place in different circumstances from those envisaged by the Old Corps leaders, but it is clear from their actions and expectations while the old monarch was still alive that they did not share the view which held that parties had been brought to an end by the war with France; on the contrary, they were prepared for a return in the elections of the political status quo *ante bellum*. But even for Pitt the support of the Tories might be retained at too high a price when his alliance with Leicester House was rapidly becoming an encumbrance. For Bute was not sparing in the demands he made. Such impractical matters as the prince's desires for an independent military command in Germany and for the protection of Lord George Sackville after his disgrace at the Battle of Minden could be parried, but they left a coolness which provoked from the young heir to the throne the outburst to Bute that Pitt 'seems to forget that the day will come, when he must expect to be treated according to his deserts'. The final straw was provided by George's demand that Bute should be given the Treasury in the next reign. When Pitt made clear that he could not do without Newcastle in this office the prince was deeply mortified. Well before the prince's accession to the throne Pitt had cut all but formal links, while remaining unaware of the full extent of the antipathy he had aroused.[31]

From the strained relations of Leicester House with the ministry only the Tories could hope to benefit, and they were not unaware of their opportunity. The prince's indifference to the fate of Hanover had for some years been demonstrated by his 'family' in Parliament as openly as he dared. In this respect, therefore, the Tory party found Prince George even more congenial than his father, for Frederick's parliamentary opposition had usually stopped well short of overlooking Hanoverian interests. For the rest, some of Frederick's promises had already, as in the case of support for the militia, been honoured by his son; the remainder, including the all-important removal of the ban on Tory officeholders, could reasonably be expected. The journey back to favour which had begun for the Tories with their appearance in Frederick's lists of proposed appointments, and was continued by Pitt's provision of some increased local influence and place, was now approaching its long-awaited last stage – the removal of all proscription in the coming reign.

Notes: Chapter 5

a Despite the use made of this agitation by other opposition elements, its role as a party issue for the Tories and High Church clergy is emphasized by its historian, Perry, *Public Opinion, Propaganda, and Politics*, pp. 37, 70, 73, 85, 118 and *passim*.

b Notable was the stance taken by the Tory *Monitor* and *Critical Review* in pointing to ministerial rather than naval responsibility in the failure to relieve Minorca (Peters, *Pitt and Popularity*, pp. 48–9).

c J. R. Western, *The English Militia in the Eighteenth Century, the Story of a Political Issue 1660–1802* (1965), pp. 127–54. Professor Western also pointed out a meeting of parliamentary supporters of the militia in 1759: 'George Onslow sent Newcastle a list (which survives) of those who attended. The members of parliament present numbered forty-five, whom Onslow classified as twenty-three

Tories and twenty-two Whigs. Sixteen were county members and nine others came from "popular" constituencies with sizeable electorates. The proportion of Tories and of representatives of counties and "popular" constituencies was very much higher than in the Commons as a whole' (p. 123).

d   Holderness later recorded complacently that his resignation on this occasion, following Newcastle's line, was looked upon by their opponents as 'the declaration of the Party, and they concluded the whole strength of the nation was joining against them' (Add. MS 6832, f. 181).

e   Sir Lewis Namier drew from Kinnoul's letter, which he quoted extensively, the conclusion that his 'distrust of coherent groups, even when moved by Whig principles, was typical of Newcastle and his associates' (*England*, pp. 187–8), but does not appear to have taken into account Newcastle's actual reaction on the subject of the Scottish and English militias quoted above from his letter to Hardwicke of 16 August 1760.

CHAPTER SIX

The End of Tory Proscription 1760–65

> The ministry continued . . . the only difference of conduct I adopted was to put an end to those unhappy distinctions of party called Whigs and Tories, by declaring that I would countenance every man that supported my Administration and concurred in that form of government which had been so wisely established by the Revolution.

George III's private memorandum, with its close similarity to his late father's several statements of intention, sets the tone for the opening of the new reign on 25 October 1760. George believed, as had his father, that only by breaking the party pattern could the political independence of the crown be restored and the power of the Whigs broken. The time was ripe for ending the unequal alliance between this party and the monarchy. Ties which had held them together since 1714 were slack since Jacobitism had ceased to be a practical threat. A greater danger, the new king believed, lay in the Whigs' ever-increasing control of government patronage, not only perpetuating their own power but tainting political life. Salvation for the nation could come from rationalization at the hands of 'a good Prince', a brother ruler of the enlightened Frederick II of Prussia and Austrian Archduke Joseph. George's first preoccupation, though with no thought of reviving 'the iron rod of arbitrary power', was to establish his right to appoint and retain the man of his choice as his minister. That the Earl of Bute had no practical experience of politics was of little account beside the consideration that he seemed fitted to clear up the miasma of public life. Neither monarch nor peer was evidently gifted at this point with a vision of the continued national patronage machine twenty years later, by then generally designated 'the influence of the crown'. In George's mind, wrote Sir Lewis Namier, there dwelt only a dream of cleansing the national Augean stables:

> In fact, practically everybody was to him ungrateful, faithless, and corrupt, and this poor, immature boy, in speaking of the oldest and

most distinguished statesmen of the age, would say how some day he would treat them 'according to their deserts', make them 'smart', etc. From morbid self abasement he would pass to exultation such as that of the Emperor William II, and feel himself in a partnership with God; only in the case of George III, even for that partnership Bute was indispensable.

Thus one of George's first actions was to give his friend a place in the Privy Council, marked for future promotion. But if Bute were to be elevated to an effective office either Newcastle or one of the Secretaries of State would have to go, and the wartime coalition ministry be discredited.[1]

For the further composition of any future ministry George had only general ideas when he came to the throne. Whigs willing to put the king before party, often like Bute himself descendants of Tories, were to be the raw material of the new dispensation, aided by such Tories as were fit for household, minor governmental and provincial posts.[a] But the king's intention to replace the ministerial Whigs by more agreeable politicians was known only to a few, and there was no detailed scheme of changes such as those drawn up by Egmont a decade earlier for Prince Frederick. Opportunity was to be the guide, and caution the watchword, for as the veteran schemer Dodington reminded Bute: 'Remember, my noble and generous friend, that to recover monarchy from the inverate usurpation of oligarchy is a point too arduous and important to be achieved without much difficulty and some degree of danger, though none but what attentive moderation and unalterable firmness will certainly surmount.' The views and ambitions of able politicians had to be explored and exploited carefully, with a view to seeing who would serve most usefully, and the process was to be a painful one during which the king and Bute burned their fingers on a number of occasions over the next few years.

That the king intended to rid himself of the ruling ministers does not mean, as was once thought, that he wished to replace them with a Tory ministry. Nothing was further from his thoughts than to place himself in the hands of a single party. Initially appointments were limited. New Tory Grooms of the Bedchamber were former allies of George's father: William Northey, grandson of the Sir Edward Northey who had been Attorney-General in Anne's Tory ministries, and Norbonne Berkeley, brother-in-law of the late Jacobite leader, the fourth Duke of Beaufort. Among the new Lords of the Bedchamber appeared the ominous names of Harley and Bruce. Other Tories were encouraged to appear at the king's levees. Moreover, the new wind from court met no check from Pitt, who even claimed to have advised the household appointments, though in fact they appear to have been made without his being consulted.[2] The knowledge that George was willing to have about his person men of Tory views, even those whose families had been known Jacobites, rapidly brought about a new atmosphere, and other aspiring Tories waited hopefully. But in accordance with circumspection there was no removal of Whigs from the Household, and dismissals from government offices proceeded slowly. Moreover, where such removals occurred the Tories did not immediately benefit. Their lack of administrative experience and shortage of men of ministerial calibre, the result of desertion by their traditional service families since 1714, would have made their elevation to a government party impossible even if the king had wished for it.

The further myth that George III had the intentions of a tyrant is even wider of the truth, though his famed obstinacy and his frequent errors of judgement often caused his opponents to see tyrannous purpose where only firmness and rectitude were intended. That he intended to destroy party distinctions and to use his constitutional powers to that end is, however, well evidenced in both his words and his actions; and to this end the destruction of the Whig ministerial edifice and raising of the proscription of Tories were essential preliminaries. From the early days of the reign, so sensitive a political weathercock as Newcastle could not fail to register not only the new direction of the wind but also further impending changes in the air. His first fear was of a Tory revival in Parliament. With a general election due in 1761 the duke had, even before the death of the old king, expressed anxiety lest 'the Tories would be stirring *as Tories*', and Pitt's attempt to curry credit for the new Household appointments may have added to his worries. These arrangements were made, as the old duke informed Rockingham, 'without the least previous notice given of it to any of us'. He believed that he had received an assurance from Bute that he should manage the elections as usual, but 'the measure of introducing their Tories was taken principally to defeat any assurance of that kind, which they gave me to induce me at first, to remain in the Treasury'.[3]

Newcastle exaggerated, but his fears were not imaginary. Appointments were indications of the royal pleasure, and if gestures encouraging to Tory candidates were to be concerted with Pitt they could upset many of the Old Corps' electoral calculations. Nor were the duke's suspicions eased when he heard of Bute's proposal for removing Lord Powis from the lord-lieutenancy of Shropshire, a scheme threatening the arrangements which had long contained that border county's strong intrinsic Toryism. But Newcastle's objections merely provoked from the favourite an angry reminder of the king's right to make such appointments as he wished. Of this interview Newcastle wrote to Devonshire: 'When I found . . . that I was to have the King's name put upon me in every Tory election they pleased to favour I . . . told him very plainly that I could be of no use to the King if I had it not in my power to serve my friends.' Newcastle had consulted Hardwicke and other friends already, and it was their opinion that: 'If the King gives me any orders as to elections, either to favour the Tories or any scheme which may be contrary to what I had concerted with our Old Friends, that I should desire to be excused in not executing it, and then leave to them the part of turning me out.'[4] The threat of withdrawal proved enough, though for the last time. Bute was as yet sufficiently in awe of the Old Corps to promise to refrain from supporting Tories. However, the earl was not without ability at bargaining. In return for giving Newcastle a free hand to block Tory electoral aspirations, he insisted that the duke should abandon opposition to elevations of former Leicester House men. At 76, William Pulteney, Earl of Bath, became Lord-Lieutenant of Shropshire while his veteran associate, Samuel Sandys, was made First Lord of Trade; further down the scale Sir Francis Dashwood became Treasurer of the Chamber and John Evelyn, of once-Tory family, joined the Board of Green Cloth.

Newcastle's compliance in such appointments marks a new stage in court tactics, for the king and Bute perceived that having somewhat quietened his fears concerning the Tories they might be able to use him to undermine Pitt. The lever which could be used to divide the ministry was a future peace negotiation for which, as Bute had carefully ascertained, Newcastle had more enthusiasm than the Secretary. Bute pointed out to his confidant Dodington, as the latter recorded: 'That I always talked of them as if they were united, whereas they neither were nor could be; that the D of N most sincerely wished peace and would go great lengths to attain it – that Mr. Pitt meditated a retreat, and would stay no longer than the war.' Pitt had added to his offences in refusing to weaken the war-time ministry by intriguing with Bute against the Old Corps leaders. Newcastle had no such scruples. He was now jealous of Pitt's fellow Secretary, Holderness, fearing in him (as the latter believed) 'a predilection for Mr Pitt', and consented to a suggestion that Bute might be brought in to replace Holderness. The latter was thus summarily discarded after many useful services to his party and the new appointment took place in March 1761. It cannot be said that Newcastle was alone among the leading Whigs in sanctioning this momentous step, for Hardwicke, Devonshire and perhaps others were privy to the elevation of Bute. Their excuse to their followers was that 'it was better for the public and for us, that [Bute] should be in a responsible office, than to do everything and answer for nothing'. They thus took the first step in the breakup of the ministry with their eyes open.[5]

As a result of Bute's agreed forbearance in the general election the results were satisfactory to Newcastle. In all about 113 Tories were returned, including some 21 new members, but even the excitable duke could see no more threat from them than in recent times. The relatively mild revival of old party animosities which had marked the 1754 election was missing in its successor, and electoral compromises prevailed in many seats, other than those for large constituencies where Tories were usually returned. In the City of London two of Pitt's closest supporters, William Beckford and Sir Richard Glyn, were beaten into third and fourth places by an independent Whig and by a Tory newcomer, Thomas Harley, brother of Edward, fourth Earl of Oxford who had recently been appointed among the new Lords of the Bedchamber. For the rest there were few electoral surprises and Bute's moderate demands for seats appeared to have resulted in little threat to Newcastle's arrangements from either Tories or courtiers.[6]

The meeting of the new Parliament was heralded in October 1761 by the fall of Pitt. The immediate cause of his removal was his advocacy of energetic measures against Spain when a new Bourbon pact made that country's entry into the war almost inevitable. 'I would say let that mad Pitt be dismissed', penned George to that individual's fellow Secretary. But there were problems: in particular 'what are we to do for system in the House of Commons, and if we have none what shall not we be exposed to?' Happily the means were at hand in the form of Pitt's colleagues, for the Old Whigs agreed with the court that opening hostilities with Spain was undesirable. Pitt and his brother-in-law Temple, finding themselves alone in the Cabinet, resigned. Their isolation was complete even within their own family circle, for George Grenville agreed to take over government leadership in the Commons and successfully recommended as Secretary of State his other brother-in-law, the Earl of Egremont, son of the great Tory Sir William Wyndham and a Leicester House man of over twenty years standing. To complete the new arrangements Bedford later agreed to take Temple's place as Privy Seal. The swiftness of Pitt's fall ensured that it went unchallenged except for some grumbling in the City of London where Pitt was still, as Bute enviously remarked, 'Our Darling'. But even in Pitt's strongholds his popularity was on the wane. Some cities drew up addresses of thanks to him but there was by no means the massive support which had been characterized by the 'rain of gold boxes' in 1757. The loss to Pitt of six Tory corporations, who failed to display such enthusiasm as on the earlier occasion, pointed to the transfer of their party's support to the king and to peace.[7]

With the influence of the court and the Old Corps combined, Grenville rightly anticipated that his task in the Commons would not be a difficult one. Hardwicke had a conversation with him on 15 October and reported to Newcastle:

> He did not imagine that Mr Pitt would have any great following of the Tories, that Ald. Beckford and Sir John Philipps pretended to answer for them but could not; and that Sir Charles Mordaunt and the soberer part of them were sick of Mr P——'s measures of war, more especially continental, and of the immense expense. That Lord Bute had gained my Lord Lichfield and Lord Oxford and Lord Bruce who had great credit with the party, and in short had made a great inroad amongst them.

In the Commons debate on the Address, Beckford found himself opposed by two other Tory speakers on the war issue, and subsequent debates confirmed the shift in their party's support towards the court. Other than Beckford few Tories adhered to Pitt, and while the Old Corps continued an uneasy alliance with the court through most of the session of 1761–2 clash he preferred to avoid a fruitless clash with the ministry. In the longer run the desertion of Pitt by most of his ministerial colleagues was to have far-reaching effects on personal relationships, considerably aiding the king's plan of breaking up the old Whig party. Pitt long remembered his sense of isolation at the time of his resignation when, as he complained, 'out-Toried by Lord Bute and out-Whigged by the Duke of Newcastle, he had nobody to converse with but the clerk of the House of Commons'.[8]

In the factionalized political world of the reign's first decade the actions of those who had helped to bring Pitt down rebounded upon them when their own turn came to quarrel with the monarch. The first to suffer was Newcastle. Even before Pitt's removal Newcastle had drawn the conclusion that he was either to be subordinated to Bute or forced out, in which case 'the Whigs, as a body, will not come much under consideration'. He found that patronage was again being taken from his hands, even in the ecclesiastical sphere where he had for so long played a leading part. In the appointments of autumn 1761 Bute ignored the suggestions of this 'crazy old man', though considering him now innocuous enough to leave in office for a further year or two. Newcastle unsuccessfully attempted to assert himself by objecting when the speakership made vacant by the retirement of Arthur Onslow at 69 was offered to Thomas Prowse, the first time a Tory had been so honoured since 1713. In the upshot Prowse refused to take on the burden of the Chair, which duly went to a Leicester House man, Sir John Cust. Newcastle next had to swallow the purchase of Fox to support Grenville in the Commons, reporting to Devonshire that 'Mr. Fox is to act, speak, or not speak, when and as my Lord Bute will advise'. By April 1762 the king and Bute felt strong enough to propose a measure known to be unacceptable to the Old Whigs, the reduction of the subsidy to Frederick the Great preparatory to forcing an end to the Continental war. Now Newcastle, Hardwicke and Devonshire found themselves alone, as Pitt and Temple had been, in opposing a policy endorsed by the rest of the Cabinet. A few weeks later Newcastle resigned, though his friends waited to see the effect of this gesture.[5] Indeed, Bute's resolution wavered and he tried in the following months to entice Newcastle and some followers back. For the duke's long experience put him, for once, in the right; the precipitate abandonment of Prussia and its ally Russia later led to over three decades of British isolation in the European scene and to the loss of the American colonies in alliance with Old World enemies. Newcastle resolutely refused to consider return to office unless assured of preserving the connection with Prussia and Russia 'in war and in peace', and thus Bute's overtures came to nothing.[b]

In the ministerial reconstruction which followed Newcastle's fall, Bute himself took the Treasury, while Grenville consented to take Bute's place in the northern secretaryship. But as political manœuvres began, in preparation for what the court intended to be the crucial session endorsing the conclusion of peace, all was not well within the ministry. Grenville and Egremont were less eager than the king and Bute to make concessions to France or Spain. Grenville's talents could not easily be dispensed with in the Commons, where the adherents of Pitt and Newcastle had to be encountered. An attempt to remove Egremont to Ireland met his refusal to budge and aroused the antagonism of both Secretaries. Bute's endeavour to conciliate the Old Whigs was intended to obtain the removal of Grenville, but simply hardened them in their stand. Newcastle became friendly with the king's old bogey man, Cumberland, began to consider active opposition and hearkened to Hardwicke's suggestions of a reconciliation with Pitt. Nevertheless, as autumn drew on, the court decided to go ahead as planned and remove Grenville who, despite his protests, consented in October to transfer to the Admiralty and be replaced as Secretary by the more amenable Halifax. Peace preliminaries were signed in November. To carry them in the Commons, Fox took over the leadership from Grenville and joined the Cabinet, the king's first major step down the slippery slope to 'corruption' despite his dislike of using so tainted a tool. Another ministerialist, the Earl of Shelburne, had recently complained that 'the great body of the Tories are by no means assured' and that 'there is no detail established among Lord Bute's friends'. Fox's would be the task of pulling these bodies together.[10]

To ensure that the Tories and Whig placemen should be in no doubt as to his intentions, the king took the step at the beginning of November of dismissing Devonshire whose failure to attend Cabinet meetings since May sufficiently indicated his view of the peace negotiations. Newcastle immediately sprang to his friend's defence by trying to organize a mass resignation on the lines of that which had cowed George II in 1746, but this time circumstances were different; with every prospect that a war-weary Commons would endorse the royal policy only seventeen of the thirty-three men approached by the duke actually gave up their offices. Whig professional junior ministers and placemen had little love of the amateur Bute but they had a living to earn and it could no longer come from Newcastle. Typical of the type was the able 30-year-old Lord North, grandson of a Tory minister of Anne's reign, who owed his first steps in office to Newcastle and Pitt. Faced with the choice between following his inclination to be loyal to Newcastle and his desire to retain his commissionership of the Treasury and thereby support a large and growing family, North could not hesitate for long; he chose security and service to the crown in spite of bad personal relations with Bute. North was not uninfluenced by a suspicion that the Old Whigs' mass resignation announced 'a fixed resolution to oppose the measures of government', and in this opinion he was not alone – Temple, too, surmised it. These two men, and many others, shared the common aversion from 'formed opposition' which Newcastle himself had until recently professed to hold. Such Whig officeholders and Pittites had their own political morality and personal motives for holding off from the Old Whigs' activities.[11] The king's action against the Old Corps, by the removal of Devonshire, thus provoked an ill-considered and ineffective response and may be considered to have won him the first round in his parliamentary campaign for peace. It also made political war unavoidable.

Both court and Old Whigs now began to calculate their strength and look for allies. The allegiance of the Tories was crucial. Bute had already been angling for their support, through his Secretary, Charles Jenkinson, during the summer. Fox reckoned upon rallying 'the Tories, the Scotch, and the loaves and fishes'. The potential opposition were divided. Pitt, recognizing the Tories' solidarity with the court on the peace issue, hoped to retain his remaining influence with them by avoiding commitment to the Old Whigs. In reply to a feeler from Newcastle via Cumberland, he stated that he intended to respect the Tories' feelings by not opposing the Address and could not agree to renew their proscription. But even Newcastle was willing to angle for Tory support, though he received a chilling reply to his overtures through Sir Charles Mordaunt and William Bagot. They stated, he wrote to Hardwicke, 'that they found themselves in a very disagreeable situation – that if they were proscribed (meaning by us) was it to be expected that they should assist in running down the present ministers for whom they did not show any great regard?' When Parliament assembled, however, Bute's offers proved to have been more attractive to these, as to most Tories, than the lofty summons of Pitt or any hard-won promises of Newcastle. Fox diligently sought their alliance, asked their advice and finally invited them to the traditional meeting of the court party in the Cockpit on the eve of session.[12]

The first weeks of this session showed that on the peace the Old Whigs had far less support than the 150 or more members for which they had hoped. Richard Rigby forecast that 'the Tories will certainly be with the court'. So it proved on the Address. Lord John Cavendish, ablest of Devonshire's brothers in the Lower House, wrote with only slight exaggeration that 'the Tories all went against us'; though in fact at least five Tories voted with the opposition. In the key debate on 9 December, opposition numbers sank to sixty-seven, of whom only twelve were Tories. Pitt came to the House on crutches, delivered a long and mixed judgement on the peace preliminaries, disclaimed any connection with the Old Whigs and left before the vote was taken. On the following day the opposition numbered only sixty-three. Bad organization accounted for some absentees but could not disguise the fact that not only the Tories but also some more Old Whigs had left the opposition side, including Hardwicke's sons. Even Hardwicke himself, in the upper chamber, was no more enthusiastic in opposition than he felt called upon to be.[13]

The lines were drawn and were emphasized, in the weeks which followed, by a savage government purge of Whigs on a scale unknown since the ousting of the Tory officeholders in the autumn of 1714 – the court had nothing further to lose in alienating Newcastle's remaining friends, and anything less would hardly have succeeded in securing the Tories.[c] Fox had his lists ready even before the parliamentary rout, and those dismissed in the 'massacre of Pelhamite innocents' included not only members who had voted against peace in either House, but also many of Newcastle's men who had not voted at all together with the whole range of his appointees at every level of government, central and local. The court's action went far beyond anything that the Old Whigs could have anticipated. They passed among themselves, with relish, a newspaper pleasantry that the ministry had turned out everyone Newcastle had helped to bring in except the king. It was a smile among tears. Some of Newcastle's worst expectations at the time of George III's accession were now proved to be justified. Within two years both Pitt's clique and the Old Whigs had been ousted and deprived of the positions of privilege carefully built up since Walpole's time. Looking back in 1764, Charles Townshend was to conclude that the game had been lost well before the massacre, that 'the gradual overthrow of the Whigs at court was too quietly submitted to in the several preliminary steps'. Tories had been appointed first to court places then to other offices, and by 1763 most of them were regularly attending Treasury managers' meetings before important debates.[14] For the more senior positions, those Whigs had been selected whose earlier family histories often showed service to the crown rather than the Whig tradition of Walpole and the Pelhams. At the opening of 1763 the Old Whigs' reversal of fortune was complete, and shorn of their less steady or less financially independent brethren they were ready to form the basis of a leaner but more vigorous party.

Several modern historians have pointed out how, soon after the dismissals of November–December 1762, the followers of Newcastle adapted themselves to standard opposition behaviour; Dr O'Gorman has further shown that it was not only the 'boys' of Wildman's, the newly established Whig social club, but the leaders themselves who were set upon a formal opposition.[15] What perhaps remains to be pointed out is that there is nothing particularly surprising in these facts taking into account the deep-seated opposition instincts of the Old Whigs which were born in the stormy times of the Popish Plot, nurtured in the reign of Anne, revived by Walpole in his period of judicious opposition to Stanhope and never more than skin deep even under so eminent a manipulator of court methods as Newcastle himself. Newcastle's avowed abhorrence in the later years of the last reign of 'formed opposition' could spring from the comfortable belief that he was not likely to be called upon to indulge in any such activity himself, and that it was indeed reprehensible in others. But when called upon to seek their lost offices the Whigs not only took up easily the old habits of opposition but slipped equally smoothly into the well-oiled routine of a party obtaining strength through unison. Their need for strength in opposition was stressed in March 1763 when Bute agreed to give government support to a Tory call for a Select Committee on the expenses of the late war; such a move could only be aimed at Newcastle. Even Hardwicke, least party-minded of the Whigs and now intending to detach himself from his old friends, could assert that 'they would never come into office, but as a party and upon a plan concerted with Mr. Pitt and the great Whig Lords, as had been practised in the late King's time. That King William had been forced to a change of Ministry, so had King George the Second.' And the sentiment did not come any less plangently because spoken by one who was noted for his caution and experience.[16]

Party opposition, however, might seem hollow and factious unless accompanied by acceptable points of principle and underpinned by Pitt's prestige. Opposition to the peace treaties was useless as an issue, having proved unacceptable not only to Tories but also to many Whigs; indeed, the spectacle of the Old Whigs opposing terms which were not seriously opposed even by Pitt could not enhance their appeal to popular esteem. A more generalized opposition to the unconstitutional activities of the crown, real or alleged, offered more hope and had the advantage that it could arouse sympathy from most of the political class, especially if directed against Bute rather than George himself. The minister had quarrelled not only with the men he had found in power in 1760 but with many on whom he was forced to rely in their stead. Above all, Bute's activities continued to give offence to Pitt. Without the Great Commoner's assistance, opposition would continue to be self-interested in the eyes of independent observers; and without his voice in the Commons any oratory would be futile. Pitt's position, however, was seriously misunderstood by the Old Whigs. Newcastle could comprehend Pitt's anger at himself, and was willing to step down from the limelight if this was the price of alliance. But deeper-seated than Pitt's displeasure at the events which had brought about his fall was his distrust of party itself. He had been an opponent of Whig doctrines as promulgated by Walpole, and a sufferer from Old Corps exclusiveness for many years under the Pelhams. His own family's Tory origins, his early period of co-operation in opposition with the Tories and their support for his ministries in the later 1750s, all made his experience of parties very different from that of Newcastle and his friends. On the other hand, he was no Tory himself and disliked the new authoritarian trend in royal policies. For the moment he was willing to work with the Old Whigs, but he would never be able to reconcile himself to the doctrines of party which manifested themselves ever more strongly as the years passed.

The emissaries chosen for Newcastle's first attempt to conciliate Pitt after the fiasco of the peace preliminaries were Devonshire and the Marquis of Rockingham. The marquis had been marked out as one of the rising men of the party. He was among the first and most eager to resign his Household post in November 1762 and his place in the inner circle of the Old Whig aristocracy was unquestionable – a Rockingham had seconded a Devonshire in bringing in the Septennial Act in 1716. A moderate and conciliatory man within the party, Rockingham was on the best of terms with its younger members as well as its leaders.[17] His qualities were already recognized, not least his firmness on matters of party import as distinct from his affability in personal relations. The outcome of the overture to Pitt was to enhance this firmness, for when the two spokesmen met only polite rejection Rockingham was left with an understanding of Pitt's basic lack of sympathy with the Old Whigs which made him for ever distrustful of alliance. Pitt, as Devonshire reported in February 1763, would come to the House 'upon any national or constitutional points, but to enter into a direct opposition was what he could not do'. As to Newcastle's insistence that any ministry formed 'should be Whig, and be supported by the Whigs', Pitt at first replied 'that he would always act upon Revolution principles, expressed a regard for the Tories, and [stated] that they should not be proscribed', even though he 'owned they were all gone to Court'. Nevertheless, when he saw that the Tories' new adherence to the government was not confined to the peace issue he consented in practice to a working alliance in opposition. In February 1763 Philipps and other Tory leaders came to closer understanding with Bute, obtaining the ministry's consent to a reduction, demanded by 'most of the Tories' and some Whigs, in the number of regiments proposed in the army estimates. After such activity Pitt chose, on 27 March, to announce his own position, belabouring his brother-in-law Grenville publicly in the Commons. Pitt further 'served the whole body of the Tories in the same manner, pitying them for their understandings and their acquiescence; advising them not to be too much in a hurry *to have done with him*, as he called it, for he should certainly have them again, and very soon'. The following day Pitt attended the first of several dinners given by the Whig grandees to seal the understanding.[18]

Pitt's boast that he would 'have' the Tories again very soon was apparently based on the erroneous assumption that the government's proposal to extend the excise on cider, would permanently alienate them. There were good grounds, indeed, for supposing that the Tories, especially those of the six cider-producing western counties, would oppose this proposal; any widening of the hated excise was good ground for a popular opposition, such as had nearly overthrown Walpole in 1733. The opponents of the cider tax duly found a Commons leader in William Dowdeswell, representing Worcestershire. Defections from among Bute's independent supporters, including many of the Tories, badly shook the First Lord's confidence and were one of the deciding factors in his resignation in April. But the cider issue proved to be untypical and did not lead to a permanent estrangement between the government and the Tories; Philipps, once a leading Jacobite but now Bute's 'very warm friend', was soon to lead them in support of Bute's successor.[19]

Bute had had his fill of unpopularity. He attempted to strengthen his ministry by an offer of office to Pitt, but the Great Commoner loftily refused. Bute's last major work, the conclusion of peace, was now complete, and even the king's wishes could no longer prevail with him. George was placed in an insoluble dilemma by Bute's retirement, for there was no one else in whom he had confidence and the selection of a new First Lord thus became a choice between men of varying degrees of unacceptability. The king was currently most estranged from the Old Whigs and these were accordingly ruled out. Fox prudently refused the Treasury and was raised to the peerage as Baron Holland in fulfilment of a promise previously extracted. That left Grenville, still smarting from his recent translation to the Admiralty, *faute de mieux*. George consoled himself with the thought that Grenville and Egremont might well be opposed in the Cabinet by Halifax, Grenville's successor in the Northern Department, for 'Grenville's coming into the Treasury will so hurt Halifax that it will dissolve his union with them'. Divide and rule was already a permanent element in the young king's thinking since the successful detachment of Newcastle from Pitt two years earlier. In an evil moment for both George and Grenville the Treasury was offered and accepted. The Admiralty went to Bedford's friend Sandwich, and other Bedfordites accepted court places. But the king had no intention of giving his confidence to his ministers. As John Brooke writes in his biography of King George III: 'Bute was still his "dear friend", and despite all the evidence of his incapacity the king continued to depend upon him. The Grenville ministry was intended as a mere facade.'[20]

Although the king's treatment of Grenville during his term of office has been described by recent historians as 'spiteful hatred' and 'appalling', the two men's views on most matters were usually very close: there was only one real issue between them, lack of royal confidence, and it turned upon the crucial axis of the control of patronage. From the start Grenville took a view in support of the

Treasury's exclusive control of this function which would have pleased Newcastle himself. Almost at the same time, however, rumours began percolating through the political world that the king and Bute were attempting to retain control of government 'management', and that Bute was 'as much Minister as ever'. In April 1763 the king told Grenville that Bute's brother, James Stuart Mackenzie, must continue as 'the recommender in the Scotch affairs'. Mackenzie's control of the all-important Scottish patronage became a permanent source of rancour both to Grenville and later to Bedford, when the latter joined the ministry. Egmont, at the Admiralty, was (in Namier's phrase) 'a King's man'. Bute's protégé Charles Jenkinson became Joint Secretary to the Treasury in charge of patronage under Grenville and kept his old master in touch with government and other business. Jenkinson even had a spy about Newcastle, and was thus able to keep Bute informed of opposition affairs. The Old Whigs, wrote this spy, James Brindley, 'never suspect me of consequence enough to convey anything to his Lordship'. Many seekers of favour clearly regarded Jenkinson as the channel to Bute rather than to Grenville.[21] The apparent paradox of Grenville's stormy ministry was to be that, although his relations with the king deteriorated rapidly, the government's opponents insisted upon labelling it, in Pitt's words, 'a Tory administration', by which they meant that it was largely subservient to the king's wishes. In fact George III and George Grenville were agreed on nearly all major matters of policy. This became evident immediately upon the minister's appointment, over the activities of John Wilkes and the *North Briton*. The journal had been, along with other opposition polemic, a thorn in Bute's side. Wilkes chose the speech from the throne at the close of the session on 19 April as an occasion to air views on the Peace which coincided closely with Pitt's private beliefs. Issue number 45 contained an attack which, while ostensibly directed at the king's advisers past and present, left its readers in little doubt that George himself was also a major target. Grenville's ministry, having taken counsel from its legal advisers, decided that the piece constituted a seditious libel and authorized the issue of a general warrant, signed by Secretary Halifax, for the arrest of the publishers and printers. They thereby precipitated such a 'national or constitutional point' as Pitt had been seeking to allow him to take the offensive. The general warrant, providing blanket powers for the arrest of unnamed offenders, was a device of doubtful constitutional validity, though used by Newcastle and other Secretaries. Pitt saw the freedom of the press as at stake. 'When the privileges of the Houses of Parliament are denied in order to deter people from giving their opinions, the liberty of the press is taken away. Whigs, who would give up these points to humour the Court and to extend the power of the Crown, to the diminution of the Liberty of the subject, I shall never call Whigs . . .' When Wilkes was put in the Tower on 30 April the question of parliamentary privilege had become involved, for he was member of Parliament for Aylesbury. He secured his release in the Court of Common Pleas, with the assistance of Pitt's friend, Lord Chief Justice Pratt, but the issues involved were clearly a matter for debate in the next parliamentary session. Until then Pitt urged, and the Old Whigs more reluctantly conceded, the cause of Wilkes as a ground for attacking the government.

Before facing this opposition Grenville, though the 'Tory' of opposition rhetoric, had his initial brush with the king. He found common cause not only with Egremont but also, despite the king's hopes, with Halifax. The First Lord thus had strong support in August when he hinted at resignation unless the present 'want of confidence' and Bute's 'superior influence' ceased. The king then sounded Bedford, but was told that the price to be paid for the entry of this grandee to strengthen the ministry was the exclusion of Bute's influence and the withdrawal of his person from London. At this point Egremont died, precipitating an immediate ministerial crisis. Both Bute and the king now interviewed Pitt, but found him in a Whiggish and libertarian mood refusing to serve, as Sandwich heard, unless widespread removals were undertaken: 'not only the Duke of Bedford and all those who had been in any way concerned in the Peace, but the Tories and all but men of *Revolution principles* were proscribed'. Moreover, Pitt would not consider taking office except in conjunction with the Old Whigs, and demanded Bute's retirement from London 'till everything is forgot'. Faced with such an ultimatum, the king chose to capitulate instead to Grenville, promising the withdrawal of Bute from court and leaving the minister to negotiate for Bedford.[22] In September, Sandwich became a Secretary of State and Bedford himself took the office of Lord President which had earlier become vacant by the death of Earl Granville. On the whole, the politicians who had endured the yoke of Bute so unwillingly since 1760 exerted themselves successfully against him, though both Grenville and Bedford remained rightly suspicious of his unseen influence throughout the nearly two years remaining to the ministry.

Pitt's refusal to serve without 'the great Revolution Principle families' endeared him greatly to them for the moment. Nevertheless, he remained insistent that 'he was not for a general opposition like that of my Lord Bath [Pulteney]; but upon proper points he was ready'. With this the Old Whigs had to be satisfied. They needed all the help they could get, for Grenville did not waste time in establishing support before the opening of Parliament in the autumn of 1763. He ensured that the main body of Tories who had aided Bute would continue to follow the new ministry. They remained, as ever, resentful of the Old Whigs. Philipps reported to Grenville that he had told the king:

> I knew their scheme was directly opposite to His Majesty's, which was to abolish all party distinctions, and to be King over all his people, whereas theirs was to take the throne by storm, to foment divisions, to proscribe all his Majesty's subjects from his service but themselves and their creatures, and to rule with an absolute sway, as they did in His Royal Grandfather's time; and I went so far as to say, that if His Majesty suffered that faction to prevail, he would be a King in shackles. His Majesty said he was sensible of the truth of what I told him . . .[23]

In general, Grenville was as assured of Tory support as Bute had been though in two issues, general warrants and a new attempt to revive the cider proposals, he came close to losing divisions. A renewed attack on the cider tax was led as before by Dowdeswell. The parliamentary Minority, a term of the 1730s revived and often used to describe Grenville's various opponents, managed at their highest point to obtain 152 votes against the government's 172. For the general warrants affair the ministry were better prepared but on more than one of the many votes they were run even more closely, as on 17 February 1764 when a defeat was averted by the narrow majority of 232 to 218 with 43 Tories voting among the Minority.[24] Here an issue of great constitutional importance, no less than the freedom of the subject from arbitrary arrest, was at stake. But in other votes less relevant to British liberties, even those concerning Wilkes, the opposition were far less successful in detaching Tories and dinting the government's solid phalanx. Wilkes himself was expelled from the Commons in divisions which produced only around sixty votes for the opposition.

Heartened by the few near-successes, rather than deterred by the many setbacks, the Old Whigs determined for 1764/5 upon a wide-ranging attack upon general warrants, the dismissal of serving officers for political reasons (as had happened after the vote of 17 February), the lack of foreign alliances, and the absorption of the sinking fund by current expenditure. If Pitt held back from so general an opposition, as seemed likely, they agreed with Devonshire's judgement that it was 'incumbent upon us to try, and to attempt the removal of an Administration which had conducted the King's affairs in the manner they had done, without waiting for the concurrence of any particular man, or set of men'. Devonshire's death in the autumn of 1764 left his wishes to be carried on strongly by his brothers. The new mood of confidence was manifested in the Old Whigs' attitude when a group of West Country Tories asked for 'an hearty coalition . . . making the removal of the [cider] excise the common centre of union'. The prospect of acquiring allies was tempting, but the Tories in question would not agree to regular opposition. Rockingham, to whom Newcastle increasingly turned for advice, pertinently observed that Tory 'hankering' to support the government would not be easily overcome by temporary agreements. The Tories' help must be wholehearted to be acceptable. Rockingham's misgivings proved to be justified when the session began in January 1765. A motion by the Tory Sir William Meredith declaring general warrants to be illegal obtained only 185 votes to 224, a less close vote than that of the previous session. Newcastle's correspondent reporting the defeat thought it 'too serious,' and opposition sagged thereafter. In February when Grenville brought his resolutions to impose new taxes upon the American colonists there was little objection except from Pitt's follower Colonel Barré in the absence of Pitt himself through illness. The fall of the Grenville ministry in July 1765 owed little, in fact, to the Whigs' immediate activities or to misgivings about his most famous and fateful measure, the American stamp tax.[25]

The change was precipitated by a short illness which the king suffered in late February and early March, a precursor of the longer periods of disability from which he was to suffer in 1788–9 and at later periods. With a Prince of Wales barely 3 years old, the experience was sufficient to determine George III to provide against a renewal of the crisis by means of a Regency Act such as that passed in 1751 during his own minority. His plan, when he presented it to Grenville demanding immediate legislation, differed from the earlier one in that the king proposed to reserve for himself at a later date the nomination of those members of the royal family who, together with ex officio members, would sit on the Council of Regency. Though the king's motive for this variation was probably quite innocuous, many politicians on both sides considered the whole matter somewhat sinister. Grenville had already been worried by reports that Bute had visited the king during the illness and all his long-nursed suspicions flared up again. These were correct in one respect, for the king was setting in motion clandestine negotiations, conducted through Cumberland, for the formation of a new ministry.[d] George's first suggestion, to replace Grenville by Bute's daughter's father-in-law, the Duke of Northumberland, was quickly abandoned when it became obvious that neither Pitt nor other major politicians would tolerate any of Bute's relations. Pitt's own conditions for heading a ministry, when approached, included unacceptable demands for the final removal of Bute's influence, the abandonment of general warrants and the reappointment of officers dismissed for voting in Parliament against the use of such warrants. With Grenville and Bedford the king at least had common policies, and for the moment he preferred to accept these men's terms, including even the dismissal of Stuart Mackenzie and authority to make known that 'Lord Bute is to have nothing to do with His Majesty's councils or government in any manner or shape whatever'.[26]

Within three weeks of this event, however, Bedford again had to remonstrate about Bute's influence and the king was spurred in desperation to try the opposition again. On 19 June, Pitt had two interviews with the king who appears on this occasion to have conceded Pitt's terms on points of policy and agreed to the Old Whigs' having places in the new ministry, including Newcastle as Privy Seal. 'You can name no Whig families that shall not have my countenance', George told Pitt, and he stipulated only that 'where Torys come to me on Whig principles let us take them'. The Old Whigs, tired of exclusion from place, made no objection. Newcastle confided to Rockingham: 'All that I wish . . . is to see such an administration settled as may support the Whigs and carry on the King's business and that of the public with ease, honour and success, which I think cannot be done without Mr. Pitt and the Great and Little Whigs, I mean the whole Whig party. There is my heart; and there shall be my wish.' But the vision of a reunited Whig party, which was to dominate Newcastle's thinking for the rest of his life, remained a vision for an unanticipated reason. Temple, who was to have been the keystone of the new arrangements as First Lord, refused office for reasons which are still a matter for conjecture. Without Temple, Pitt would not form a ministry in which he might be overborne by his Old Whig colleagues. The king had no recourse but to turn to Newcastle and Rockingham.

When Pitt declined office the Old Whigs had to decide whether to manage without him. Their decision was not long delayed. Newcastle reflected that if they held back the king would have no alternative but to 'fling himself entirely into the hands of my Lord Bute, and the Tories'. On 30 June 1765 the leaders of the party decided, by twelve votes to six, to accept the king's offer. They stipulated, as what Newcastle called 'conditions *sine qua non*', the dismissal of some of Bute's principal adherents and the continued exclusion of Mackenzie. The king agreed that Bute should not be allowed to interfere 'in the least degree in any public business whatever', and he also conceded the party's nomination of a First Lord and other ministers. Newcastle, after half a century of active political life which had begun when he threw his energies into the Whig cause in the general election of 1715, decided to give way to younger blood. By general consent the party leaders selected Rockingham for the Treasury. Newcastle himself chose to occupy a Cabinet place as Lord Privy Seal. As a first step Rockingham presented to the king on 9 July a 'list of removals, humbly submitted' together with a memorandum concerning lord-lieutenancies and 'a restitution to the lower boards'. These matters settled, Rockingham himself took office four days later.[27] The Old Whigs' return was the outcome of holding together since 1762 and refusal to enter office, with or without Pitt, except as a party and on their own terms. With these attitudes Rockingham was fully in accord. A radical pamphlet stated of Newcastle that 'party was both his delight and his support'.[28] The same was true of Rockingham.

Notes: Chapter 6

a   See above, pp. 42–3.
b   Professor Brewer's account of Newcastle's stand is a corrective to Namier's scathing account of Newcastle's position. Brewer points out that the duke's conditions were 'completely unmentioned in Namier's account of these months' (Brewer, *Party Ideology*, pp. 123–4).
c   Urging Bute to distribute some 'plunder' from the government's opponents among its new supporters, Shelburne wrote that without such encouragement: 'The Tories, as well as other more material ones, will suspect you leave the door open for those against whom they were brought to shut it' (Fitzmaurice, *Life of Shelburne*, Vol. 1, p. 182).
d   The extent to which George III used the Regency Bill to deceive and outmanœuvre his ministry is brought out by Derek Jarrett, 'The regency crisis of 1765', *EHR*, vol. 85 (1970), pp. 282–315.

PART THREE

**Party Tradition versus
Court Tradition**

CHAPTER SEVEN

Whig Revival and Court–Tory Assimilation 1765–73

'Necessity not choice has made me take several steps that cut me to the soul.' With these ominous words the king concluded his memorandum on the change of ministry in July 1765. Defeated over Bute's and Stuart Mackenzie's continued exclusion, he retaliated by refusing to give control of Scottish patronage to Rockingham's nominee or to promise the minister full use of the royal influence in a general election. Failing a new and more favourable House of Commons Newcastle counselled 'doing the best you can with this Parliament'; but neither he nor Rockingham appear to have considered resignation at this point. Anxious to retain their new offices they did not realize until later that MPs owing allegiance to Bute were determined from the beginning upon, in Stuart Mackenzie's words to Jenkinson, 'the King's friends connecting themselves together closely, and acting in a body as occurrences shall happen'. With reports by late August of George showing 'no great marks of cordiality' and being 'more and more hurt: obliged to absolute submission' it is not surprising that 'the King's friends', both those ejected from office and those remaining nominally as Rockingham's subordinates, were encouraged to act as described in one such report: 'Some, I can say, that are personally attached to the [King], and do not chuse to take their mark from any other gnomen, avow their having no liking for, no confidence in, our present steersmen, and so much so that they have abstained going near them . . .'[1] In later years the Rockingham Whigs were to lay much blame upon George for failing to give them necessary support while in office. The state of violent irritation in which he commenced their ministry might have been considerably allayed if they had permitted the restoration of Stuart Mackenzie to the office of which he had been deprived by Grenville, but this acknowledgement of Bute through his brother they thought impossible. Rockingham's retention of some other Buteites, intended as a sop to the king, neither satisfied the latter nor pleased the Old Whigs. Though both sides showed signs of intending to make the best of the arrangement for the moment it was, for both, the best of a bad job.

If the composition of the incoming ministry showed the desire of the Rockinghams to conciliate the king as far as they deemed possible, even to retaining the assiduous courtier Northington as Lord Chancellor, it displayed even more sign of being intended to obtain the support of Pitt. The two Secretaries of State, Grafton and Lieutenant-General Henry Conway, were both on good terms with the Great Commoner and desired his presence in the ministry. In addition, the appointment of Dowdeswell as Chancellor of the Exchequer reflected a desire to please the country gentlemen in the Commons; he had voted with the Minority on a number of occasions over the last two sessions, led the campaign against a cider tax and was popular with both Whig and Tory backbenchers. Another appointment, that of Charles Yorke as Attorney-General, steadied the wavering Yorkes, who had shown many signs of unwillingness to put party before the attractions of office. Cumberland, who had acted as intermediary with the king, brought a few personal followers, mainly army officers, to this administration along with the aversion of all Tories. In the lower places, Newcastle's wish for sweeping removals gratified the Old Whigs with places on the boards and commissions. The entire Treasury Board was changed; one of the former members, the capable North, might have kept his place but refused both this and later offers, perhaps expecting the early downfall of the ministry.[2]

Despite some high appointments made with a view to pleasing others, it was a party which took office, with Cumberland as the figurehead, Newcastle as the doyen, Rockingham in control of Treasury patronage, and the Old Corps staffing the many boards and lower offices. 'The Rockingham Whigs', writes their historian Dr O'Gorman, 'were not a "new" party in 1765. Furthermore, it certainly cannot be maintained that the Rockingham Whig Party was created by the Rockingham ministry.' The party had just over a hundred members in the Commons, the same strength as it had enjoyed since mid-1764. Their policies were modest in twentieth-century terms but considerable and clear-cut by contemporary standards: the restoration of the status quo *ante* Bute in domestic affairs, the repeal of the cider tax to please the country gentlemen, and the obtaining of a renewed defensive alliance with Prussia to end Britain's isolation in Europe. In addition, general warrants were to be illegalized, admittedly a departure from practice under the Pelhams but one which was consonant with the late Minority's reviving Whig stress upon the liberty of the subject. All these points had been agreed to by the king in his negotiations with either Pitt or the Old Whigs. The ministry had, as yet, no policy concerning American colonies; this remained to be formulated in the light of events.[3]

The first problem the ministry had to face was the death of Cumberland less than four months after his appointment. Though thrown together with the Old Whigs by mutual need rather than shared ideas, he had become a useful adjunct in cultivating some sections of parliamentary opinion as well as in negotiating with the king. 'The enemy will rejoice', wrote Rockingham to his wife on hearing of Cumberland's death. Immediate thought had to be taken on strengthening the weakened ministry. Newcastle urged an approach to Pitt, but before much was done the full force of another and much more important crisis began to take effect. The results of Grenville's Stamp Act in the colonies had taken some time to be felt in Whitehall, but reports of rioting in American cities, of petitions from colonial legislatures, and of an unofficial and unprecedented 'congress' of their representatives at New York, portrayed a picture of American dissatisfaction on a scale unknown in the days of Walpole and the Pelhams. While the ministry wavered, Pitt declared his support for repeal of the Act and rejected co-operation in Parliament, advising one of his followers to refuse Newcastle's request to second the Address in December. Rockingham faced a major crisis. Any suggestion of repeal or modification of the Stamp Act roused the opposition of the Grenville and Bedford groups while, as the king agreed with them, the attitude of the court placemen and Tories remained in doubt. In the end the ministers were influenced by pressure from English merchants and others suffering from the disruption of their trade in the colonies. By January 1766 the final decisions still had to be taken, though Rockingham was able to give Newcastle an outline of preliminary party discussions which indicated that 'giving the colonies every possible relief in trade and commerce should go hand in hand with declarations of authority'. Newcastle replied perceptively that 'the idea of *authority and relief* going hand in hand . . . will be found very difficult'.[4]

So it was to be, but the plan was an expedient born of necessity. The Rockinghams found themselves pinned uncomfortably between Pitt, on the one hand, and the king and an outspoken Grenville on the other. Pitt's impassioned declaration in the Commons on 14 January of his rejoicing at American resistance, and his refusal to accept Parliament's right to lay internal taxes upon the colonies, made some immediate ministerial action imperative. The king reluctantly permitted Rockingham and Grafton to attend Pitt with an offer of office but the negotiation fell down on Pitt's

insistence upon the unacceptable proposition that the 'Administration must be dissolved' in order to make way for Temple as well as
himself. Rockingham summarily refused to consider the offer as
other than one of including Pitt in the existing ministry. The
minister determined to go ahead with the American policy they had
already worked out in outline despite the likely opposition of the
king to one aspect of it, relief for the Americans, and Pitt's forcibly
stated rejection of the proposed statement of parliamentary
authority.[5]

The first problem was raised by the activities of the king, whose
attitude had hardened during the negotiation with Pitt because of
Rockingham's obvious willingness to concede a repeal of the Stamp
Act. In a long letter of 10 January George poured out his heart to
Bute, authorizing 'my friends' to differ from the ministry 'where
they think their honour and conscience requires it' adding, lest this
were not clear enough, his opinion that 'it is their duty to act so; nay
I think that it is also incumbent on my Dear Friend to act entirely
so also'. The core of such 'friends' within the ministry was led by
Chancellor Northington, Egmont at the Admiralty and Barrington
as Secretary at War, and included a large number of lesser officeholders of the same type. The king kept Northington informed of
every stage of the Pitt negotiation. In Parliament waited all those who
held their allegiance to be to the king, ready in Stuart Mackenzie's
words to 'act all together in a respectable body . . . as prudence
shall direct'. And throughout the country were those of like mind
who responded to the guidance of King's Friends in the know. Thus
Sir William Meredith, a Tory currently supporting Rockingham,
found that when he had to re-contest his seat at Liverpool consequent upon his appointment to the Admiralty he was up against the
influence of a recently dismissed member of Grenville's Board of
Trade, Bamber Gascoyne. Amongst his opponents there, wrote
Meredith on 1 January, 'there are two who hold good employments
under the Treasury, but are persuaded by Gascoyne of the short
livedness of the present administration'. The king's hints were more
than enough to stir up those who thus waited.[6]

The first opportunity for an overt demonstration of King's
Friends' independence came on the last day of January, when they
pressed for the hearing of an election petition which Rockingham
wished to defer and came within a dozen votes of success. The
Minority, reported Newcastle's informant in the Commons, included 'the combined forces of Lord Bute, Tories and late Ministry'.
The dissidents also carried with them several prominent officeholders, including Charles Townshend, Lord George Sackville and
Jeremiah Dyson. Worse was to follow a few days later, when the

Rockinghams' American policy came under discussion in the Lords. Here the opposition was led by Bute himself, supported by Northington and several other officeholding peers, and the ministry sustained two narrow but shocking defeats. The Rockinghams immediately discussed resignation, but guided by Newcastle decided to soldier on. The slenderness of their victory in the Commons, together with the defeats in the Lords, had been partly due to their being taken by surprise and full ministerial strength had not been displayed. Moreover, on 12 February, Rockingham at last obtained the king's reluctant consent to announce his support for repeal of the Stamp Act; George had considered forming a ministry of his own friends around the hesitant Northington, and on being disabused of a belief in the practicality of that plan had even opened a negotiation through Bute, with Grenville and Bedford, only to be told that the price for their support was 'to tread the same paths we had before taken'.[7] In the following weeks a Repeal Bill passed the Commons with large majorities, while better ministerial 'management' took it through the Lords. But opposition in the Commons continued to include not only the Grenvilles and Bedfords but also Bute's followers and the majority of ministerial Tories who followed their lead.[8] And the king significantly refused to discipline either the dissident officeholding and household peers or Commons placemen such as Dyson.[a]

The Rockinghams' decision not to resign enabled them to carry most of the parliamentary business they had determined upon. Even without the dissident members of the court party their strength was considerable, and their policies were usually assured of the support of some other groups. Thus the cider tax was at last repealed, with the support of the Pittites and Tories, and many of the latter also joined in persuading the Commons to adopt a resolution condemning general warrants, albeit by a margin of only two votes in a crucial division. And a Declaratory Act, asserting the authority of Parliament to legislate for the colonies, was passed with the approval of the king and of Grenville and Bedford, though it was to remain for a decade a barrier to close understanding between the Rockinghams and Pitt. But without the assured support of the court and administration party the ministry was clearly weak, and even before the end of the session the king and Pitt began to come at last to an understanding based on George's acceptance of the *fait accompli* of Stamp Act repeal. Pitt made the first move, by praising Bute in the Commons on 10 March. Six weeks later he went on to declare himself 'independent of any personal connections whatever'. Within four days, after Rockingham had stubbornly reiterated his refusal to serve with Pitt on the latter's terms, Grafton resigned and went over to Pitt. Conway likewise wavered but stayed in office for the moment.[9] If their preference was a union with Pitt, however, Rockingham was also under pressure from Northington and Egmont to turn to the Buteites; but though he was now ready to envisage the restoration of Stuart Mackenzie, he was agreed with Newcastle in refusing any other concessions to that group. Stuart Mackenzie and his friends, the Buteites, out of office felt strong enough to refuse, as Egmont reported to the king, to support Rockingham on this 'narrow bottom'. By this time, too, George had already asked Bute whether 'if I call on those who call themselves attached to you, I cannot form something out of that chosen band' without the Rockingham Whigs. But Bute, he found, 'had in a manner left those who were attached to him formerly to their own discretion'.[10] The earl, despite his recent active intervention in politics, had enough wisdom not to attempt what he had failed in three years earlier. For the future the King's Friends would be that alone; Bute was now a spent force, by his own choice neither their leader nor the king's crutch. His final withdrawal from the brink of a ministry of courtiers made George III's dream finally and obviously unworkable.

Nevertheless, the ministry's end was also near and waited only the result of Pitt's signals to his monarch. While the two men drifted slowly to an understanding, the Rockinghams' pleas for marks of the royal confidence, by the dismissal of dissident placemen and the creation of peerages for supporters, continued to be refused. With the king's approval Northington absented himself from Cabinet meetings in June and resigned on 6 July. George thereupon informed Rockingham that he had sent for Pitt.[11] His long search for a minister who was both amenable to his own views and strong enough to control Parliament had taken him into many unfortunate situations since 1760, but the worst was still to come when Rockingham and many of his colleagues resigned to make way for the new regime.

By what combination of calculation and intuition Pitt reached the conclusion that the time was ripe for his intervention must remain a matter for speculation. One important factor had emerged since his refusal to serve in 1765. Temple continued to refuse the Treasury but, because of Grafton's adherence to Pitt, there was no longer the same pressing problem of finding a man of sufficient ability and prestige for this office. Grafton carried with him some of the Old Whigs, including Conway. With these additions there appeared to be enough support for a ministry based upon Pitt's own followers, the Tories and the King's Friends. Further, there was enough talent for government to be managed without much active participation on the part of Pitt himself, who was in poor health. He accordingly took the unexacting post of Privy Seal and moved to the Lords with the title of Earl of Chatham.

In his first conversation with the king on 12 July concerning the formation of the new administration, Chatham firmly repeated his desire 'to see the best of all parties in employment'. The resulting ministry, later to be described scornfully by Burke as a 'tessellated pavement', contained much individual talent and even brilliance but little cohesion or unity of intention.[12] Grafton at the Treasury was flanked by Conway and Shelburne as Secretaries. Townshend was appointed Chancellor of the Exchequer. Pratt, elevated to the peerage as Lord Camden, became Lord Chancellor replacing Northington, who was made Lord President and continued to head the royal contingent. The Grenvilles were vetoed by the king and the Bedfords were represented only marginally by Gower on the Treasury Board. Although the two main groups favouring a hard line against the colonists were thus excluded there still remained a wide diversity of opinion in the Cabinet. Even more serious was the fact that Chatham could rely upon none of the leading Whig groups from whom the ministers were chosen, other than his own, and was thus heavily dependent for voting strength on the Buteites and Tories. These crowded back into the administration, led by the triumphant Stuart Mackenzie as Scottish Privy Seal and with Lord North as Joint Paymaster. On the appointment in December of Nugent as First Lord of Trade and Jenkinson at the Admiralty Board, the rehabilitation of the King's Friends was complete. Only the greatest of them all, Bute himself, was absent. Chatham's restoration of the political element which he had, until lately, been among the loudest in denouncing, was not entirely deliberate. Only the appointment of Stuart Mackenzie seems to have been in ful-filment of a prior promise to the king. Such other early appoint-ments as that of North were a sensible recognition of parliamentary ability or administrative talents. A substantial number of the Rockinghams remained in office after July 1766 by their own wishes and with their leader's consent, and only the deteriorating rela-tionship of Rockingham and Chatham brought about late in the same year the vacancies which were filled by further Buteites.

At first Rockingham had been disposed to encourage all members of his corps who were acceptable to Chatham to remain and form a leaven in the new administration, remarking on Lord John Cavendish's precipitate resignation from the Treasury that he wished his friends had been 'more temperate'. Dowdeswell, deprived of the Exchequer to make way for Townshend, might have had a lesser post but refused. Many other men appointed by

Rockingham, however, were willing enough to accept his advice and remained in office to buttress Grafton and Conway. Rockingham was thereby committed to avoidance of opposition, a fact which he was the first to recognize. The Rockinghams were strengthened in their initial decision to assist Chatham by a comfortable consciousness that their popularity in the country since their legislation of the spring had actually been enhanced by their removal, while Chatham's reputation had suffered further by his acceptance of a peerage and by the reappointment of Bute's brother. Such a reversal of the state of public approval served, however, to make Chatham more conscious than ever of the danger of dependence on the Old Whigs. From the beginning of his ministry he began cautiously to weaken their position. The climax of several slights came in November, with the removal of the Rockinghamite Lord Edgcumbe from the treasurership of the household. A meeting hurriedly convened at Rockingham's house on the 19th concluded that 'if nothing was done, the Party and all the friends of the late Administration would be weeded out by degrees'. Portland demanded 'absolute security to all the party . . . and that they shall be treated with as a party and as a party only'. He, Scarborough, Bessborough and Monson agreed on resigning their posts immediately. Newcastle's protest that the gesture would be futile, revealing the weakness of their party by the refusal of lower officeholders to follow the peers' lead, was swept aside, not least by three of the four Commoners present, Cavendish, Dowdeswell and Burke, though Dowdeswell cautiously thought that the resignations should be presented as individual actions rather than as a 'party plan'.[13] Newcastle's fears were, however, justified, and the *démarche* flopped badly. Apart from the peers who had agreed to resign, few who had until recently been encouraged to remain in office now saw the need to relinquish it. Some of the members of Newcastle's Old Corps, who had followed him loyally out of office in 1762 and into it again three years later, refused to face the wilderness a second time, and these included the old campaigner John Roberts, the two George Onslows and even Newcastle's cousin, Thomas Pelham. Worse was to follow when other Old Whigs drifted over to the government during the next two sessions. But though the party now reached its lowest point its members were to become less heterogeneous and more united than they had been while Chatham's fickle alliance had been an important consideration in their thinking. By his injudicious rejection of their support and preference for relying upon a revived court party he effectively set them on the path which led them eventually to revive the Whig party without his aid.

Before this took place, however, the Rockinghams engaged in a new negotiation with Grenville and Bedford in a last attempt to patch together the old Whig party. The breakdown of relations between Chatham and the Rockinghams was the signal for an exploration of the common ground between the latter and the other rejected elements. Newcastle, anxious as ever for reunion, pressed his view upon his younger colleagues but found Rockingham at first reluctant to compromise his hard-won popularity in the country by precipitate agreement with groups who differed strongly from him on American affairs and suffered from the reputation of factious self-seeking. Both Rockingham and Portland thought that to 'ensure us the continuance of the public good opinion' it was necessary that 'we should wait for, and not be the makers of overtures'. This attitude ensured that an initial negotiation with the Bedfords came to nothing in January 1767. In March a major concession came from Grenville when he agreed not to press for a renewal of the Stamp Act and other measures repealed by the Rockingham ministry, though he remained, in general, hawkish towards the colonists.[14] Meanwhile Grenville's and Bedford's followers in the Commons supported a successful motion by Dowdeswell for a reduction of the Land Tax from four to three shillings, a move which also succeeded in temporarily detaching many Tories and independent Whigs from their usual support of the ministry. The Rockinghams, for their part, now deferred to the feelings of Bedford and Grenville and did not oppose the duties upon colonial trade introduced by Townshend to offset this loss to governmental income. On the other major issue of the session, Chatham's desire to institute a searching inquiry into the affairs of the East India Company, the opposition groups again found themselves united in April in attempting to obstruct the proceedings; but this time they failed to win over any significant numbers from the ministry's supporters and lost the key division by 157 votes to 213.[15]

The session which saw an emergence of some common ground between the opposition Whig groups also exposed rifts in Chatham's ministry. With its leader ill and much absent from the capital his followers quarrelled. Townshend's duties were unwelcome to Chatham's personal friends, while the East India policy had little sympathy from Conway and other ministers. Against this background of an unstable government there appeared to be a chance of a new ministerial arrangement if the Whig groups could come to an agreement. This, however, proved impossible and in July a further complex negotiation broke down after having at times involved discussions even with Whig elements of the ministry. All opposition groups shared a genuine desire to unite, but they showed little sign of playing down the policies which had emerged to separate them since 1762. Rockingham was willing to compromise with Bedford but found Grenville's views on current American unrest too different from his own. Bedford would not join any union without Grenville and both men insisted, uncomfortably to Rockingham, that Conway should be excluded from any new ministry and that a 'capital measure' should be 'asserting and establishing the sovereignty of Great Britain over its colonies'. Rockingham's own insistence upon the Treasury and a majority in the Cabinet for his friends, based upon his contention that they were the main Whig party, pleased no other group. Thus the final will for unity was lacking even though the Rockinghamite Lord Bessborough thought that 'the grand and only view is to form a right strong and lasting administration of Whigs', while Grenville was for 'an extended comprehensive administration as the likeliest to be a permanent one' and even Bedford felt juncture desirable as a means 'for rooting out that maxim of Favourites . . . *divide et impera*, and of changing administrations almost annually, in order to retain their unconstitutional power'. Like the Whigs in the ministry itself, the Whigs in opposition were hopelessly divided by issues and new leading personalities which had appeared since the golden age of Whiggery for whose return they yearned in vain.[16]

The multiple negotiations of mid-1767 proved to be the last major attempt to reunite a substantial majority of the old Whig party. Hopes continued to be harboured by most Whig groups for several years, but so good an opportunity did not again present itself. Instead the tottering administration was given a reprieve by the sudden death of Townshend, and North took over as Chancellor of the Exchequer in September providing a loyal and less erratic leadership for the court party and stiffening the administration's strength in the Commons. Before the end of the year Bedford, caught on the rebound from his abortive negotiation with Rockingham, allowed his followers to enter the ministry. His price was high and was largely paid by Chatham's personal followers. A new secretaryship for the colonies was created for the anti-American Hillsborough, who thus divested Shelburne of responsibility for American business. Gower became Lord President while Weymouth replaced Conway as Secretary and Bedford's lesser supporters were well provided for.

The remodelled administration did not have matters all its own way in the parliamentary session which preceded the general election of 1768. Although Grenville clashed with the Rockinghams over their respective positions on American affairs, February found them again achieving a measure of co-operation over Dowdeswell's proposed clause, in a Bribery Bill, to deprive revenue officers of their votes. Neither the clause nor the bill itself, despite the deathbed good wishes of the respectable former Speaker Onslow, met any success, but more promising was another cause which drew support from many members who usually supported the government. The background to this affair was a claim by the Cumberland magnate, Sir James Lowther, to wrest territory, and hence voters, from Portland. The property in question constituted a grant from William III to the first Duke of Portland of lands which Lowther claimed should have reverted to the crown. The case had wide implications, for many landowners in possession of former crown lands had no better title than Portland. On 17 February 1768 Savile made a motion to bring a *Nullum Tempus* Bill, to void crown claims to former possessions which had been in other ownership for sixty years or more. A telling point with many independent Whigs and some Tories was Savile's contention that party self-interest was not involved as his proposal was not retrospective and could not apply to Portland's case. By this move the proposal became a point of principle such as the Rockinghams constantly sought, and its popularity was demonstrated when it was rejected by only 134 votes to 114. By the end of the session, and of the Commons elected in 1761, the Rockinghams had a minor cause which they promised to revive in the new House. The election, as it happened, provided them also with an issue of liberty to outshine that of property.[17]

In the run-up to the election there was little sign of national issues. Townshend's duties were a bone of contention for the unrepresented American colonists but caused little stir at the British polls. For the first time since 1714 self-acknowledged Tories did not constitute a separate party, for the court party which enjoyed the support of the great majority of these did not acknowledge its opponents' description of itself under the Tory title. This attitude was given some colour by the election at Oxford University, where the stiff old Tory Newdigate acquired a true-blue partner to defeat Charles Jenkinson and another ministerialist. But such events were now becoming distinctly unusual. Jenkinson fell back upon Lowther's borough of Appleby, but elsewhere in the north-west Portland benefited from advances in Cumberland and Carlisle with a modest gain of three seats for his followers. Apart from these advances, however, the hard core of Rockingham Whigs took little advantage from the election; their increase in strength would depend upon the attraction of their policies for the uncommitted independent Whigs. On the whole, the party were well content to face the future believing that 'attending solely to national points . . . will procure us the good opinion of the public'. In the first session their confidence received an initial boost from the Middlesex election dispute. In this middle-class, urban county constituency the forty-shilling freeholders returned as their chosen representative John Wilkes, highly unwelcome to the court party and still technically an outlaw.[18]

From its outset the new Parliament gave or promised several issues suitable for opposition. Spring and summer of 1768 saw mounting protests from the colonies, first literary then riotous. In October, Shelburne, deeply critical of the Bedfordites' heavy American policy, resigned and at last provoked his leader to the same action. The death of old Newcastle removed at the same time one of Chatham's objections to working with the Rockinghams. The American issue, however, proved hard to use immediately, in view of the difficulty of securing much independent support for the American cause; moreover, the Rockinghams' themselves leaned over backwards in order to avoid compromising their own stand on the right of Parliament to impose taxation. A strongly supported *Nullum Tempus* Bill was accepted by the ministry, and the issue was thereby defused. More useful was Wilkes's cause. The killing of demonstrators outside the prison at St George's Fields, where Wilkes was imprisoned on giving himself up soon after his election, provoked from Rockingham the opinion that the court party 'think if they can accustom the nation to have all mobs quelled by military force it may accelerate the coming forth of that party', and he determined to resist this.[19]

The best opportunity for attack occurred in February 1769 when the new Grafton government sought the Commons' consent for the expulsion of Wilkes from the House. His removal and re-election by the Middlesex freeholders, and the continued refusal of the government to allow him to sit, brought together the Rockingham, Chatham and Grenville Whigs in impassioned denunciations of governmental infringements of liberty. Wilkes had already been punished by Parliament for the seditious libels which were the nominal reason for his expulsion. And, by continuing to resist the wishes of the electors and finally declaring Wilkes's unsuccessful opponent duly elected, the ministry and its supporters put themselves formidably in the wrong in the eyes of the public.

In the summer recess of 1769 pressure was kept up by the opposition, with a campaign to obtain petitions up and down the land asserting liberty and the rights of electors. In public and in private they urged that the constitution was being overthrown by the king's dependence on what was variously called 'the court party', 'the King's Friends' and 'the Bute party' constituting a favoured inner

group among 'the Tories'.[b] The more respectful opposition pamph-
leteers depicted the king as misled by evil advisers rather than
personally culpable, though conventional disclaimers of this type
deceived no one. In this and other ways the Whigs were taking a
stand reminiscent of their predecessors who had defied earlier
monarchs. The Grenvillite lawyer, Alexander Wedderburn, at a
county meeting for the adoption of a petition concerning the
Middlesex elections, 'continued to apply to his arguments almost all
the disputed points that fell out between the Whigs and Tories in the
reigns of King William and Queen Anne, and took the Whig side of
all of them in the highest tone. He concluded by affirming that to the
petitions in 1701 we owed the preservation of the liberties of Europe
and the Protestant succession'.[20]

It was with a good expectation of bringing down Grafton's
belaboured and unhappy administration that the opposition Whigs
prepared themselves for Parliament in the autumn of 1769. The
attack on Grafton was assisted from within the ministry by the
resignation of Camden, who thus returned to the Chathamite fold.
In both Houses the government's use of parliamentary power was
questioned; Chatham called for an increase in the number of county
representatives, the 'incorruptible' element in the Commons, while
Dowdeswell moved on 25 January 1770 that in electoral matters the
Commons were bound to judge according to the law of the land.
Though the opposition, with 180 votes, were defeated by 44 in
North's amendment reaffirming Wilkes's incapacity to sit in the
House, Grafton had seen enough. His decision to resign had
already been taken, and the king raised North to First Lord while
allowing him to remain Chancellor. The promotion was a wise one
from George's viewpoint: North's record proved him loyal and
capable, and he was to hold office for twelve years.

Over the Wilkes issue many of the government's supporters had
wavered. The change of minister rallied them. After a decade in
which the court party and its independent supporters had been
forced to follow first the unpopular Bute, then the disrespectful
Grenville, and finally the absentee Chatham and the immoral
Grafton – of whom only Grenville was in the Commons – the
popularity, ability and respectability of North and his physical
presence in the House breathed fresh life into the government side.
By February it was obvious from increasing voting figures that
North was more than acceptable to them, and he was able to make a
timely concession to the libertarian instincts of some independent
supporters before the end of the session by obtaining parliamentary
repeal of most of the Townshend duties. He retained the duty upon
tea, defeating by a solid 204 votes to 142 an amendment for its

repeal supported by the Chathamites and Rockinghams.[21] The tea duty was defended by government speakers on the ground that this commodity was of a different type from the other items taxed; in fact, the duty was retained partly for its income and partly as affirmation of Parliament's right of taxation. North's compromise between expediency and the constitutional claim of right which had been upheld in the Declaratory Act cut the ground from under the Rockinghams' feet and ensured that North heard little more of the tea duty in Parliament for three years, though a ground swell of dissatisfaction continued to run in the colonies.

The years which elapsed from the appointment of North until the Boston Tea Party exhibit a lull between periods of exceptional parliamentary excitement. Savile's annual motions for securing the rights of electors and Dowdeswell's attempts to disfranchise revenue officers aroused no great debate, for the government's majority ensured in advance their easy rejection. At the end of the 1770 session the only success which the opposition had been able to obtain, by detaching a sufficient number of the government's Tory and Whig supporters, was the passing of Grenville's bill regulating the procedure in dealing with election petitions. This cause, many decades overdue for implementation, proved to be irresistible, despite North's opposition, when it was found that 'all the Tories and many of the court were in the majority'. For the first time petitions were largely removed from the control of the majority party and given relatively impartial treatment. But though Chatham enthused that 'the temper of the people seems at this moment, as the friends of the constitution could wish, the spirit of firm opposition to slavery', libertarian issues were harder to come by under the cautious North. Attempts in the summer of 1770 to revive the successful petition campaign of the previous year met little success. Moreover, the brittle alliance of Rockingham and Chatham was not assisted by the publication of Burke's *Thoughts on the Cause of the Present Discontents*, a work whose asides on Chatham's political philosophy, as embodied in the ill-fated ministry of 1766, had been sanctioned by Rockingham in spite of their obvious offence. Chatham ventured to express to Rockingham his dislike of the pamphlet as extremist and divisive, pleading that 'the whole alone can save the whole'. This mild criticism elicited the stiff reply that only the political line acted upon by the Rockingham Whigs had been 'constant, steady and uniform'. Even worse for the prospects of opposition, the death of Grenville in November removed the king's main objection to his followers and was soon followed by the merging of these, headed by Wedderburn as Solicitor-General, with the government party.[22]

In the succeeding session the two groups remaining in opposition often fell apart, ignoring or even hindering each other's preferred schemes. When there was near-unanimity, as in attempts to make capital out of the ministry's handling of a dispute with Spain over the possession of the Falkland Isles, there was little success in drawing off government supporters.[c] In the key vote of thanks on 13 February 1771 the opposition rallied only 157 voters against North's 275. A continued search for libertarian issues produced even less success and exacerbated misunderstanding between Rockingham's and Chatham's followers. Dowdeswell, whose frenetic activity as leader of his party in the Commons exhausted him in coping with incipient tuberculosis, complained that Chatham had 'declared himself against' details of his scheme to improve the rights of juries in cases of seditious libel. Rockingham, for his part, gave little encouragement to his rival's desire for increasing the number of county seats in Parliament. The difficulties of working together lay not so much in the details as in basic differences over principles. For the Rockinghams, Whiggism was becoming increasingly reidentified, as in the early eighteenth century, with the united endeavours of committed party members. For Chatham, it was a more vaguely conceived adherence to 'Revolution Principles' embracing all who would embrace his current conception of those principles. He wrote: 'The narrow genius of old-corps' connection has weakened Whiggism, and rendered national union on Revolution principles impossible; and what but such an union can have any chance to withstand the present corruption?'[23]

The next two years continued to display little sustained co-operation between the two groups. During 1772 the parliamentary scene was quiet, though important for the future of the Whigs in that it saw the first quarrel between the government and one of its ablest younger men, Charles James Fox, over the Royal Marriages Act. This unpopular measure was demanded by George III in order to ensure that marriages should not take place in the royal family without the monarch's approval. Despite opposition which might, in Rockingham's opinion, have amounted to a majority in the Commons, the bill was carried as a result of the failure of his party to obtain an understanding with the Chathamites, or to agree over details. Richmond wrote wearily after the division of 13 March, a government victory by thirty-six votes, that 'we have long lost all hopes from numbers. Character alone must support us, and that will give us great inward satisfaction, but never bring us into power.' Such despair led some Rockinghams in the summer of 1772 to consider a party secession from Parliament, believing that such a gesture would win them attention and national support, though

Rockingham himself believed that 'constituents in general will rather incline that their representatives should try to thwart bad ministers'. The idea hung in suspense, but it resulted in lower than usual attendance in the following year.[24]

The principal debates for 1773 centred upon a series of measures proposed by North to regulate the affairs of the East India Company. Chatham's followers largely welcomed, as a logical development of his scheme of 1767, proposals that the company should accede to the placing of Bengal under a governor-general and council nominated in the first instance by Parliament. The Rockinghams were at first divided among themselves. Some were beginning to see a need for reform of the company's weak and ineffective government in India, others still adhered to the view that the company's charter was sacrosanct. The consensus of their views, however, favoured resistance to any measure which, in Rockingham's words, would have the result that the company's offices and appointments 'will virtually fall into the patronage of the crown'. Their activities were accordingly directed towards trying to prevent this outcome, with all the implications that such a development would have for strengthening governmental influence in Parliament.

Differences between the opposition Whigs over India brought the possibility of a combined opposition to its lowest point. Rockingham, indeed, had come to believe that his party must regulate its actions independently of other members who could never 'act cordially and fairly with us'. Shelburne, as Chatham's deputy, was equally disillusioned with the Rockinghams.[25] Before the summer recess, however, a government measure slipped through which was to provide a fresh stimulus to American protests, and hence ground for opposition unity. The Tea Act introduced in May 1773 was intended to give assistance to the East India Company, by permitting it to export tea cheaply to the colonies without payment of the usual duties in the English entrepôt. Little thought, apparently, was given to the effect of this measure on existing colonial importers and on American public opinion, which still smouldered sullenly at the continuance of Townshend's duty upon the import of tea into the colonies. Dowdeswell's sensible proposal that the Townshend duty should now be withdrawn was swept aside by North with the ominous words, 'the temper of the people there is little deserving favour from hence'.[26] With the Boston Tea Party in December the government's hardening attitude was reciprocated. The colonial issue blazed forth, not only resulting in American independence but also bringing a new sense of direction back to party politics in Britain.

Notes: Chapter 7

a   Jeremiah Dyson, formerly Clerk of the House of Commons for fourteen years and the acknowledged expert on its procedures, had been given a government appointment by Bute on Newcastle's resignation in May 1762 and had held office ever since, being one of those officeholders whom Rockingham did not dislodge. 'Except during the Rockingham administration he rarely gave an opinion on procedure against the Government' (*History of Parliament, 1754–1790, sub* Dyson).

b   As has been pointed out earlier, Tory was by now used by the opposition as a generic term for all supporters of the court, though many Old Tories normally in close alliance with the ministry voted with the opposition on Wilkes's causes as libertarian issues. See above, pp. 40–2.

c   The literary campaign against the government's alleged pusillanimity in dealing with Spain brought out in its defence the archetypal Old Tory, Samuel Johnson, earning the pension he had obtained from Bute, in *Thoughts on the late Transactions respecting Falkland's Islands* (1771). Johnson, though an ardent ministerial supporter, was also a typical Tory who hailed Grenville's Controverted Elections Act as an important 'advance in democracy' (Donald J. Greene, *The Politics of Samuel Johnson* [New Haven, Conn., 1960], p. 208).

CHAPTER EIGHT

Court Party and Whig Party 1774–82

The main effect of the American problem on British politics from 1774 until the end of the War of Independence was to polarize parliamentary conflict into two clear camps. On the government side there was little of the defiant voting by Old Tory and independent Whig supporters which had characterized the previous decade or more; conservative opinion closed ranks in face of the national emergency. Among the opposition the bickering of Rockingham and Chatham Whigs was temporarily submerged in increasing support for the colonists, whose cause both groups identified with that of British liberty. Only after the loss of Cornwallis's army late in 1781 did the solidarity of both sides begin to crumble. First, some influential country gentlemen, led by the Tory Thomas Grosvenor, decided to withdraw support from North in view of the hopeless military situation. Then, in the course of the subsequent Whig ministry, Rockinghams and Chathams fell apart again, over the terms of peace and the degree of parliamentary reform needed.

The session which began in January 1774 was the first in which the American problem bulked large. News of the Bostonians' act of dumping the East India Company's tea into Massachusetts Bay produced in the minds of many parliamentarians a strong reaction in favour of disciplinary action; even Chatham and Rockingham felt that the colonials' case had been sullied by criminal action, though both men refused to contemplate the use of force against the colonies. From the government side it was reported that 'the Bedfords and the remains of G. Grenville's friends are very loud' against the colonials, and North himself came to the conclusion that 'we must control them or submit to them'. The outcome of the government's deliberations was a series of measures intended to bring Massachusetts to heel. In the prevailing atmosphere of general indignation the coercive legislation passed without arousing much concerted opposition, for the Rockinghams were, on the whole, content to give only partial or passive support to Chatham in his objections during the passage of the Boston Port Bill, the Massachusetts Bay Bill and the Administration of Justice Bill. The

Quartering Bill, which did much to arouse colonial feelings outside New England against the government as smacking of military tyranny, appears to have roused no opposition in the Commons and little in the Lords.[1]

If the usual opposition was disunited and ineffective, the American cause began to receive support from a new and powerful quarter. Charles James Fox had for some time been on bad terms with the king and with North, and in February he was dismissed from his Treasury commissionership. His treatment removed his last inhibitions about criticizing his former colleagues, though several years were to pass before he fully threw in his lot with the Rockingham Whigs. In the meantime he acted as an independent critic of the government's policies, joining the Rockinghams for the first time on 19 April in calling for the repeal of the duty on tea. The same debate produced the first of a great series of speeches by Edmund Burke on the American problem. In it Burke not only supported a motion for the repeal of the duty but also discussed the whole question of misgovernment of the colonies by successive ministries; doctrinaire government and unprecedented forms of taxation, he maintained, were destroying the good relations built up with the colonists by Whig management before 1760. Together the voices of Fox and Burke were more than enough to offset the decline of Dowdeswell, who was reported 'very deaf this year' as well as handicapped by the illness of which he died soon after.[2]

As the coercive acts began to take effect in the summer of 1774 American criticism became vociferous, and violence trembled beneath the surface. The ministry's expectation that further firm measures would be required led to a decision in September to hold a general election before the next session in the hope of obtaining a better House of Commons. The Treasury Secretary responsible for patronage, John Robinson, had been engaged upon calculations and preparation for several months; but secrecy was so well maintained that Rockingham confessed himself taken 'very much unaware' by dissolution six months before expected.[a] He was by no means ready to put the government's colonial policy forward as a contentious issue, and the election when it came showed little sign that the affairs of America were foremost in the minds of the electors. More prominent in many constituencies was the cause of Wilkes, who was returned for Middlesex together with another Radical. London elected four men of the same stamp while Bristol, too, returned one Radical. Bristol's other representative was Edmund Burke, who thereby gained for himself and his party the considerable prestige of representing a large and important constituency. Despite government losses in popular constituencies, however, the ministry's preparations brought a comfortable government margin; North spent £50,000 to assist his supporters, twice as much as Newcastle had distributed in 1754, in a notable departure from the high ideals which had caused the king to restrain Newcastle's Treasury distributions in the 1761 election. North and his assistants calculated that they had 321 certain supporters for the new Parliament. And if government candidates had met some setbacks, the principal opposition Whigs led by Rockingham had difficulties of their own. They were seen to be out of sympathy with the Radicals and still reluctant, despite Burke's speech on American taxation, to exploit the American problem. In addition, Portland lost some of the gains which he had made in the last general election. The hard core of the Rockingham Whigs was thus reduced from fifty-five immediately before the election to forty-three after it, though they had the expectation, based on experience in the last Parliament, of regular support from twice that number of Whig independents.[3]

The most pressing problem before the new Parliament when it assembled in November 1774 was the actions of the colonials' recent Continental Congress, which had included representatives of all the mainland colonies except the youngest, Georgia, and had drawn Americans together in a united body. The congress called unequivocally for the repeal not only of the recent coercive legislation but also of all taxation and regulation of revenues since 1760. These demands were backed by fresh non-importation agreements, and reports indicated that the colonists were drilling and training their militias energetically. The opposition chose the occasion of the Address, infrequently used in recent years, for a division on 5 December. The amendment was moved by Lord John Cavendish for the Rockingham Whigs and called for accounts received by the government from America to be laid before the House. But although Barré gave strong support on behalf of Chatham, and Fox spoke vigorously on the same side, the amendment gained only 73 votes against the ministry's solid 264. The pattern was drawn up which was to persist for several years; the opposition groups were acting in close co-operation, carefully playing down their outstanding difference over the Declaratory Act whose principle the Rockinghams remained unwilling to abandon, but most of the independents were stiffened in support of the ministry by anger and resentment of the colonists' strong stand.[4]

The mood of the ministry's supporters was such, indeed, that when North decided on an attempt at conciliation rather than a further show of force he found himself with a minor revolt on his hands, including dissent of some of his junior colleagues. His plan

involved the principle, strenuously denied for a decade, that individual colonies might be exempted from government taxation if
they would raise sufficient supplies through their representative
assemblies to pay the costs of their own administration and defence.
North's Propositions were carried in the Cabinet and in the
Commons, but they came too late to conciliate the Americans. Not
even schemes of conciliation brought by such colonial sympathizers
as Chatham in the Lords on 20 January 1775 or Burke in the
Commons on 22 March could now influence the course of events.
Chatham was willing to give up parliamentary control of taxation
altogether and made an impassioned plea that the Americans' cause
should be considered to be based on true Whig tradition: 'The cause
of America is allied to every true Whig. They will not bear the
enslaving America. Some Whigs may love their fortunes better than
their principles; but the body of Whigs will join; they will not
enslave America' ran the somewhat disjointed account of his
speech, which however conveys the passion of his oratory, even
though it fell dead upon the ears of all but eighteen of the eighty-six
peers present. Burke brought forth his greatest imaginative understanding of the colonists' problems in his better known speech *On
Conciliation*. But soon after the end of the session the news of the
first military clashes at Concord and Lexington arrived in Britain.[5]

As dispatches brought confirmation of the colonists' intransigence the armed forces were put on a war footing. Refusing to
recognize the Continental Congress and its so-called 'olive-branch'
petition, the Cabinet displeased some of its own members including
Grafton, who spoke against the government on the Address in the
Lords at the opening of the next session in October and, followed by
Conway, was reconciled with Rockingham. Grafton was relieved of
the Privy Seal, making way early in November for Dartmouth
who had no stomach for directing a war against the colonists as
American Secretary. Dartmouth was succeeded by Lord George
Germain, a favourite of the king and a forceful speaker in the
Commons for a strong coercive policy against the rebels. At the
same time, the advocates of a tough policy were strengthened by
the reappointment of the Bedfordite Weymouth to the southern
secretaryship.

With the government front bench thus stiffened in the Commons
and public opinion running ever more strongly in favour of harsh
measures, North experienced little difficulty with Parliament. Such
was the despondency among the Rockinghams at what their leader
called 'the quintessence of Toryism (which may synonymously be
called the Kings Friends system)' that they decided upon a
secession from Parliament until general opinion should come closer

to their own. The decision was not acceptable to Chatham or Fox, or even to some of Rockingham's own closest followers including Burke, who believed that his own proposals of conciliation had been 'far from being ill received by the house'. On 16 November, Burke rose to put forward his second plan. This went considerably further than the first by calling for a renunciation of Parliament's right, though not of its overall authority, to tax America. This compromise represented the first retraction by a Rockingham Whig of the principle of the Declaratory Act. But the Americans were now moving towards the solution of total independence, and Burke's proposal was, in any case, still in advance of his friends' thinking on the subject.[b] Early in 1776 most of them drifted back into desultory attendance, but their behaviour reflected their indecision, being weak and ineffective.[6]

In July 1776 the Americans declared their independence, forestalling a further half-hearted attempt by North to negotiate a settlement. But the Rockingham Whigs were in no better position, and the best course they could decide upon was a renewal of the partial secession. Even Fox now lamented that 'to complain is useless and I cannot bear to give the Tories the triumph of seeing how dejected I am at heart'. There was thus little prospect that those who remained in Parliament to champion the Americans' cause would make much headway. Burke loyally tried to defend his colleagues' decision in his *Letter to the Sheriffs of Bristol*, but did not succeed in restoring confidence in the dichotomous attitude to America which had characterized the party since their legislation of 1766. The secession broke down finally when a renewal of the problem of the king's Civil List debts offered a better chance of striking a blow at the government's majority, and Rockingham was forced to give his followers in the Commons their head. It was thus that the opposition were able to score on 19 April 1777 their best division figures since the outbreak of the war with 109 votes to the ministry's 137, a result which reflected the absence or defection of many of the government's usual supporters on an issue which combined accusations of excessive royal expenditure and secret political management. For the moment, however, the close voting was only an indication of what might happen if war expenses went on too long, rather than a serious critique of the government's intransigent attitude towards the Americans. On 30 May Chatham's motion for an address to end the war, carefully planned with Rockingham, was lost by 99 to 28 in the Lords.[7]

The first turning-point of the war, for British politics as well as for military calculations, was the arrival late in 1777 of news of General Burgoyne's surrender to colonial levies at Saratoga. This event made imminent the entry of France into hostilities on the side of the Americans, for which the way was already prepared by secret negotiations and subsidies, and the ministry's more vociferous supporters began to speak of a pre-emptive declaration of war. The opposition, however, viewed the prospect of a long-drawn-out struggle with horror, and stepped up its campaign in the country against ministerial policies. This trend, visible in county meetings and counter-meetings from 1778 onwards, was to continue and gather strength as war costs soared.

The first tangible result of the defeat at Saratoga was an attempt to strengthen the ministry by the inclusion of Chatham. The project was made necessary by North's talk of resignation and was deemed possible because Chatham had never, despite his long-standing defence of the colonists' rights as he conceived them, contemplated the complete independence which they now asserted. And on this point Chatham found himself in fundamental disagreement with the pragmatism of Rockingham, who was moving rapidly towards the viewpoint already adumbrated by Burke. But the negotiation broke down upon Chatham's insistence on a general reconstitution of the ministry. Relations between Rockingham and Chatham were not seriously affected, though the king perceived and noted for the future a potent difference between their two outlooks.[8] For the moment, however, he had other matters to see to. Angered by North's 'desertion' he nevertheless believed that the minister, for all his hesitation in the cause of subduing the Americans, was irreplaceable as government leader in the Commons. But the king henceforth began to rely increasingly on North's junior colleagues to keep their superior in office and to direct his course of action, a sleight of hand pleasing to no one.[c]

In Parliament the combined opposition took new heart after the failure of Chatham's negotiation with North. Aided by a crescendo of party rhetoric, they achieved better results in divisions early in 1778 than they had managed before, rarely falling below 100 votes and rising, on Fox's motion of 15 February that no more troops be sent to America, to 165 against a ministerial 259. Encouraging to Fox was his private observation that on this occasion 'we had several Tories with us'. Several years were still to pass, however, before the ministry's independent supporters deserted in sufficient numbers to aid the opposition.[9]

The death of Chatham in May 1778, and the succession of Shelburne to leadership of his group, made no change for the moment to their recently improved relations with the Rockingham Whigs, while the expected entry of France into the war provided fresh material for attacking government. The ministry was accordingly steadied by a reshuffle which promoted vigorous and committed adherents of the king, Edward Thurlow as Lord Chancellor and Jenkinson as Secretary at War. Both government and opposition made energetic preparation to get their followers to Westminster in the autumn, urged on by the king personally and by Charles James Fox. The latter was now striving hard to overcome the Rocking-hams' distrust of him by showing zeal and by acceding gradually to the idea of party unity which they obstinately refused to modify in order to purchase his powerful support. In the event, the debates of the session centred mainly upon a naval *cause célèbre*, involving a dispute between Admiral Augustus Keppel, a member of the parliamentary opposition and descendant of William III's Dutch favourite Albemarle, and Vice-Admiral Sir Hugh Palliser, who enjoyed the support of king and ministry. The issue was the naval disaster of 27 July 1778, when the French fleet was allowed to escape by Palliser's disobedience of Keppel's order. Lengthy trials of the two men and subsequent parliamentary debates justified Keppel. Public opinion in his support, through the extensive coverage of the case by the press, aided the opposition in further assaults on the conduct of the Admiralty under Sandwich. In March 1779 the voting strength of the opposition rose briefly to over 170, giving them considerable satisfaction. The ministerialists, on the other hand, were considerably shaken, with the Bedfords discontented and Germain and Sandwich increasingly unpopular. With the entry of Spain into the war now imminent North was urging the king to conclude peace, but came up against George's adamant resolution never to give up the American colonies. Failing peace, North again considered negotiation with the opposition, and Jenkinson was provoked to write: 'Let me advise your Lordship to shut your ears to all intrigue and negotiation whatsoever; you cannot negotiate in the present moment but to great disadvantage. The claims of all mankind will be extravagant; instead of this use your endeavours to recover your former majorities.' The more subtle North was aware that such a mechanistic view of politics, in terms of the greed of opposition politicians and of the government's patronage efforts, was becoming increasingly irrelevant to the situation of the nation and the climate of opinion both outside and within Parliament. But a further series of developments was needed to bring the king, and the junior ministers upon whom he relied, to some awareness of this situation.[10]

The first major parliamentary setback of North's ministry and challenge to his majority was preceded, in October and November 1779, by a Cabinet crisis. Most of the former 'Bedfords' decided to pull out, headed by Gower, avowing 'a want of activity, decision, or subordination in every department' and in the Cabinet such things 'that no man of honour or conscience could any longer sit there'. The loyal workhorses, Bathurst and Hillsborough, were brought back as Lord President and Secretary respectively to replace Gower and Weymouth, who followed his friend out. But the new arrangement had a makeshift look. North wrote desperately to Thurlow, for the king's eye, 'My wish (and what I really believe would be the best measure in the present moment) is, that His Majesty would call to his assistance a part of the opposition, or indeed the whole.' But George remained adamant, so long as North could be prevailed upon to carry on, remarking to Robinson with blithe confidence that 'if government business is well organized I shall yet with credit get out of the present difficulties'.[11]

If the ministry was again shaken, the opposition was ostentatiously united; Shelburne had been approached by Thurlow from the king at the height of the crisis, but refused assistance. War weariness was strengthened in December, on the initiative of a Yorkshire landowner, Christopher Wyvil, when an historic meeting of gentlemen, clergy and freeholders of that county called for 'economical' and parliamentary reform. Their example was soon followed by many other county meetings producing petitions and by a widespread provincial newspaper campaign. A new stage of dissatisfaction with the war had been reached. In its early stages the movement of associated counties showed every sign of adding strength to the arm of parliamentary opposition, and the Rockinghams were willing to join Shelburne in using this new lever, though they felt disquiet at some of the more radical proposals put forward by the associators. Rockingham set out his view that the Yorkshire petition should aim at 'stating the necessity and loudly calling for a reduction of the power and influence of the Crown. I much wish speculative propositions might be avoided – short parliaments or more county members, or diffusing the right of voting to every individual, are at best but crude propositions whereof no man perhaps can well ascertain what the effects may be.' And Burke early in 1780 broached a plan for reducing the number of placemen and otherwise limiting crown influence.[12]

Torn between an overwhelming desire for peace and the increasing probability of extended European conflict, the ministry's independent supporters, Tory and Whig, oscillated violently. Thus it was that while March saw Burke's bill 'so thoroughly plucked', in his own later disgusted words, 'that not one clause is left standing in it', the Chathamite spokesman, John Dunning, so far roused the Commons early in April as to secure the passage of a series of motions hostile to the government, the most famous of which claimed that, 'the influence of the crown has increased, is increasing, and ought to be diminished'. But government waverers then rallied and refused support for the opposition when it further sought to reduce governmental patronage. On 13 April, Crewe's bill for disenfranchising revenue officers was rejected by 224 votes to 195, and this encouraging majority for the government was improved eleven days later when Dunning, reacting to pervading rumours that the government was contemplating an early general election to improve its position, unwisely moved for an Address requesting that there should be no prorogation or dissolution until proper measures had been taken to diminish the influence complained of. This suggested invasion of royal prerogative brought about a reaction and was rejected by over fifty votes.[13]

The ministry's position was further stabilized by the timely appointment of a committee of accounts in the Lower House, a traditional panacea for backbench discontent. By the end of May, moreover, the opposition were beginning to fall out among themselves again, over the demands of the Association Movement. The Chathamites were well able, by the precedent of the great Chatham's own former statements, to accept increased county representation, some borough reform and triennial parliaments. But the Rockinghams, with the partial exception of Fox who was closely involved in the radical politics of his Westminster electors, became ever more conservative and cautious as the more extreme policies of the Wyvilites were revealed. This caution was furthered by the Gordon riots early in June, which found Rockingham joining vigorously with the king in the restoration of law and order after Lord George Gordon had stirred up mob feeling against recent wartime amelioration of penal legislation against the Roman Catholic population.

The opposition's activities in the June rioting encouraged the ministry to attempt a coalition with Rockingham before acceding to the prompting of Robinson for an early general election. Here, however, both king and ministers seriously miscalculated the Rockinghams' attitude. The party had come a long way since 1765, and had no intention of taking office while depending partly upon the support of the court party; Dowdeswell's teaching on the need to make specific prior conditions was not forgotten. Their terms to the king were economic reform as recently demanded in Parliament, the replacement of the most warlike ministers by leading Rockinghamites including Fox, and independence for America if the Americans would accept no less. Such terms the king was by no means ready to accept, and the Cabinet, stiffened by some good

military news from America, began to consider a general election
which Robinson was confident of winning by the usual patronage
means available to him.[14]

Although Robinson's desire for an early election, and rumours
that this was in prospect, dated at least from March, the critical
Cabinet decision in August to dissolve the existing Parliament
succeeded in taking the opposition by surprise. 'The dissolution of
the Parliament', wrote Jenkinson to a confidant on 20 September,
'has been for some time resolved on, and the day fixed, but everything was done to keep it secret.' Rockingham professed himself
'exceedingly vexed' at the news. The government's patronage managers thus had the advantage of an early start in the short campaign
which followed. With Sandwich and other ministers mistakenly
confident of public support and Robinson predicting a vast majority
of 128 in the ensuing Parliament, king and ministers congratulated
themselves on their strategy. Their optimism was soon dissipated by
the results. Public opinion was aroused to a much greater extent
than in recent general elections, but not on the side of government.
In contrast with the relatively fluid state into which the Commons
had fallen in the 1760s and early 1770s there occurred in 1780 what
Professor Christie has called 'the clear, abrupt division which
sundered two groups of parties in parliament'. A growing national
discontent with fratricidal strife in the colonies, escalating
European war and inevitable wartime taxation made itself especially clear in those constituencies, such as the English counties and
large-franchise boroughs, which were capable of responding
directly to such feeling. According to the same writer's careful
calculations the election yielded the government a 'notional absolute majority of 26 . . . so that Robinson's estimate was out by more
than a hundred'. The number of county members favourable to the
government was reduced from twenty-six to fifteen, and the overall
ministerial majority was actually weakened by five or six votes as
the result of the dissolution.[15]

Despite these results, the opposition had their own difficulties.
The Rockinghams had increased their hard-core membership from
forty-six to eighty-three, but these now included some seventeen
Foxites whose ideas, though invigorating, introduced a powerful
radical element which was not always consonant with the traditionally aristocratic and conservative outlook of the older members.
The new dichotomy was emphasized by the fate of Burke, who had
been forced by lack of support at his Radical constituency of Bristol
to take refuge in one of Rockingham's Yorkshire boroughs. And
the existence of some thirty members attached to other opposition
groups, including Shelburne's, was not always a source of strength

to Rockingham, who began in the new Parliament on worse-than-usual terms with Shelburne himself concerning the latter's desire to add the creation of new county members to any reform programme. Shelburne wrote angrily to his leading assistant in the Commons, Barré, 'the head of the Whigs, as he styles himself . . . stands obstinately stopping the free course of popular spirit, which alone can ever oppose the Court'.[16]

Above all, the prospects for opposition were hampered, in the absence of any further decisive military setbacks, by the failure of the government's independent supporters to repeat their unrest of the last session. An opposition amendment to the Address moved and seconded by friends of Fox, Thomas Grenville and Richard Fitzpatrick, was lost by 212 votes to 130, a discouraging start. The speeches of the opposition spokesmen, including one of an hour and a quarter from Fox himself harping on the result of the county elections as 'the fairest criterion of the people's sense', had little effect on the voting of members. With the second reading of a new bill for 'economical' reform from Burke in February 1781 a some-what better opposition vote of 190, against the government's 233, was obtained by the detachment of some ministerialists. One such, Philip Yorke, explained that 'had it been proposed by Fox, I should have been less inclined to approve of it', and noted that only a few county members had voted against the bill. Nevertheless Crewe's bill to disenfranchise revenue officers followed Burke's to destruction in March, and Yorke reported two days later that 'the opposition are extremely languid and out of spirits' – as well they might be after a session of anticlimax. The one redeeming feature for the opposition in general was the support, on his first appearance in the Commons, of the younger William Pitt. But Chatham's son, though a critic of the government's American policy, was no admirer of the Rockinghams' concept of united party and refused 'to call myself anything but an *Independent Whig*'. This refusal, inherited from his father, was to be upheld by Pitt throughout his life.[17]

Almost until the eve of Parliament's meeting in the autumn of 1781 there seemed little reason to suppose that the pattern of the last session would be reversed. On 19 November Rockingham confided in Portland 'that there was no indignation arising among those who had long comprised a majority in Parliament', and he made his own task as leader of the opposition no easier by continuing to refuse Shelburne's proposals for co-operation in support of the Association Movement's reformist proposals, being willing to commit his followers only to 'an union on the ground of the American war'. But the prospects were completely changed on the 25th by the arrival in London of news that a British army under General

Cornwallis had surrendered to Washington at Yorktown, leaving the British cause in the colonies beyond redemption. The opposition was spurred into activity, with a summons going out to secure general attendance at a rally of MPs held by Fox at Brooks's Club on the eve of session. On 12 December, North would probably have sustained a defeat in the Commons but for his assurance that the government did not intend to proceed in the war 'on the same scale, and with the same plan' as before. Germain unwisely declared on the same day that the ministers were unanimous for continuing war on some lesser scale and, with pressure mounting from several sources within the ministry, was dismissed in the Christmas recess.[18] But even so the New Year brought doubt about the value of North's assurance, and a series of attacks was launched upon Sandwich as the most recalcitrant of the remaining ministers. These attacks culminated in a motion by Fox on 20 February 1782 which was defeated by only twenty-one votes in a full House. Two days later a motion from Conway for an Address to end all military endeavour in America was defeated by only a single vote, 194 to 193. When the old soldier carried a similar motion by 234 votes to 215 on the 27th, with about 20 of the ministry's usual supporters abstaining and the same number actually voting for the motion, the end of North's ministry was in sight. Yorke probably echoed the feelings of many of the government's wavering supporters when, after voting for Conway's motion of the 22nd, he wrote in explanation: 'I should be sorry that it should be attended with the consequence of placing Mr Fox in Lord North's situation . . . yet I could not avoid voting for the address.' Many members, having supported the government while suppression of rebellion seemed possible, now took the practical view that the war was lost, and there remained only the task of convincing the king of this fact.[19]

A further three weeks were to pass before George III could be brought to concede a change of measures and men. In the meantime he made efforts to bring some, at least, of the waverers back into the government fold by constructing new governments under Gower and Weymouth, Shelburne, or Grafton, or by reconstructing North's ministry, but all such attempts proved abortive. With an opposition motion to remove the ministry down for 20 March interim divisions offered little prospect of a governmental success, and North renewed his endeavours to have his resignation accepted. But on the evening of the 18th, after another such attempt the same morning, the minister was informed by Grosvenor, as spokesman for a group of members who had supported the administration until recently, 'that they shall think it their duty henceforward to desist from opposing what appears to be clearly the sense of the House of Commons'. They had supported the sovereign as long as they could; their defection, conveyed to him by North, convinced him as nothing else had done that he must accept peace and with it the downfall of the existing ministry. On the 20th, before the removal motion could be taken, North arose in the Commons to announce his retirement.[20]

Though the opposition, aided by inexorable circumstances, had forced North's removal, there remained the problem of what terms could be obtained from the king. Rockingham demanded full control of the ministry together with royal authority to obtain peace on the basis of American independence and to bring in a programme of reform intended to diminish the influence of the crown in Parliament and in parliamentary elections. George, on the other hand, had refused to consider a total removal of ministers to accommodate new party appointments, and would offer only to consider an arrangement 'on a broad bottom'. In favour of Rockingham was the support of Parliament and the nation for removing the ministry and ending the war; in the Commons, on the 20th, Fox regretted that the opposition's motion had been forestalled by North's announcement of resignation, because a vote in its favour would have made clear that the retirement was not 'for any of the common reasons which ordinarily occasion the resignation of Ministers, but because it was the sense of Parliament that they should retire, because that House had expressly called upon the Crown for their dismission, and because the good of the country made it absolutely necessary'. But the king had, in his favour, the traditional concept of a sovereign's right to choose and appoint new ministers without acceding to their terms, even though such terms might be forced upon him at some later stage of their relationship. Moreover, George was able to call upon the assistance of Shelburne, whose own policies differed considerably from those of Rockingham.[21]

Shelburne recorded that on 21 March the king summoned him to ask him to form a ministry, in which the Rockinghams might or might not be included, speaking of his 'bad opinion of Lord Rockingham's understanding; his horror of C. Fox; his preference of me'. Shelburne prudently declined the suggested honour, admitting to Rockingham that 'you can stand without me, but I could not without you'. But the king confided to Jenkinson on the interview with Shelburne: 'his language is fair. He dreads the R[ockingham] party and will, I believe, offer to take a secondary part if he can gain them. He knows I will not treat personally with Lord R[ockingham].'[22] Shelburne, as expected, consented to act as intermediary, and Rockingham was induced to give up his claim to treat personally with the king. Shelburne's intervention appears, by the Rockinghams' own account, to have been responsible both for the retention in office of Lord Chancellor Thurlow, at the king's request, and for the inclusion of a far stronger element of his own followers in the Cabinet than his support in the Commons warranted. It is difficult to resist the conclusion that Rockingham was outmanœuvred by George and Shelburne together and that the king, though he complained that on appointments 'the number I have saved except my bedchamber is incredibly few', had in fact done better than he might have expected. Apart from Rockingham himself, as First Lord, only Fox, Keppel and Lord John Cavendish in the new Cabinet can be counted as definite Rockinghamites. Shelburne secured the admission of himself and the old Chatham-ites Camden and Dunning, in addition to Thurlow, while Con-way, Richmond and Grafton had often sided with Chatham rather than with Rockingham in the past.[23] The government which took office at the end of March 1782 was thus, while overwhelmingly composed of former opposition leaders, far from representing a united party. It was destined to carry the measures of reform upon which most of its members could agree, but to fall asunder as the ancient quarrels of Newcastle and Chatham lived on in their successors, bedevilling the chances of a united Whig ministry almost as effectively in 1782 as in 1765.

Notes: Chapter 8

a   The government's abandonment of the 'septennial convention', whereby Parlia-ment was allowed to go to its full seven-year term, was unusual, though there was a precedent in 1747.

b   Thus even Burke's friend Richard Champion was writing to his Philadelphia correspondents at about the same time: 'The Whigs in England are the only body which the Whigs in America have to trust to, if they do not mean Independence; for if they have any such views, the Whigs of England must equally be her enemies with the Tories who are now in power' (*The American Correspondence of a British Merchant*, ed. G. H. Guttridge [Berkeley, Calif., 1934], p. 62).

c   The principal colleagues in question were Charles Jenkinson and John Robinson. Their task was to stiffen rather than to rival North, but the effect of their efforts was to underline the breakdown of understanding between a single-minded monarch and an intelligent minister. See Butterfield's *George III and the His-torians*, pp. 277–9.

CHAPTER NINE

Foxites and Pittites
1782–90

The second Rockingham administration lasted for only three months, cut short by the death of its leader, but achieved important and, in the long run, permanent changes in British government. Despite the weaknesses implied by the king's discontent and by the inclusion of a strong Chathamite contingent in the Cabinet the terms imposed upon George were formidable, humiliating and a startling precedent which was not lost on contemporaries. That the legislation actually passed was less formidable, except as showing the way for similar and more effective reforms under the younger Pitt, is undeniable. But the existence of such a programme of legislation, planned ahead, pressed upon the monarch against his will and carried fully into execution was a new departure. The appointment of the party's leaders as a group against the king's wishes was equally new and, in the eyes of many, revolutionary. Former instances had occurred, but none with the parade of constitutional self-justification which accompanied the Rockinghams' assumption of office.

One innovation was reached by sensible agreement between ministry and king. The late opposition were committed to abolishing the colonial secretaryship, and in the division of its duties between the remaining Secretaries an opportunity was taken to make them responsible for home and foreign affairs in place of the older distinction of northern and southern foreign departments with shared home responsibilities. Shelburne took the Home Office and was also assigned to colonial administration. Fox became Foreign Secretary and was to clash with his colleague in matters connected with making peace with the colonies of the North American mainland. Fox was in a stronger position by being in the Commons, where he was flanked by Lord John Cavendish as Chancellor of the Exchequer and Burke as Paymaster-General.

The programme outlined by Rockingham was implemented without delay. Burke's Civil List Bill, Jennings Clerke's bill to make the holding of government contracts incompatible with a seat in the Commons, and John Crewe's bill to prevent revenue officers from voting in elections were all reintroduced and passed with the minimum of delay. Concurrently with these expected reforms, Burke produced legislation to remove the opportunities which the office of Paymaster-General gave its holders to line their pockets at the public expense. Of previous holders only one, the elder Pitt, had refrained from using this facility. The Civil List Act abolished a number of obsolete offices, together with others such as the commissionerships of the Board of Trade. Equally importantly, in the Rockinghams' eyes, the Act also limited the king's expenditure on the Civil List, attempting to curb the suspected use of the 'secret service' allocation for patronage purposes. In addition, the ministers, amid general approval, gave a lead to the Commons in passing resolutions permitting the Parliament of Ireland virtual independence from British oversight. This statesmanlike attempt to end the subordination of the Irish legislature, and thus to learn the lesson taught by the colonial assemblies' grievances, was to give a golden period of independence. But the government of India, also notoriously in need of amendment, was barely discussed and hardly put in hand before Rockingham's untimely death, which took place on 30 June.

Already by this time some rifts had come to light and were threatening to destroy the ministry. The younger Pitt had the distinction of making these fissures clear. A reformer on the pattern of his late father in requiring an expansion of the number of knights of the shire by reduction of representatives of close boroughs, he chose on 7 May to bring a motion for an inquiry into the state of representation. Defeated only by the narrow margin of twenty votes, he succeeded in delineating the difference between the Chathamites and the main body of the Rockingham Whigs who voted against him. But Pitt also drove an early wedge between the more conservative Rockinghams and those newer and usually younger members of the party who favoured some parliamentary reform. Burke had strong feelings against the motion and, though induced to be absent on this occasion for the sake of amity, managed an indirect oratorical lunge in the House soon after, thereby provoking Richard Brinsley Sheridan to write vituperously that Burke 'attacked W. Pitt in a scream of passion, and swore Parliament always was and had been precisely what it ought to be, and that all people who thought of reforming it wanted to overturn the constitution'.[1]

Any overt rift between the Foxites and those who adhered to Rockingham's line on reform was still some years away: that between the Chathamites and Rockinghams was more immediate.

The king made clear from the start that he considered Shelburne, despite his much smaller following in the Commons, to be virtual co-head of the ministry with Rockingham. Fox told Shelburne bitterly 'that he perceived this Administration was to consist of two parts – one belonging to the King, the other to the public', and to Portland he wrote that 'I can hardly see one favourable circumstance in our situation'. The Rockinghams' well-founded suspicions only increased the Home Secretary's disruptive manœuvrings. As tension grew over patronage and over the king's scarcely concealed favouritism, a major difference opened between Shelburne and his fellow Secretary over the policy to be pursued in making peace with the Americans. Close voting in the Cabinet in May left Fox with the impression that he had secured a victory for his view that a negotiation should be pursued with the Americans on the basis of complete independence to be offered before any general treaty. He rejoiced too soon for, in the last week of June, Shelburne succeeded in getting the Cabinet to reconsider its views. Grafton, sensing disaster, urged a meeting between the First Lord and the two Secretaries to sort out their differences. Without this: 'I plainly saw that we should break and undo what we had been labouring for years to establish in a Whig Administration. For if this system was broken, the purposes of the Court would be completely answered, and from thence would proceed a Ministry actuated by the same principles as the last.' But he was too late. Rockingham was on his deathbed, and Shelburne succeeded during his absence in winning his point of not conceding independence before concluding a formal treaty. Even before news arrived of Rockingham's death Fox had notified his other colleagues of his intention to resign.[2]

The resulting crisis was one which the king knew well how to exploit with a view to breaking the Whig wartime alliance. In calling upon Shelburne, rather than either Portland or Fox as leaders of the majority element in the ministry, George succeeded in his aim and also initiated a period of party confusion and realignment which was not completed for many months. His use of his prerogative in the choice of a minister was challenged by Fox and a few of his associates, who nominated Portland as First Lord. But the novelty of Fox's move, and perhaps the absence of Portland himself in Ireland as Lord-Lieutenant, ensured that even those who had little love of Shelburne failed to protest when the king contemptuously ignored the rival applicant. Fox resigned on 4 July, and together with Burke took a place on the opposition bench the following day. A meeting of rank-and-file party members at Rockingham House supported the resigners and called upon other officeholders to follow; but while there was a good response from such lesser officeholders as

Althorp, Frederick Montagu and Sheridan the only member of the Cabinet to resign, other than Fox himself, was Cavendish. Portland's resignation came as soon as the postal service allowed. But Grafton, Richmond, Keppel and Conway decided to retain their places for the moment either to favour Shelburne or in the hope, to use Grafton's words, of 'seeing the Whigs once more united' by the readmission of the Foxites.[3] On 9 and 10 July Parliament had a chance to debate the matter. But it was in vain that Fox declaimed on royal influence; without a united resignation Shelburne's position was hard to shake. Many MPs must have privately echoed the new First Lord's complacent remark that forcing a Rockinghamite into the Treasury would have been 'taking the executive altogether out of the King's hands, and placing it in the hands of a party, which, however respectable, must prove a complete tyranny to everybody else'.[4]

The nub of the resigning Foxites' problem was the weakness of their constitutional argument against the king's right to choose ministers. Moreover, Shelburne's new team was by no means weak in talent; with Pitt at the Exchequer it had an already powerful Commons orator to face Fox, and in Thomas Townshend, reviled by the Foxites as a deserter, it had a competent new Home Secretary. Pitt's cousin, Temple, replaced Portland as Lord-Lieutenant of Ireland, taking with him his brother, William Wyndham Grenville, as Chief Secretary. Above all, the ministry was known to have the king's confidence. But, in the last count, Shelburne needed to secure a permanent majority in the Commons. The last days of the session, which was prorogued on 10 July, did not produce any clear indication of the new government's strength. One hundred or more members continued to look to North for a lead, in the expectation of his return to office or in gratitude for past favours. This group for the moment held aloof from both Shelburne and Fox.

During the summer and autumn intensive manœuvres took place to determine which way North would throw his weight. While he delayed, some of his less-devoted followers could not be prevented from deserting. One of the ablest, Henry Dundas, was among the first to go, tempted by the treasurership of the navy and a life office. Jenkinson and Robinson were ordered by the king to give Shelburne the benefit of their assistance. On the other hand, Eden and Wedderburn favoured an alliance on terms with Fox, and urged their leader in that direction. North himself remained enigmatic, encouraging the bidding in July by letting Robinson know that he had received overtures from Fox.[5]

As the new session approached, various estimates were made of party strengths. Two of the best were in close agreement in putting

Shelburne's following in the Commons at 140, Fox's at 90 and North's at 120. By this assessment North clearly held the balance, but Shelburne's calculations, based upon over-optimistic lists supplied by Robinson, made the mistake of classing most of North's following as 'hopeful' and thus greatly underestimated the potential opposition. Several factors were in fact driving North inexorably towards Fox. Shelburne was being forced by the colonists virtually to recognize their independence unconditionally, and North was concerned that the Foreign Secretary was taking the 'cruel and dishonourable' course of failing to insist upon the payment of indemnity by the United States to those American Tories who had been dispossessed or exiled by their fellow Americans. Shelburne, indeed, was prepared to give way on more than this, and had been deterred only by fear of public opinion from taking the king's insistent advice to give up Gibraltar. Finally, Shelburne and Pitt were known to favour some kind of parliamentary reform, and North professed himself, as always, 'determined to oppose amending the representative body'.[6]

The opening of Parliament on 5 December found the Northites still not finally decided. Fox's brilliant opening attacks on the last ministry found no sympathy from North, who even saved Shelburne on the 18th on a motion for the production of the independence clause of the preliminary peace terms. Indeed, the magnitude of this opposition defeat by 219 votes to 46 served to give the king and Shelburne greater confidence than the case justified. George felt himself relieved of the need to make any more gestures in North's direction than he had already made.[a] Shelburne continued, and even increased, his habit of riding roughshod over his colleagues, thus finding himself with a near mutiny on his hands soon after Christmas. Finally, both king and minister were influenced by Pitt, who was a committed critic of North's former government.[7]

At the beginning of 1783, therefore, North moved towards reconciliation with the Foxite Whigs; for if they, too, had been virulent detractors of his government they were more disposed to attribute its worst features to the king, and Fox had remained on terms of friendship with North. A Shelburneite approach to North through Dundas, prompted by ministerial quarrels including the resignations of Keppel and Carlisle, produced nothing substantial in the way of new offers. Almost simultaneously a similar ministerial approach to the Foxites revealed that they would act with Pitt, but only if Shelburne were removed. When Dundas informed North that Pitt was likely to join with Fox he provided the final nudge: North hurried to come to terms with the Whigs himself. Meeting three days before Parliament was due to reassemble, Fox and North lost no time in agreeing their terms for coalition. The question of parliamentary reform was to be left open, and even the role to be played by the king in forming a new ministry proved to be no sticking point.[8] North's long and humiliating years as minister had left him no doubts as to the expediency of reducing the monarch's future power.[b]

The opening debate, on 17 February, virtually destroyed the ministry. In the Lords the attack on Shelburne's conduct of peace negotiations was led by North's friend, Stormont, supported by Keppel and Carlisle. Shelburne, aided by Thurlow, was able to obtain only a hollow victory by seventy-two votes to fifty-nine: 'the smallest majority', remarked the king, 'I ever remember in so full a House'. In the Commons, where Cavendish moved an amendment to the Address, North followed with a further sweeping condemnation of the peace. Although Pitt and other government speakers made the best they could of the incongruous juncture of former opponents they failed to make any significant break in either Foxite or Northite ranks but lost a number of their own supporters who scented the ministry's imminent fall. The amendment was carried by 224 votes to 208, and Shelburne resigned on the 24th.[9]

After Shelburne's withdrawal following upon his loss of control in the Commons the formation of a new ministry was a protracted process. George III tested every expedient, possible and impossible, before bowing to the inevitable by accepting the Fox–North Coalition. Pitt was approached first but found that, apart from facing the Coalition, he would lose the support of such influential peers as Grafton and old Camden 'as the Ministry would no longer be reckoned to be the body of the Whigs called up to administer the King's government'. As any such union of Rockingham and Chathamite Whigs had arguably ceased to exist after the death of Rockingham, such refusal of support showed that any government Pitt formed would have to be of new material rather than of the last generation's luminaries. Such a government could not be formed overnight, and Pitt again prudently declined advancement to certain failure. With Robinson's aid the king tried to construct a ministry under Gower, but failed to find support. A royal approach to North revealed him refusing to be detached from Fox or to serve under any peer except Portland.[10] From that point a coalition ministry became inevitable, and Portland was not slow to exploit his strength in forcing even more stringent terms upon the king, in the matter of ministerial and other appointments, than Rockingham had insisted upon a year earlier.

The king's reluctant acceptance of the Coalition on 2 April was prompted by the need for a ministry of some kind. The concessions, however, were not only on his side. Fear of alienating independent opinion by asking too much induced Portland to take office without adequate assurance of future favours, particularly in the creation of peerages. From the start George was advised by Thurlow to withhold such 'marks of confidence' as were usually accorded to a ministry by this means. To this advice the king adhered throughout the ministry's short life, leaving the political nation in no doubt as to his views of his 'servants'. Pitt foretold the Coalition's downfall on this score alone. George wrote to Temple: 'I hope many months will not elapse before the Grenvilles, the Pitts, and other men of abilities and character will relieve me from a situation that nothing but the supposition that no other means remained of preventing the public finances from being materially affected would have compelled me to submit to.' Until the Grenvilles and Pitts rallied, however, the Cabinet contained Portland at the Treasury, Fox again at the Foreign Office, Keppel at the Admiralty and Cavendish as Chancellor of the Exchequer. North as Home Secretary was flanked by his friends Stormont and Carlisle as Lord President and Lord Privy Seal respectively. Outside the Cabinet the Northites had a slight preponderance of offices, as befitted their numbers.[11]

If the new ministry's prospects of obtaining the royal confidence were slender it also lacked any concerted plan for inspiring public opinion. The Whigs had no further reforms to offer in the first session, after their recent burst of legislation under Rockingham, while North's followers were strongly averse to constitutional change. Pitt's motion to increase the number of county members by at least a hundred and gradually to reduce the number of pocket boroughs was ensured a resounding defeat of 293 to 149 by the objections of most of North's followers, the more conservative Whigs and many independent members.[c] Burke, especially, distinguished himself by outright resistance to the idea of parliamentary reform in a manner which would have gratified his old mentor Rockingham, but offered little to the Yorkshire and other reformist associations. Nor did the ministers evoke any public sympathy when they attempted to obtain for the profligate Prince of Wales, a new ally, an annual allowance of £100,000. They eventually had to settle for the more reasonable sum of £50,000 offered by the king out of his Civil List. So incensed was the king by what he called his son's ministry that he was deterred from dismissing them only by the Pitt–Grenville view that the Coalition had not yet sufficiently alienated public opinion. At the height of the crisis the ministry, too, considered resignation but decided against it because, according to the Northite MP, William Adam, 'the opinion has prevailed that this would have been prejudicial, because the apparent ground of the resignation would have been such as would have injured them with the Country'. The ministers had, indeed, an issue which they hoped would be the ground upon which to base their showdown with the king: this was the reform of Indian government which, by general consent, was long overdue but which by reason of its complexity could not be introduced until the autumn session of 1783. When it came on, the bill did indeed produce a confrontation, but with a result very different from that which the ministers anticipated.[12]

As a measure of reform the proposed India legislation drawn up by Burke and Fox and presented by them in November was generally unexceptionable, except to the East India Company which it proposed to deprive of political control of government in India. The aspect of the measure which gave rise to general unease, and was seized upon by the king and Pitt as a means of overthrowing the Coalition, lay in its proposal that political control should be vested in seven commissioners appointed for four years in the first instance. The proposed commissioners, headed by Rockingham's heir, Earl Fitzwilliam, were naturally nominees of the ministers, and their irremovability during their term of office was generally taken as likely to give sufficient time to establish a fount of Coalition patronage. Further, such patronage would continue to be in the hands of the Coalition during the next general election even if, as was quite possible, George III rid himself of his present ministers. A press campaign, much of it backed by the funds of the East India Company, portrayed the Foxites as betrayers of their own crusade against influence. In the Commons, where the second reading of the controversial bill was carried by 229 votes to 120 on 27 November, with good independent support, the criticism had little effect. But in the Lords the king's personal intervention through his intermediary Temple, who produced a written declaration of the royal opposition to the East India proposals, ensured that the bill was beaten on 15 December on an adjournment motion by eighty-seven votes to seventy-nine. The declaration stated 'that His Majesty allowed Earl Temple to say that whoever voted for the India Bill was not only not his friend but would be considered by him as an enemy' and was enough to influence voting by the more timorous peers. In vain the Coalition protested that the king had communicated to them no open criticism of the bill. In the Commons they carried, by majorities of about two to one, motions questioning the constitutional propriety of the proceedings. The king's supporters attempted little constitutional defence of their master's action; but it was not illegal, and he followed it on 18 December by dismissing his leading ministers without granting them a prior audience.[13]

In the events leading up to the Coalition's fall William Pitt must bear part of the responsibility, for, as Professor Cannon has shown, he made the use of the king's name the *sine qua non* of his agreement to take office. But Pitt had other grounds, too, for thinking the time ripe for a change of ministry. Early in December the veteran election forecaster, Robinson, produced 'states' of the present and estimated future Commons giving every hope that a new government would be able to expect good support after a general election. When Temple showed other peers the king's declaration against the India Bill he did so in the expectation, shared at that time by his friends, that a dissolution of Parliament would follow immediately upon the dismissal of the Coalition. Although Temple accepted the seals as Home Secretary he did so with trepidation and even fear of impeachment, and he resigned within two days on discovering that there would be some delay in the dissolution while the necessary election arrangements were made, that financial supplies were still needed by the Treasury and that these would have to be sought from the existing Commons. Pitt, who became First Lord and Chancellor of the Exchequer, was made of stiffer material than his cousin. He had made Fox a very tentative and unsuccessful offer of Whig reunion, specifying the exclusion of North and some amendment to the India Bill. He now determined to face a hostile Commons while going ahead with the Treasury's preparations for an election to be held three years before it was due.[14]

The young Prime Minister at once demonstrated his political maturity by choosing to be the only member of the Cabinet in the Commons, a decision the more remarkable in that the Coalition's principal orators were in that House. Thomas Townshend, now Baron Sydney, resumed the post of Home Secretary which he had held under Shelburne, while the appointment of Carmarthen to the Foreign Office signalled Pitt's intention to be that department's Commons spokesman. Both Secretaries were solid if not outstanding statesmen. Pitt's friend Rutland took the Privy Seal but later left to become Lord-Lieutenant of Ireland. On the whole, however, the Prime Minister's contemporaries were considered too young for the highest posts and his cousin, William Wyndham Grenville, had to be content with the paymastership though he was eventually to occupy both secretaryships in turn. Viscount Howe, a professional, became First Lord of the Admiralty, while the king was again represented in the Cabinet by Thurlow, as Lord Chancellor. Other king's men, however, were noticeably excluded. Shelburne became Marquis of Lansdowne, but his devious relationship with the closet and his general unpopularity excluded him from office under his former subordinate. Pitt, like Walpole before him, appears to have believed that colleagues of ability who were on a footing of near-equality with himself were dangerous, especially if they were also in the Commons, though an exception was later made for Henry Dundas, the most trusted of his associates over the years. In general, the Cabinet was workmanlike and politically neuter, a basis upon which could be gradually built a body increasingly Pittite in complexion.

In December 1783 the new government's weak point was the House of Commons where the Coalition's majority was, as yet, little diminished. But Pitt was sustained by the belief that the power of government patronage would assist him to a majority in an early general election. In fact it was his own popularity, or at least acceptability to the nation, which saved him. In face of the Coalition's unpopularity beyond the walls of Parliament he stood out as a saviour of the nation, and even in the House his position was less unsatisfactory than the Whigs could have wished. Much damage had been done to their reputation by their juncture with the Northites. That Lord North had never been personally on bad terms with his late opponents meant little to the man in the street; nor did evidence that his loyalty to the king during a time of national emergency had been qualified by a respect for Parliament equal to Rockingham's. In the public mind North was associated with humiliating, unsuccessful war and unbending opposition to reform, while his followers were renegade conservatives and placehunters. Nor had the former Rockinghams benefited from the alliance, except by the acquisition of votes in the Commons. The Coalition of 1783 had sent a shiver through the nation, bringing with it a realization that the parliamentary Whigs might in some ways be separated by little but the rhetoric of debate from those 'Tories' whom they had lately portrayed as the betrayers of English liberties. The patronage provisions of the East India proposals, coming hard on the heels of the 'infamous' juncture of leaders and providing evidence of the Whigs' disregard of their own strictures against patronage management, completed the process of national disillusionment. When Fox opposed the idea of an immediate general election he had a shrewd idea of his party's situation. But even he can hardly have been aware of the extent to which the Whigs had lost their appeal while Pitt stepped into the vacancy as champion of reform and retrenchment. The election campaign which the new government was already preparing achieved little by its use of the traditional means of influence but much by its appeal through the press to an existing surge of public feeling.

Even the three months which elapsed between Pitt's appointment and the dissolution of Parliament saw a decline of the Coalition's majority almost to an equality of voting, caused by immediate patronage management, by defections in the expectation of government election success and by a rally to Pitt of those influential independents whose withdrawal from support of government had caused North's downfall in 1782. From the outset Pitt enjoyed the support of the king in patronage appointments and honours; royal favour by the creation of peerages, denied to the Coalition ministry, was signalled in December by the elevation of Thomas Pitt to the Upper House as Baron Camelford. And although Pitt intended to abolish many sources of government patronage, other than peerages, he did not hesitate to use them while they existed. Those members who feared for their seats were encouraged by the government's election managers to change their allegiance to Pitt. But the most telling manoeuvre in securing support came from Pitt's approach to Fox, on the eve of Parliament's reassembling on 12 January 1784, to detach him and other Foxites from the Coalition. Fox's predictable refusal to allow his following to be thus split was a key factor in the independent group's decision to remain in support of the government. Fox's decision, though received with relief by the Northites and marking a coming-of-age in adversity by the Coalition, could easily be construed by the independent mind as a failure in a politician's primary responsibility for maintaining the king's government.[15]

Within two weeks of Parliament's assembling the ministry was seen to have made very considerable inroads upon the opposition's theoretical majority in the Commons. A wide-ranging opening debate on recent events, especially royal influence, found the Coalition majority reduced to 39 in a House of over 400. On the 23rd a revised India Bill from Pitt was rejected by the even smaller margin of eight votes. Below this the opposition's voting did not sink for some weeks, and in a nearly deadlocked House where supplies were voted only with infuriating delay and scrutiny the group of independents operating, as in 1782, from the St Alban's Tavern worked to reconcile Pitt and Fox. Rising from thirty or forty members in December to nearly eighty late in January the size of this group was enough to make both sides listen. But the Foxites' obdurate demand for the present ministry's removal, together with Pitt's scarcely more amenable if blander approach, showed a new hardening of party lines. 'The *independents* . . . as ineffectual as ever', wrote Pitt with contemptuous underscoring of the offending term after nearly a month of negotiation with them, comfortably aware that most of the St Alban's Tavern group had been, and still were, government supporters at heart and would eventually come down on his side if he made a display of falling in with their initiative.[d16]

While this negotiation was afoot there was growing evidence in newspapers, petitions and addresses that the ministry's campaign against the Coalition was meeting a favourable reception in the country. This development took a further toll of the opposition's strength as members prepared to face their constituents. A steady trickle of by-elections, resulting in a net gain of six for Pitt, pointed the same way. By early March the Coalition's voting majority, after a small revival in the previous month, was down to single figures. The time was ripe for dissolution, and on the 23rd Pitt wrote that 'our calculations for the new elections are very favourable, and the spirit of the people seems still progressive in our favour'. With patronage consideration and public opinion pointing in the same direction the Parliament which had begun disappointingly for North in 1780 ended on a note of justified optimism from Pitt.[17]

The clear two-sided alignment which had characterized the last election, over the issue of America, was repeated in 1784 over that of the Coalition's formation and activities. Gone was the three-way split which had begun with the appointment of Shelburne as First Lord in July 1782. Jenkinson stated the position accurately in February 1784 with the words, 'Mr Pitt is at the head of one party and Mr Fox at the head of the other, under whom Lord North acts'. The subordination of the Northites to Fox was increased because they had little experience of opposition and because most of the desertions from the Coalition were by North's followers. The same two-way pattern was visible in families torn by conflicting loyalties, including the royal family itself with the prince in opposition, the Grenville clan of whom Thomas Grenville was an ardent supporter of Fox, and the Bedfords who were now in the Whig camp but whose old ally Gower was in Pitt's Cabinet. Such a decline of the 'natural connexions' seemed sad to such a conservative as Philip Yorke, and he had reason to deplore it since his own immediate family was as firmly in Pitt's camp as its one-time inseparable associates, the Pelhams, were now in the Whig party.[18]

Pitt's first general election, in April 1784, took place amid a publicity campaign unprecedented since the 'excise' election of 1734. Government and opposition both manipulated public opinion, the former rather more effectively. But, as in the previous months, it was the ardent interest of the people themselves which set the tone of the occasion.[e] Many constituencies usually dominated by local affairs were rent by Pittite appeals to loyalty and

Foxite counter-claims of parliamentary liberty in danger, polarized on the issues of the Coalition's formation, Fox's India Bill, the king's part in its defeat and the propriety of Pitt's minority government. But government's polemic prevailed, and as the election results came in over five weeks they provided shock after shock for the opposition. In English counties and large boroughs 'Fox's Martyrs' were mown down. Lord John Cavendish, recently Chancellor of the Exchequer, lost his seat at York to Pitt's friend, the still unknown William Wilberforce, testifying to the discontent of the Yorkshire Association at its birthplace with Whig reluctance to reform Parliament. From Norfolk came the news that Thomas William Coke, of whom Robinson had written that 'his connections carry him dead', was likewise defeated. The Foxite William Windham, returned for Norwich, was one of his party's few successes, for being a newcomer he had been able largely to avoid publicizing his connections. Carmarthen wrote that 'the elections went more favourably for government than its most sanguine friends could have imagined'. Pitt made a net gain of about seventy, slightly exceeding the number forecast by Robinson. That election manager had, however, overestimated the effects of patronage and seriously underestimated the extent to which the Coalitionists would lose in the open constituencies. Of sitting members only 83 among 130 Foxites and 69 of 112 Northites were returned again.*f* The now substantial margin in favour of government was reflected in a vote on the Address as soon as Parliament met, when only 114 members opposed the assertion that the king's recent actions had preserved the constitution. Subsequent divisions improved the opposition performance by only about a score of votes.[19]

The six-year life of the Commons elected in 1784 was, so far as concerned party development, a quiet but not uneventful aftermath to the excitements the previous decade. Issues raised by the American colonists' revolt simmered on after Independence and increased demand for parliamentary and other reforms in Britain. In the Commons the new lines drawn by Pitt's accession to government remained largely unaltered between the election of 1784 and that of 1790, the only spectacular change of side being that of the able Northite William Eden who transferred his allegiance from the opposition to Pitt in 1785. Both sides had to explore the situation left by the constitutional crisis and the swing of public opinion away from the Whigs. Pitt's majority was diverse in character and unsettled by the reformist issues unleashed during the struggle with the Americans. For the Whigs a drastic reassessment was needed now that the success of America's cause had deprived them of an ideally libertarian issue but left a legacy of reformist aspirations, many of which were unacceptable.

Pitt's voting strength was derived from placemen, from the government-oriented independents, and from his own modest following. This heterogeneous government party was by no means easy for its young leader to control in face of what he called the 'clamour from without doors'. Within a year of the election he was writing to his friend Rutland: 'Our majority, tho' a large one, is composed of men who think, or at least act, so much for themselves, that we are hardly sure from day to day what impression they may receive.' Pitt's most spectacular early failures were on his attempt in April 1785 to provide for the transfer of some seats from small boroughs to counties, his manœuvres to prevent Fox's return in the disputed election at Westminster, and his proposal in the Irish Parliament in 1785 to integrate Ireland into the British trading system. But such early setbacks did not seriously shake his parliamentary strength which was in May 1788 estimated at 280 members including 52 attached to the minister himself. Further, Pitt succeeded in dishing the opposition by passing in 1784 a reform of Indian government which placed the sub-continent under the ultimate political management of a Board of Control in London, and thus obtaining the approval of a broad consensus of British public opinion.[20]

Pitt's strength in the Commons was such that his defeats were transient. Only by falling into the trap of seeming to betray his ideals, or by the king's action, could he be removed. He skilfully avoided the first in 1786 by giving support to the opposition's impeachment of Warren Hastings, thus avoiding odium in the eyes of the nation while going against the king's wishes. Of withdrawal of royal support for his ministry there was no question: George was only too well aware of the likely alternative. The king, it is true, contributed to the defeat of the Reform Bill by letting his opposition be known to the placemen, many of whom voted against it in unholy combination with the Whigs.[21] The direct approach to reform was clearly non-viable but Pitt began, with the aid of recommendations from the Commons committees set up during North's last two years, to make a far-reaching overhaul of administration which ultimately reduced government influence in the legislature to a fraction of its former position. He succeeded, by greatly reduced use of sinecure offices, leases of crown land, government contracting and many other forms of patronage, in virtually eliminating the 'influence of the crown' by the early years of the nineteenth century. Pitt may not have deliberately set out to remove the crown's influence and replace it by ministerial dependence upon party, but the effect of his desire to clean up politics was to have this result before the death of George III.

Pitt's increasing assurance in the Commons and his overhaul of patronage were to have important effects in the later development of a new Tory party. But, for the moment, the main interest in party history still centres upon the Whigs. At first the omens for a further advance on Rockingham's steps towards a revived party were not propitious, though numbers grew gradually from about 130 in 1784 to around 144 by the end of the Parliament.[22] The aftermath of the War of Independence was accompanied by a new clash of ideas and personalities within the party. After the Coalition it was a less coherent body led in the Commons by the near-reformer Fox but containing a large anti-reformist element of Rockingham's stamp together with the even more conservative North and his followers. In addition, party was now openly joined by the Prince of Wales upon his coming of age in 1783, representing a royal 'reversionary interest' almost unknown under Rockingham. This new diversity of personalities made unity upon shared principles more difficult. In its place, however, came new advances in party organization which, for the moment, served to cover a growing tension within the party and provide some substitute for clear party principles.

The origin of the new organizational developments probably lay in the Westminster Election Scrutiny from which Fox finally emerged triumphant as representative for that constituency. In the course of the bitter struggle for their leader's seat the Foxites provided themselves with a potent instrument of party organization in the Whig Club founded in May 1784, which soon outgrew its local importance and became the centre of both parliamentary and national activities. At the same time, the defeat of the former unofficial party Whip, George Byng, at neighbouring Middlesex left the way open for a more active and resourceful organizer, William Adam. This Scottish member, a former Northite, had already flung himself into the task of unifying and regimenting the two elements of the former Coalition into what, in writing to North as early as January 1784, he now simply called 'the party'. Modern research by Dr Frank O'Gorman and Dr Donald Ginter revealed the importance of Adam's work in the later 1780s in giving the party new institutions of central office, party funds and nationwide election management which for the first time paralleled those long enjoyed by government party. This structure formed the basis, after some backsliding in the 1790s, for the party's nineteenth-century organization. Taken together with a serious and massive marshalling of the newspaper press by Fox and others, Adam's work was to be crucial for the party's ultimate survival.[23]

Institutional developments served to paper over the cracks among the Whigs until the onset of the French Revolution, but personal differences and underlying divergences upon fundamental ideas caused disquiet to some of the party soon after the general election. Fox was the most active Commons leader and his seemingly radical attitudes were increasingly shared by the younger members of the party who entered Parliament in the 1780s, notably Richard Brinsley Sheridan and Charles Grey.[g] Against their pressure stood Burke, the self-appointed guardian of conservative tradition, and Portland, Rockingham's successor as leader in the Lords and nominal leader of the party. Portland, indeed, tried to keep a façade of impartiality, and his reluctance to come out openly on the side of Burke, his personal friend and Buckinghamshire neighbour, until well after the onset of the French Revolution evidences his close adherence to Rockingham's own most important party principle: unity and loyalty among party members. But he failed to conceal a growing distaste both for parliamentary reform and, later, for the reformist agitation supported by Fox for the repeal of the Test and Corporation Acts.[24]

Emerging differences were reflected from the opening of Parliament in a number of ways. All the leaders were agreed upon the party's loss of public support, as reflected in the elections, but they were by no means agreed on the tactics to be employed in the face of this situation. Burke looked for issues involving political principles such as had served Rockingham. Fox preferred to proceed by *ad hoc* opposition, often of questionable consistency, while he built up party organization in Parliament and prepared the ground for a new election. In 1784 their differences emerged over Pitt's new India Bill. Fox withdrew himself from the debates, claiming that the party's present unpopularity was actually serving to advance the bill. Portland and Burke favoured active opposition as an opportunity to maintain that Pitt's former objections to their own bill had been factious rather than principled. Burke indeed took the opportunity to go further and state his undying intention to punish, in the person of Hastings, the past misgovernment of India. Further differences arose in the following session over Pitt's proposals for parliamentary reform. This time it was North who spoke loudest in opposition and achieved so much sympathy among the Whigs that Fox, committed not to split the party on this issue, was reduced to the point where he 'spoke against and voted for the motion' on the crucial division.[25]

At this stage the differences between the conservative and radical wings of the Whig party should not be overstressed. They worked together loyally on the routine of opposition, and Pitt himself testified ruefully to their 'indefatigable energy, sharpened by disappointment, watching and improving every opportunity'. But Fox's opposition principle of keeping up unrelenting pressure on all government business in Parliament could make little headway without some prominent issue on which the party could unite, and this may well have helped to precipitate his decision to fall back upon Burke's crusade against Hastings, despite Burke's scepticism as to the usefulness of this issue 'in a party light'. The scepticism proved justified: Pitt refused to be trapped into supporting Hastings and, together with Dundas the leading light in the new Board of Control for India, was conspicuous in voting against the former governor-general.[26] With dilatory impeachment proceedings in the House of Lords allowing only two of the twenty charges of Hastings' impeachment to be completed by 1788, Fox, Sheridan and Grey soon tired of the pursuit. By this time, too, Beaufoy's first motion for the repeal of the Test and Corporation Acts, though warmly supported by Fox, had found Portland and Burke withholding support and North unequivocally hostile.[27]

Mounting constraint within the party ranks appeared to be dispelled in the autumn of 1788 when the king's illness and signs of mental derangement opened the possibility of a regency under the Prince of Wales and a Foxite ministry.[h] But Fox, hastily recalled from a holiday in Italy, handled the matter badly in debate during December. When the Commons heard the doctors' reports on the 10th, Fox startled the House by arguing the prince's inalienable claim to unrestricted regency, basing his case on a doctrine of right which many of his listeners thought suspiciously like traditional Toryism. His political flexibility had carried him too far, and Pitt was not slow to 'unwhig' him by bringing forward a rival and more apparently Whiggish plan for a modified form of regency in which the regent would be prevented by parliamentary restrictions from carrying out many of the royal functions, especially in the field of patronage. Aided by Fox's imprudence, Pitt was smugly able to base his proposals on parliamentary supremacy and Revolution principles, pointing for precedent to the limitations imposed on the crown by Parliament in the legislation of 1689. Finding a limited regency unopposable, Fox began at once to back down, but in so doing he further alienated Burke and the party's leading lawyer, Loughborough. Burke roundly told the House that he was for an Address to the prince to assume unlimited administration of government immediately, adding that 'whether his sentiments would be considered as favouring of Whig or Tory principles, he was very indifferent'. Fox was thus forced openly to renounce the extreme position which he had lately held, and his planned ministry under the prince's limited regency pointedly excluded Burke from the leadership of the Board of Control for India and allotted him only his former office of Paymaster.[28]

Before this new government could come into effect, however, the king recovered. Pitt had prolonged the debates successfully. He had his reward in the king's increased trust and, at the same time, planned to continue or improve his majority in the Commons. Secret preparations were put in hand for an election a year early, in 1790. Public opinion had rallied to Pitt and to the stricken king during his illness, away from the too-obviously grasping behaviour of the prince and the opposition. Subsequent developments did little to improve their position. After Burke forced the continuance of the impeachment proceedings in the spring of 1789 against the wishes of most of his colleagues, at the same time failing to support Fox on Beaufoy's second attempt to repeal the penal legislation against Dissenters, rumours of the quarrels could no longer be concealed. The rift deepened in the summer and autumn as revolution burst out in France and found eager support from many Britons.[29] In January 1790 Burke became acquainted with the Unitarian Richard Price's *A Discourse upon the Love of Our Country*, a popular eulogy of the recent events in France, and began to prepare the reply which was to become his most famous publication, the *Reflections on the Revolution in France*. In the debates of February 1790 concerning the army estimates, Burke's differences with Fox and Sheridan over their public support for the French Revolution were openly aired for the first time. On the eve of an election such dissension was not lost upon an increasingly observant public. The unity based upon some 'particular principles in which they are all agreed', laid down by Burke himself in the *Thoughts* twenty years earlier as the basis for Whig party action, was no longer present. In its place had come two new unities, for and against revolution in France and reform at home, to be the basis of revived Whig and Tory parties.

Notes: Chapter 9

a   The king was unjustifiably incensed with North over election debts incurred in 1780 by North on behalf of the government. In the opinion of North's biographer the king's action was 'at best inconsiderate, at worst spiteful'; in any case, it did not improve relations in 1782–3, though the king later consented to meet the sums outstanding (Thomas, *Lord North*, pp. 134–5, 144).

b   See above, p. 29.

c   An analysis giving some idea of how the parties split is provided by Professor

John Cannon, showing 47 per cent of Foxites, 40 per cent of Shelburne's former following but only 6 per cent of Northites favouring reform (*Fox–North Coalition*, p. 92, n. 2).

d   The basically pro-government sympathies of the leaders of the St Alban's tavern group is described by Dr P. Kelly, 'British politics, 1783–4: the emergence and triumph of the Younger Pitt's administration', *BIHR*, vol. 54 (1981), pp. 62–78.

e   Mrs E. George, 'Fox's Martyrs: the general election of 1784', *TRHS*, 4th ser., vol. 21 (1939), pp. 138–68.

f   The figures quoted are from Cannon, *Fox-North Coalition*, pp. 215–18 and 244–5. Somewhat varying figures are provided by O'Gorman, *Whig Party and the French Revolution*, pp. 244–6, and Mitchell, *Charles James Fox*, pp. 244–5.

g   The former better known as a playwright, the latter as Lord Grey of Reform Act fame after 1832.

h   The king's madness was thought at the time, and for long after, to be congenital. Some modern medical opinion, based on contemporary reports of the symptoms, has suggested that the king's illness was porphyria, which can have side-effects akin to mental derangement.

PART FOUR

The Revival of
the Tory Party

CHAPTER TEN

The Rebirth of Ideology
1790–1801

The decade of the French Revolution was for Britain a period of revived reformist activity, often led by Protestant Dissenters, more widespread and virulent than the Wilkite and Wyvilite movements which had preceded it. This activity stimulated an often violent reaction from most of the propertied class and Anglican clergy, spreading upwards to become a more disciplined organization of the forces of order under Pitt. The first effect of these developments on parliamentary alignments was to widen the already latent rift within the Whig party, with Fox remaining in favour of the Revolution in France but Burke, by 1792, the figurehead for a formidable body of conservative Whigs. Portland's decision to come out openly in favour of the Burkeites two years later and lead them into Pitt's camp divided politics into the Pitt–Portland government party, including about half the former opposition, and the rump of Whigs remaining under Fox. So drastic a realignment did not come about without major heartsearching, a process which led to the emergence of new and permanent party ideologies dividing the political nation into two parties over the desirability of reform in Britain. For the Foxites reform, as has been emphasized before, did not at this stage necessarily include parliamentary reform; there were many lesser reformist paths to pursue.[a] But by the end of the 1790s the main lines followed by both Whigs and Tories after the overthrow of Napoleon were already present.

The dissolution of Parliament in June 1790 brought little change in the balance of government and opposition in the Commons. For over a year both sides had been making their preparations, the Whigs with the aid of their new election funds.[1] Election management made headway when used resolutely, as in Scotland by Dundas or in Yorkshire where Fitzwilliam was determined to repair the damage done in the last election. The French Revolution was not yet a major issue but the Whigs succeeded, thanks to Fox's stand on the repeal of religious tests, in detaching many Dissenters who had swayed to Pitt on the reform issue in 1784. Any advantage thus gained by the Whigs was offset, however, by the continuing unpopularity of religious reform with much of the rest of the electorate.[b] Also in the minds of many loyal voters was the opposition's unscrupulous use of the prince's claim to regency during his father's illness, to which recollection the government press added reminders of the revelation in 1787 that the prince had made an illegal marriage with a Roman Catholic, Mrs Maria Fitzherbert. On the other hand, Pitt's popularity was unshaken, thanks to his decisive stand on the question of a limited regency and the circumspection with which he had borne himself on the earlier questions of parliamentary reform and Hastings' impeachment. Government held its ground and even slightly improved its position by a net gain of three seats.[2]

In time for the meeting of the new Parliament, was published Burke's *Reflections on the Revolution in France*. His ideas had begun to take shape in the autumn of 1789 as a result of his private information about the nature of social upheaval in France and his indignation at the common assumption in Britain that this event was similar to the revered Revolution of 1688. In particular, Burke took objection to Price's comparison of the two revolutions in a 'sermon' delivered on 5 November 1789 to the Revolution Society, a staid body which celebrated the 1688 Revolution by an annual dinner on the anniversary of the Prince of Orange's landing in Torbay. The *Reflections*, a laudation of the British Constitution as the tried and tested product of slow accretion rather than an artefact such as the new Constitution of France, made an immediate appeal to conservative and moderate readers. The writer's message made explicit what had always been implicit in Whiggery: regard for the sanctity of property and existing institutions. With its themes blended, as only Burke could blend them, with supportive arguments from the sanctity of family life and from the development of English law by precedent, the book was to become the philosophical justification for future Toryism.[3]

While Burke's message was being assimilated, and his grim prognosis for the progress of the French Revolution justified by events across the Channel, members of Parliament assembled in November 1790 in an uncertain frame of mind. Pitt, like Fox, had welcomed the French Revolution, so that Burke's message had to overcome some initial resistance among the ministry's supporters as well as its opponents. While members took stock of their position the first session of the new House of Commons remained quiet before Christmas 1790 and for some time into the new year. The Whigs were unwilling to risk a display of numbers until a favourable issue could be found, and Pitt was more concerned to solve his current problems with the court's adherents in his ministry than to seek an unnecessary trial of strength with the parliamentary opposition. But an opportunity for both sides arose in March 1791 when Parliament was debating Leeds's demand to Russia for the return to the Ottomans of the Black Sea city of Oczakov, lately seized by Potemkin and deemed to be of strategic interest to Britain. The Whigs rallied energetically to attack this *démarche* as likely to involve Britain in a war she was in no position to win. The ministry were able to record substantial majorities, approaching 100 in the Commons, but behind the scenes there was no unanimity on the government side. Hardliners, such as Leeds and Thurlow, met with increasing criticism as substantial government supporters, led by Grafton, withdrew their support. Pitt's own unease at the open-ended commitment to war implied by Leeds's policy made him decide to withdraw from a position which could only weaken his ministry. By abandoning Leeds's ultimatum he also struck a blow at ministers for whom he had no love. His withdrawal of the ultimatum led to Leeds's immediate resignation and the advancement of the Pittites Grenville and Dundas to the posts of Foreign Secretary and Home Secretary respectively.[4]

The Oczakov crisis was used adroitly by Pitt but it proved to be a disaster for the Whigs by reopening differences over the French Revolution which had been glossed over during the election campaign. On 15 April, in further debate on the Russian affair, Fox decided to repeat his praise of the new French Constitution. Thus the Whigs' delight at what they chose to believe was Pitt's response to their parliamentary pressure over Oczakov was immediately overshadowed by new fears about the unity of their own party. Burke chose the occasion of a debate on the Quebec Bill to make a major reply to Fox, denouncing events in France and the doctrine of the rights of man. In his speech Burke renounced his friendship with Fox, though for many years this friendship had been no more than a political one. Fox's copious tears in the House and his protestations of continued friendship did not prevent the announcement in the Foxite *Morning Chronicle* on 12 May that Burke had, by his action, withdrawn from the party. If the Whigs were to split, Fox wished to ensure that he himself should not appear in the role of deviationist. But although the touchy Burke was pushed into making the first overt move towards schism, other party leaders had already foreseen this as a consequence of Fox's provocation. Soon after the latter's speech Portland had confided to Fitzwilliam that, as a result, 'something very disagreeable is likely to happen, and such a political schism and division as may end in the dissolution of the Party'. Portland was far closer to Burke both personally and in politics than to Fox, and a few weeks later he assured one of Burke's friends that he told anyone who criticized the *Reflections* to him that he had recommended it to his sons as the true Whig creed.[5]

Burke, however, was not to be satisfied any longer by private support which still saw the unity of the party as a reason for refusing to break openly with Fox and his doctrine. A struggle for the minds of the party began with Burke producing his *Appeal from the New to the Old Whigs*, tracing the descent of his own ideas from those of the early Whigs. The principles of Fox's 'modern Whigs' had arisen, Burke maintained in a letter to Fitzwilliam, 'out of the monstrous system which is now destroying France'. The *Appeal*, following hard upon the *Reflections*, was avowedly intended 'to compel those who approved his principles to make a public profession of them'. But although the noble leaders were willing to sympathize with Burke in private, the time was not yet come for them openly to abandon Fox. The ties of party, built up over twenty years or more, were still sufficiently binding and only the further drift of France into destruction of its own society and war with Britain could make the Whigs bow to Burke's logic when he acknowledged of his ideas that 'if they are Tory principles, I shall always wish to be thought a Tory'.[6]

The prospect of Whig schism was sufficient to dismay all concerned, save Burke, and for most of the session of 1791/2 Fox as well as Portland strove to be conciliatory. For some months, too, Pitt was again too preoccupied with his own internal power struggle with Thurlow to exploit the opposition's divisions. The beginning of the end of the quiet phase came, however, in April 1792, with the formation by Grey, Sheridan and other radical parliamentary Whigs of the Association of the Friends of the People. The principal intentions of this body were to further reform and counter Burke's influence, which its members felt was gaining ground with many of the Whig party. Following swiftly upon the inception of the Friends of the People came Grey's motion of 30 April for the reform of Parliament. The debate proved important for both opposition and government. Fox had held back from joining Grey's group out of a desire to retain an uncommitted stance on the reform issue. He was now obliged to declare himself, despite verbal equivocations, by voting with the reformers. Pitt, on the other hand, made a decisive speech against reform, both reassuring those of the government who had regarded him as uncommitted on this issue and also drawing closer to the conservative Whigs. Pitt immediately followed up this initiative by seeking Portland's co-operation in 'checking any attempts dangerous to public order', and, finding the Whig leader receptive, issued in May a proclamation against seditious writings. Having demonstrated his own renunciation of parliamentary reform, Pitt now felt strong enough to obtain the dismissal of Thurlow by threatening his own resignation. The fall of the Chancellor not only removed a critic and royal spy from the Cabinet but opened the way to the possible appointment of Lough- borough as a first step towards detaching the more conservative Whigs from the opposition side. The Chancery remained unfilled while negotiations proceeded.[7]

The barrier to juncture still lay, however, in the fact that while Pitt was willing, and indeed anxious, to dispense with the right wing of his own government, Portland was not equally willing to break with the reforming Whigs and thus split the party. So while Pitt and Grenville led their adherents in both Houses in support of Fox's Libel Bill in May, voting with the Whigs against 'all the interior Household', the approval of Fox remained for Portland the official *sine qua non* of any new ministry which might be formed as a result of Pitt's approach. When Fox declared that 'the pride of the party' demanded avoidance of 'the appearance of Pitt being at the head of the proposed admin- istration', Portland concurred for almost the last time. Pitt had gone a long way in his proposed concessions in order to win over the conservative Whigs but could hardly be expected to give up his own office. As Portland saw the matter, however, the fault for the failure of the proposed coalition lay with the government. To Burke he complained: 'They have no principle, they know not what *party* is, but for the desire of annihilating it . . . Whenever their mode of thinking is reformed I shall be willing to take them by the hand.' But even as Portland wrote, in September 1792, massacres of aristocrats, priests and many others across the Channel endorsed Burke's grim prognostications, pointing to an approaching need for a new rally of British conservatives.[8]

If the September Massacres shocked and horrified most of the political class the Foxites professed to see no reason for a right-wing defection from the party. They were aware that the negotiation with Pitt, conducted largely through Portland and Loughborough, was at a standstill. With a new session approaching, Fox confided to William Windham his opinion 'that the danger to this country chiefly con- sisted in the growth of Tory principles, and that what happened in France was likely to be useful to us in keeping alive and invigorating the spirit of liberty'.[9] And in public he reaffirmed in a speech to the Whig Club early in December his belief in the rights and happiness of the people, together with his condemnation of any obstruction to these ends. Among such obstructions he numbered the current government reaction and the vociferous loyalist associations which were springing up throughout the country to denounce revolution and reform. It was thus no surprise that in the first days of Parliament's meeting, Fox surpassed all his previous pronouncements in a systematic series of statements calling for reform and the repeal of the Test Act. He opposed the Address, calling for a recognition of the French republic and the appointment of a British ambassador to Paris. But this full-blooded acceptance of a regime which had recently seen the execution of many of its country's aristocracy was too much even for Fox's fellow Whigs, of whom only 37 followed him on 13 December, together with a few other members, to make up a total of 50 votes against Pitt's majority of 290. Again the party was thrown into turmoil with Portland issuing conflicting statements through Elliot and his own son, Lord Titchfield, respectively breaking with Fox and cleaving to him.

This equivocation was too much for Loughborough, who at last accepted the proffered chancellorship from Pitt in January 1793 and thus became the first of his party to be detached. Others such as Malmesbury, while not going so far, gave assurance of support to Pitt. The fragile nominal unity of the Whigs was barely restored by Portland's last-minute accommodation with Fox when news of the French king's execution reached England, to be followed two weeks later by a French declaration of war on Britain. Unity could survive no longer.

The first step towards withdrawal of some of the more conservative Whigs from the party came immediately upon the declaration, in February. Led by Burke's principal followers, Windham and Sir Gilbert Elliot, about twenty-six members of the party, together with twelve other members of the Commons, announced the formation of a 'third party' independent of Fox's leadership. This demonstration that they felt free to support Pitt, over war issues at least, was followed a month later by forty-five resignations from the Whig Club, the undisputed social and political centre of the parliamentary party. New demarcating lines among the Whigs were now drawn on the left by the Friends of the People and on the right by Windham's group, with the rest of the party unhappily poised between them still unwilling to recognize that disunity could become permanent. The remainder of the session saw further drifting apart as Fox continued to hold up his standard, now very close to the Friends, to rally any sympathizers who wished to remain with the party. Such was the somewhat unhappy Adam who, despite his forebodings about Fox's views on France, preferred to continue his valuable organizational work on the side of reform. Fox, in important speeches on Grey's new motion for reform in May and on his own motion for peace in June, continued to advocate support for personal liberty and some reform at home and for recognition of the French republic. Nevertheless, the paucity of Whig support for both Grey's and Fox's motions, which attracted forty-one and forty-seven votes respectively, indicated that these leaders' opinions now appealed to only a small minority of the party.[10]

The main issue which now isolated Fox's followers from the rest of the Whigs was his call for peace with the revolutionary government of France. In September 1793 Fitzwilliam wrote of Fox that 'the unfortunate turn he gave to his opposition in the course of last session, by making the principle of the war the subject of his animadversion, renders it impossible for anyone thinking as I do . . . to join in opposition with him against its management'. Even Grey's call for parliamentary reform, which in happier times would have attracted support from a greater proportion of the Whigs, was handicapped by a prevalent feeling that the time was not opportune and that any reform smacked of French influence. Not even government attacks on civil liberty, in the trials of Scottish 'Jacobins', could stir overt sympathy among the Portlandites, and Fox openly questioned whether his old friends 'have the least spark of Whiggism left in them?' Although a further session of Parliament was to pass before the party schism was made final by a coalition of Portland with Pitt, the opening of Parliament saw Fox already isolated. By December, Elliot and Malmesbury had accepted minor government posts, and although Portland held aloof this was more for tactical than for strategic reasons. In January 1794, after giving prior notice of his intentions to Fox, Portland took the decisive step of calling a meeting of leading Whigs at Burlington House to announce the end of his 'systematic opposition' and his support for Pitt's government on war policy.[11]

Portland was aware that he could not remain on this footing indefinitely without joining the government, but he was determined that his followers should join with him in strength, without allowing Pitt further to pick off individuals. Some tough bargaining followed but, by May, a negotiation was well advanced, with Pitt making difficulty only over the Whigs' proposal that the lord-lieutenancy of Ireland in the proposed coalition should go to Fitzwilliam. The earl's known preference for measures of Catholic emancipation was no more acceptable than other reforms which might rock the boat of state in troubled times. But such was Pitt's eagerness to conclude the parleying that he gave way on Fitzwilliam's appointment, leaving matters of Irish policy undefined and asking only for a deferment while he allayed the doubts of some of his colleagues. Portland and Pitt felt enough common ground to go ahead on the basis of what the former called 'the restoration of the French monarchy and restitution of property or at least a government of which property forms the basis'. Portland believed that he was saving the party, and with it the nation. Fitzwilliam saw the juncture almost as an absorption of Pitt's government by the Whig party, and he wrote to Portland of his hope that any doubters 'will think, as you do, that it will prove the cause of the renewal of power in an aristocratic Whig party, and tend thereby to the maintenance and preservation of the constitution according to its true genuine principles'.[12]

The Portland Whigs were indeed, in the longer run, greatly to influence the future development of Pitt's party, forming the basis of the Tory party under Portland after Pitt's death. But in the immediate outcome of their defection to government the Portlandites' numbers were incommensurate with their importance. Though Portland carried with him most of the Whig peers and just over fifty followers in the Commons he only strengthened already strong government majorities.[13] For such an addition, the favours received by the Portlandites looked excessive to some observers. On 11 July, Portland himself became Home Secretary, with Dundas gracefully giving him place, while Windham took the post of Secretary of War. Spencer and Mansfield also entered the Cabinet, the former becoming First Lord of the Admiralty later in the year. Fitzwilliam was made Lord President pending his transfer to Ireland. Peerages and other gratifications followed for the conservative Whigs. Many of Pitt's supporters, even among those who had not been forced to give up their offices to make way for the newcomers, were unhappy about the price paid for coalition.

Pitt himself had no doubts about the need for generous terms, but his supporters' attitude strengthened him when he had to resist the first attempt at Portlandite pressure within his ministry. This centred upon Fitzwilliam, who received the lord-lieutenancy of Ireland in December. Within a month Fitzwilliam's views were seen to be even more dangerous to the new alliance than Pitt had supposed. In the previous year the government had permitted Irish Catholics to vote in elections for the Parliament of Ireland. Fitzwilliam now proposed further to upset the Protestant Establishment by removing penal legislation and permitting Catholics to sit as members of the Dublin Parliament. Pitt declared bluntly to Portland that the new plans were inconsistent with 'the union' of their parties. The Lord-Lieutenant desired to dismiss John Beresford, First Commissioner of Revenues in Ireland, to be replaced by his own nominee as a first step towards the new Catholic policy. Fitzwilliam's old friends, notably Carlisle, Windham and Thomas Grenville as well as Portland himself, tried hard to persuade him to subordinate old Whig ideals to a higher loyalty, a party of union. On

his refusal it was Fitzwilliam himself who was dismissed, with Portland's firm but unhappy acquiescence. From now on policies had to
be agreeable not just to one element of the union but to all who
served under Pitt and Portland. A new party was coming into being,
born out of the juncture of conservative opponents of revolution in
France and reform at home.[14]

The division of parliamentary politicians on new ideological lines
which had been implicit since the outbreak of the French Revolution matured in the last five years of the eighteenth century into a
clear-cut rift between the newly constituted government party and
the much-denuded Whigs. War with revolutionary France continued to stimulate the new alignment, hardening the views of those
on both sides whose minds were already made up and, at the same
time, reducing the number of true independents who resisted the
pressure of events.[c] Gradations of voting were becoming more
apparent on both sides, with only hardliners returning votes in all
divisions while others expressed their reservations by absence
rather than deviation at a time of national emergency.

   Autumn 1794 saw a strengthening of the government's determination to suppress reform and 'Jacobinism'. The suspension of
habeas corpus earlier in that year, together with the precedent of
arrests and successful prosecutions in Scotland, led to new measures
of repression in England. With Portland's somewhat reluctant
approval, leaders of the main reformist organizations were brought
to trial. They had called for measures of parliamentary reform,
including mass suffrage. Less wisely they had tried to organize a
national convention of delegates. Parliamentary opinion was
affronted, as it had been by Wyvil's convention of 1780, though
accusations of collecting arms and plotting the government's overthrow were not substantiated. Thomas Hardy, the bootmaker
secretary of the London Corresponding Society, was chosen as the
first to go on trial. This proved to be a tactical error on the
government's part, for not only was he palpably a reformer rather
than a revolutionary but the circumstances of his arrest, resulting
in the death of his pregnant wife, aroused widespread public disapproval. Defended by the able Foxite, Thomas Erskine, Hardy
was acquitted by a jury early in November after his programme of
reform was shown to be no more radical than that of so eminent and
unprosecuted a peer as the Duke of Richmond fourteen years
earlier. Similar defence techniques organized by the opposition
brought about the acquittal of Horne Tooke, inspirer of the Society
for Constitutional Information, and John Thelwall of the Friends of
the People on charges of conspiracy and constructive treason.

But despite these successes in the courts the Foxites made no headway against the enormous government majority in Parliament. Their strenuous but hopeless objection to suspension of habeas corpus even before Portland joined the government disinclined them from further exhausting gestures in the following session. Fox's amendment to the Address to obtain peace with France achieved only fifty-nine votes. A campaign to obtain petitions outside Parliament in support of peace met little success and left the opposition further dispirited. Fox began to think that calculated absence from Parliament might be a more useful gesture than his ineffectual presence.[15] Grey, younger and more hopeful, thought that he could detect signs of sympathy outside Parliament: 'Many persons who are ready to condemn the war, are not prepared to vote a strong censure on Pitt, and we ought to unite all the opinion we can on the former point.' So in 1794/5 the Foxites continued, despite their leader's pessimism, to press for peace and campaign for parliamentary reform, relief for Dissenters and the abolition of the slave trade. Above all, in this and succeeding sessions, the parliamentary opposition fought strongly against the government's repressive measures. Numbering a little over sixty in the Commons and fewer than ten in the Lords on most issues, the Whigs still had a great deal of talent and a stiffening of important Whig grandees. Bedford, Albemarle and Guildford formed a core of opposition in the Lords, together with Fox's friend, Lauderdale. Devonshire had reluctantly followed Portland but refused to vote for Pitt, and some of the Cavendishes adhered to Fox. Also in league with the opposition were usually to be found Lansdowne, as Shelburne was now known, and Pitt's radical cousin, Stanhope. Somewhat later Norfolk, and Fox's nephew Holland when he entered the House, added strength to the ranks. Fox himself, Grey and Sheridan remained the principal speakers in the Commons, assisted by the newer orators – Whitbread, the radical son of a rich brewer, and, after the 1796 election, the lawyer George Tierney.[16]

At the opening of Parliament on 29 October 1795 a mass demonstration filled the streets of the capital and the king's coach suffered damage from a stone (some said a bullet) as he travelled to the state opening. Government immediately reacted by bringing in an already planned Seditious Meetings Bill, to control meetings of fifty or more persons, and a Treasonable Practices Bill which imposed penalties, including transportation for seven years, for speech or writing against the constitution. Of these two bills Grey immediately wrote to a supporter: 'We have determined here to use every effort to oppose them, and to obtain the opinion of the People upon this last question respecting their remaining rights.' But efforts to obtain support in county meetings met little success. Grey was forced to confess that 'we may gain little in point of numbers indoors if we meet with the same [lack of] encouragement and support from without'.[17] The bills passed by 213 to 44 and 226 to 45 in the key divisions. The judgement was confirmed in the new year when Grey's motion for opening a peace negotiation with France was lost by 189 to 50 and Fox's motion in May for an Address upon the state of the nation in regard to the war was defeated by 216 votes to only 42. The failure of further elaborate plans for a concerted campaign in the country only revealed, in the general election of 1796, that the respectable electors in counties and boroughs had little sympathy with the Foxite position. The government's majority at dissolution was confirmed and even slightly increased.

A further session of depressing performance convinced the Whigs that they had as little to hope from the new Commons as from the old. Having failed in direct assault upon the principle of war they switched their tactics and attempted to censure its management. Little improvement in voting strength resulted. Fox and Sheridan achieved eighty-one and seventy votes in divisions on the subject of Pitt's grant of a subsidy to the Austrian ally without consent of Parliament, but such results were hardly encouraging. In May 1797 it was the turn of Whitbread and Grey to fail, respectively by 237 to 63 and 206 to 60, in attempted censures of mismanagement of the naval mutiny at Spithead. This event, and the succeeding mutiny at the Nore, did, however, stimulate an abortive negotiation for a new government conducted by Lord Moira in June on behalf of the Prince of Wales.[18]

Moira attempted to capitalize upon the discontent of some of the government's independent supporters. The plan was apparently to canvass support for an administration excluding 'persons who had on either side made themselves obnoxious to the public'. Fox agreed to stand down from any such administration, but Grey and Bedford refused to consider the scheme. Moira's further suggestion that the discontented independents should ally themselves with the Foxite opposition met no success, and the matter lapsed. Though eventually unsuccessful the negotiation may have helped to gain a few extra supporters for Grey's scheme of parliamentary reform which proposed new county seats, on the pattern of Pitt's bill of 1785, in addition to seats for major unrepresented cities. Grey also advocated a copyholder vote in the counties and a uniform franchise based on the tax-paying householders in borough constituencies, thus anticipating some of the features of his successful bid of 1832. But even the relatively high vote of 91, against the government's 256, gave the Foxites no encouragement. In the summer of 1797 most of the party submitted to a majority opinion that the opposition should not attend Parliament in the next session, thereby expressing disapproval more forcibly, as they hoped, than by their continued presence.[19]

In its outcome the secession lasted for three years. Grey explained that 'to return without some material change in public opinion will hardly accord with my own feelings'. Of leading opposition speakers only Tierney continued to attend Parliament regularly, and Sheridan irregularly. In the early months of 1798, however, the party attended in strength for two issues which gave some hope of popular support, Pitt's pioneer proposal for an income tax and Wilberforce's motion for a bill to abolish the slave trade. But neither opposition to Pitt's plan nor support for his friend's humanitarian measure brought an appreciable increase in the Whigs' low voting strength, and their resolution to continue the secession was in the main strengthened. During the session of 1798/9 only Tierney continued in regular public criticism of income tax and other government fiscal measures. Fox did not attend and Grey spoke only once. Thus there was little opposition to Pitt's proposals for a union of the British and Irish Parliaments, on the precedent of the Anglo-Scottish Union of 1707, as a means of allaying the bitter religious and social strife which had broken out in rebellion in the wake of the withdrawal of Fitzwilliam's planned reforms. In February 1799 Sheridan led a handful of lapsed seceders and other critics of the scheme in hopeless obstruction which achieved only twenty-four or twenty-five votes. Thereafter opposition again almost disappeared from Westminster. Even so controversial a measure as the government's suppression of the London Corresponding Society did not stir them to overt protest. Though they did not read the complacent words of Speaker Addington they could have agreed with him when he wrote that 'Government, Parliament, and the great body of the People are at war with Jacobinism'.[20]

While Pitt's scheme of Union went forward in the Irish Parliament little more could be done by its critics in Britain; indeed many of the opposition were not entirely out of sympathy with the measure. The young Holland in the Lords and some of his friends in the Commons even offered, according to his own account, to forego all opposition to Union if it removed religious disabilities from Catholics. When serious opposition was raised it came not from Parliament but from court, and it centred on the proposed removal of those disabilities.[21]

Though not entirely unexpected, George's objections to emancipation took much of their edge from being the culmination of a series of disagreements with Prime Minister and Cabinet over domestic and foreign policies. Pitt's threat of resignation to secure Thurlow's dismissal in 1792 had been followed by his insistence on the removal of the king's own son from military command two years later. From then on, several differences over matters of strategy and over the king's objection to peace with 'French principles' at any price came to a head in 1800 with the crumbling of Pitt's second coalition against revolutionary France. The Cabinet planned several minor naval expeditions but simultaneously toyed with ideas of peace or, at least, naval armistice. George opposed the Ferrol expedition and stood down only after Pitt threatened resignation again.[22] But, as in the last war, the king remained obdurate against peace. The question of Irish emancipation therefore came as the high point of a long process during which George lost the trust in his minister which had been engendered in the regency crisis a decade earlier.

The Rebellion of 1798 in Ireland convinced Pitt, Dundas and Grenville that the problem of the unrepresented Catholic majority in Ireland must not continue under the new parliamentary Union. Through Lord-Lieutenant Cornwallis and his Chief Secretary, the rising star Castlereagh, they secured Catholic support for the Union by hints or promises of emancipation. Though aware that the king would raise every possible objection they had little doubt of their ability to persuade or bludgeon him, as on previous occasions, into agreement. In August 1800 the Cabinet decided, as a first step, that Catholics must be allowed to sit in the Union Parliament, take offices and receive other concessions. Thereafter, however, the plan went awry. Loughborough revealed it prematurely to the king, giving him time to marshal his objections and worry himself into illness. Worse still, some members of the Cabinet, uneasy at their acquiescence in a majority decision, began to feel their way towards dissent from the emancipation strategy. A measure of the degree of fusion which had taken place in the coalition since 1794 was that the split cut across the former division of Pittites and Old Whigs. The dissentients included not only Charles Jenkinson, now Earl of Liverpool, and the former Lord-Lieutenant Westmorland, but also Portland and Loughborough. The supporters of emancipation included among their number not only Pitt's personal coterie but also the Old Whigs Windham and Spencer. The disappearance of former loyalties was a sign of the emergence of a party in place of the 'union', but the new division spelt a collapse of the ministry.

The leading ministers' deteriorating relationship with George III, together with the strain of war by the autumn of 1800, may have encouraged Pitt to delay communicating the unwelcome policy to the king. The delay was fatal. On 28 January 1801 George, unable to contain any longer his displeasure at still being unconsulted on a measure about to be unfolded as a governmental *fait accompli*, broke silence. To Windham he was reported to have remarked that 'he should consider any person who voted for it, as personally indisposed towards him'. To another hearer he burst out even more forcibly, 'I shall reckon any man my personal enemy who proposes any such measure'.[23] The following day George conspicuously failed to attend in person the opening of Parliament. On the 31st Pitt wrote that having heard with deep regret of His Majesty's opposition to the proposals of Catholic emancipation, which were approved by the majority of the Cabinet, he took the liberty 'of most respectfully, but explicitly, submitting to Your Majesty the indispensable necessity of effectually discountenancing . . . all attempts to make use of Your Majesty's name, or to influence the opinion of any individual on any part of the subject'. On George's refusal to comply with this ultimatum, Pitt offered his resignation on 3 February. With him resigned Grenville, Dundas, Camden, Rose, Windham, Spencer, Cornwallis and, among the younger generation of able parliamentarians, Castlereagh, George Canning and the latter's friend, Leveson-Gower.[24]

The king lost no time in trying to form a new administration; but making good the grievous losses from the Cabinet, as well as the equally hurtful vacancies in junior offices, was not easy. Towards the end of February, George fell prey again to his previous illness and mental unbalance, and Parliament anxiously prepared for a regency. In the event the attack, though severe, proved brief. Recovery was speeded up when Pitt was induced to promise, via the doctors, never again to initiate the question of Catholic emancipation during the king's lifetime.[25] Out of respect for George's health and prerogative of ministerial appointment Pitt was to spend the next three years refraining from attacking the weak government of Henry Addington, who as Speaker of the Commons had headed the opponents of emancipation, until he could do so no longer without damaging the national interest. But, notwithstanding his humanity and loyalty, Pitt had already in February 1801 established for the future Tory party the crucial point that ministers could not remain in office unless their policies were ultimately accepted by the monarch.[d]

Notes: Chapter 10

a   By Dr O'Gorman's calculation 32 of the 66 Whigs who were eventually to remain with Fox did not vote for Grey's motion for parliamentary reform in May 1793 (*Whig Party and the French Revolution*, app. 4, p. 253).

b   Stirred up by the exhortations of the clergy. In February 1790, when Fox was again preparing a motion for the repeal of the Test Act, one London newspaper reported clerically inspired meetings 'in every quarter of England and Wales, to oppose the repeal', *London Chronicle*, 23–25 February 1790.

c The process whereby many independents were drawn into closer relationship with either ministry or opposition even before Portland's secession has been noted by Dr O'Gorman, *Whig Party and the French Revolution*, p. 129.

d See above, pp. 31–2.

CHAPTER ELEVEN

Pittite Fragmentation and Whig Coalition 1801–11

The break-up of Pitt's long-standing administration began a decade of often weak government and gave new hope to the long-excluded Whigs. Addington's period in office accentuated the splintering of the 'Pittite' party begun by Pitt's resignation. With many leading ministers excluded by their own choice the Doctor's team was weak and inexperienced. Both in Cabinet and in Parliament he depended heavily upon those who were encouraged by their former leader to place support of the new ministry before personal inclination. But Pitt's own position of benevolent neutrality was tenuous and became increasingly so while his supporters pressed for withdrawal into opposition as the only way to put an end to Addington's little-relished leadership. Because Pitt delayed overlong before deciding to force his way back into office he lost some of his most important followers to a greatly recovered Whig party. By 1804 the once overwhelmingly strong Pittite party was so divided between Pitt, Grenville and Addington that it had to struggle for years to reunite. By the time this was largely accomplished the king was permanently incapacitated, Pitt himself long dead and the Pittite image superseded by acceptance of the title of Tory.

For the fragmentation of the Pittites, like that of the Whigs after 1760, a large measure of responsibility must fall to the king's dogged assertion of his will, though on this occasion he had no wish for the break-up of the government party and would have welcomed Pitt back – on terms. The George III of 1801 was not the brash young king of forty years earlier, for though still equally determined he was more cautious. His Protestant conscience had precipitated the breach with Pitt, but having obtained the latter's undertaking to avoid further contention on the Catholic issue he saw no objection to a reconstruction of the ministry. Even Addington was willing, if a formula of accommodation could be found allowing himself some part, to stand down from the premiership. But pressure from Pitt's followers stiffened their leader in preserving his independence, and

Addington had to struggle on for three weary sessions conscious of royal approval but unsustained by any warmth of admiration or respect from the nation.

The Cabinet was not one to inspire national confidence in time of emergency. Addington himself, despite his Commons experience, was hardly of higher ministerial calibre than Bute, the king's earliest choice as First Lord. Grenville's place at the Foreign Office went to Hawkesbury, the able but untried son of Charles Jenkinson who had once been Bute's right-hand man and now, as Earl of Liverpool, continued as Chancellor of the Duchy of Lancaster and President of the Board of Trade in his fifth decade of loyal service to the crown. Eldon, a lawyer who excelled even Addington and Liverpool in his royalism and conservatism, became Lord Chancellor. The government's main reliance was on Cabinet ministers encouraged by Pitt to retain their offices, including Portland and Chatham. Such men had little personal loyalty to Addington. At the outset of the ministry Dundas wrote to Pitt: 'Our friends who, as an act of friendship and attachment to you, agree to remain in office, do it with the utmost chagrin and unwillingness, and among other considerations which operate upon them, the feeling that they are embarking in an Administration under a head totally incapable to carry it on . . .'. Though their motivation may here be overstated there is little doubt that most of the continuing ministers would have welcomed a chance to rebuild a Pitt ministry.[1]

To stabilize the ministry Addington's most urgent need was peace with France. Pitt could be relied upon to honour his concept of loyalty and refrain from opposition. The fallen minister, it is true, had early misgivings about propping up a government so little to his taste, but confided such thoughts only to his old tutor, the Bishop of Lincoln. For the moment at least Addington was secure of Pitt's acquiescence in negotiating with Bonaparte. Other adherents to this policy, of longer standing and more conviction, were the opposition Whigs. In this common ground Addington hoped for a chance of providing himself with a few useful adherents. But other than Tierney, who had recently quarrelled with some of his friends, the Foxites showed their usual objection to being detached seriatim, and held out against blandishments. Addington's approach, begun in October as Parliament met, was rejected by Grey on behalf of Fox and by Moira for the Prince of Wales. Grey demanded 'great and leading measures' of reform by any new ministry. Even the repeal of the Treasonable Practices and Seditious Meetings Acts, unless accompanied by more positive and possibly parliamentary reforms, was not enough to tempt the opposition.[2]

As usual, the Whigs' reluctance to compromise their unity and their principles came initially from the rank and file, with the leaders obeying their pressure. Even in the continued absence of Fox, still immersed in his study of the first Whigs of James II's day, the Foxites were rallying their forces after their enervating secession. Soon after Pitt's fall a motion by Grey on the state of the nation received 105 votes, with a good turnout of Whigs now that they saw some prospect of reviving an effective opposition. The next session continued their attendance and interest, their first task being to vote against the last ministry by supporting Addington's treaty with Napoleon.[3]

The peace preliminaries concluded on 1 October demonstrated Addington's haste for peace, abandoning most of Britain's military gains in return for France's withdrawal from Italy. On 3 November the Prime Minister faced criticism from leading members of the former ministry despite Pitt's approval. Grenville's reasoned stand in the Lords was based upon detailed objections to Addington's concessions, but against the forces of patronage and war weariness it gained only ten votes in a full House. In the Commons, too, peace was popular at any price though here the objectors were joined by the former Burke coterie under Windham, whose denunciation of any truckling with republican France revived the spirit of his old mentor. The appearance of such influential opponents to Addington's policy was serious. The translation of the Grenville family and Windhamites to opposition proved to be permanent, so that from the end of 1801 the term 'New Opposition' came to distinguish them from the 'old' opposition of the Foxites. Moreover, a state of near mutiny among other Pittites at their leader's refusal to allow them to oppose the peace was signalled by Canning's absence from the debate. To his friend Frere he confided: 'I have told [Pitt] plainly that after the return of peace I should consider the question of "Is this man fit to be a Minister" as a fair ground of action.'[4]

For 'new' opposition and waverers alike Pitt's stance was inexplicable. Canning waxed sarcastic at his leader's contortions over a minor dissension from a government measure: '[Pitt] *will* oppose it – but not (as you may imagine) in the spirit of opposition. No such thing.' As his discontent grew his metaphor grew wilder, venting his dissatisfaction with Pitt's position: 'Addington has managed him with masterly cunning', has 'squeezed him like an orange' and will 'pelt him at the opposition'. It was, however, Grenville's outright opposition rather than the discontent of Pitt's lesser friends which posed Addington's greatest potential problem. Against the authority of the former Foreign Secretary the ministry had no one to stand up in the Lords, where second thoughts troubled some inconstant friends of government. When the peace came up for debate again after Hawkesbury's conclusion of the definitive treaty in March 1802 it was Grenville's eloquence which did most damage. On this occasion he was followed in the division on 13 May by fifteen other peers including Spencer, Fitzwilliam and Minto of the one-time Rockingham Whigs, while old Auckland was prevented from voting against the peace only by threat of dismissal. In the Commons two days later the ministry swept the board by 276 votes to 22 but here, too, were to be seen signs of increasing discontent in the form of many members who emulated Grey and Canning in absenting themselves from the voting.[5]

Doubters as to the efficacy of the treaties were as yet few, and the summer of peace in 1802 saw a quiet general election with Addington taking advantage of the popularity of his peace. There was no clear issue and few surprises, though a signal of revived radicalism in peacetime conditions came from the return of the reformer Sir Francis Burdett for Middlesex, once the scene of Wilkes's activities. Windham's newest reversal of allegiance cost him the seat he had held at Norwich since 1784, forcing him to fall back on a Grenville borough. Another sign of the times was Canning's decision to find himself a seat without the assistance he had previously received from Pitt, thus preparing himself for independent action if the great man continued to shore up Addington. Many Britons took advantage of European peace to travel abroad, but the unfavourable impressions they received of French intentions presaged new attitudes. Few believed that Bonaparte's ambitions were sated, and before the end of the year the annexation of Piedmont to re-establish his control of Italy gave solid substance to fears. Nevertheless, Addington went ahead with economies while at the Admiralty St Vincent worked to reduce the navy laboriously built up by his predecessor. Even the Doctor, however, could not totally ignore the signs of French war preparations, and when Britain was called upon to fulfil her treaty obligation to evacuate Malta the demand was met by refusal to abandon the strategically important island.

When the new Parliament assembled the shape of possible political developments began to emerge. The Grenvilles now appeared 'on the opposite lower side of the House' in the Commons, while Canning and a few friends occupied 'the old hill fort behind the Treasury Bench'. Both groups spoke against the Address and both continued to urge Pitt to abandon support for Addington. Grenville found in Pitt's attitude 'room for volumes of reflections', and was not mollified even when his cousin expressed dissatisfaction with Addington's retrenchments by failing to support the minister's budget in December. Although Grenville was not yet ready to throw in his lot with the Foxite opposition he hoped to replace

Addington by a strong coalition under Pitt, preferably including Fox. But, as renewed war loomed, Pitt failed to obtain any such terms. In March 1803 he received and declined Addington's suggestion that they should both take secretaryships under a nominal Prime Minister. A month later Addington went further, offering the Treasury, only to be told in terms reminiscent of Portland's in 1783 that Pitt would not consent to come back unless his own 'plan of arrangement' for ministerial appointments were accepted.[a] The king was still not ready to capitulate to this extent, and the negotiation came to nothing.[6]

But the end of Addington's ministry was assured, in the longer run, by the renewal of war in May. Though Pitt continued, against the pressure of his friends, to refuse 'to give any concurrence or countenance to any plan of forcing out the Government by pressing upon them in Parliament' Addington's own deficiencies and the ruin of his policy of peace and retrenchment spoke for themselves. In August, Charles Yorke, about to assume office as Home Secretary in a minor reshuffle of the ministry, confided to his brother the opinion that the Prime Minister 'is not equal to the crisis in which we stand. In truth I think there is but one man among us who is, I mean Pitt.'[7]

Nevertheless, eight more months elapsed before Addington could be prised from the king. This interval proved too long for Grenville's patience and ensured that when the event took place Pitt would be weakened and Fox strengthened. Pitt's reluctance to oppose, and thus to upset the old king once again, was to cost the nation dear. Fox was ready to accept Grenville and 'to act in a manner that may lead to the forming of a party against *the Court*, composed of the Old and New oppositions'. Grenville carried with him the Windhamites as well as his family and friends. The main basis of the juncture, when finally agreed in January 1804, was that the old and new oppositions agreed that they thought 'alike on Irish affairs'. Catholic emancipation was the common ground when Grenville decided, as he punctiliously announced to Pitt, to go into 'declared and regular opposition'.[8]

The defection of Grenville together with another crisis in which Pitt was threatened with the loss of Canning and his friends brought to the king's mental condition the new stress and turmoil which Pitt feared. But on this occasion George's early recovery removed any last scruples. On 15 March, Pitt attacked the government on its naval management, achieving 107 votes against the government's low 128, with over 120 government supporters leaving before the vote. On 21 April he called for Addington's removal, and by the end of the month the minister informed the king that he could not continue. Pitt took office but in deference to the perilous state of the king's health felt obliged to repeat his undertaking not to raise Catholic claims. Thus the new ministry was deprived of any hope of resecuring Grenville whose views on this subject were as implacable as the king's. Pitt had forced the closet but did not, out of humanity, annihilate the king. As a result he began his second ministry without the parliamentary support of either those who supported Addington or those who had recently allied themselves with Fox.[9]

Though Pitt regained office for the short remainder of his life the main beneficiaries from Addington's fall were the Whigs. These, together with some 23 recent Grenvillite recruits, now numbered about 150 in full opposition. Such a body was not only a great improvement in size on the Whig rump before its secession from Parliament in 1797 but also represented a more solid party than the combination of old and new opposition which had confronted Addington's government. At the time of the formal juncture with Grenville even so eminent a Whig as Grey voiced considerable unease about alliance with conservative renegade Pittites.[10] But Grenville's loyalty to his new friends brought about acceptance by the Foxites, especially as he brought substantial improvement to their effectiveness in Parliament. Grenville himself gave a fresh and authoritative lead in the Lords to the weak and hitherto rather dilettante opposition of such peers as Bedford, Norfolk and Holland.[b] In both Houses the Grenvillites set a moderate tone to opposition debating, giving a new strength which was not simply the result of enhanced numbers but arose from a greater appeal to independent opinion. Moreover, unlike Fox's earlier coalition with Lord North, that with Grenville was not entirely a juncture of old opponents. The new opposition brought back into the Whig party not only old friends such as Spencer and Tom Grenville but even Burke's sometime supporters Windham and Sir Gilbert Elliot, now Lord Minto. The Whigs rejoiced at a substantial element of reunion after the decade of schism which had begun in 1794.

Pitt's Cabinet was based on his personal followers from exile together with some of the members who had served under Addington. Camden and the faithful Dundas, now Viscount Melville, were brought in as Secretary of War and First Lord of the Admiralty; their task was to keep Pitt in close touch with the conduct of the war. The Addington survivors included Portland, Hawkesbury, Eldon and Castlereagh. Whatever annoyance these adaptable politicians might cause to such as Canning, who was rewarded only by the non-Cabinet post of Treasurer of the Navy, their presence was essential in order to keep intact the body of government voters who had first served Pitt, then Addington, and were now expected to follow Pitt again. Even so, over threescore members of the Lower House continued to look to the Doctor for a lead. The first major sign of this challenge to the new ministry came over the Additional Forces Bill, revising Addington's plans for the raising of a reserve army. The subject was one on which many politicians had strong if mutually exclusive ideas, and Pitt found himself strongly opposed not only by Addingtonians but also by the Whigs spurred on by Windham. On 18 June, with nearly 500 members present in the Commons, a key vote was won by the government with a majority of only 42. The margin was too close for comfort, and despite Rose's view that of those who followed Addington on this occasion 'few would be with him on any other question', Pitt felt that his rival had to be bought off before another major disagreement arose.

In January 1805, accordingly, it was announced that Addington was to replace an ailing Portland as Lord President and go to the Lords as Viscount Sidmouth. His friend Buckinghamshire would receive the next vacant Cabinet place. Such an arrangement was a marriage of convenience, and the irrepressible Canning did not disguise his scorn at his new 'miserable colleagues'. While the new alliance lasted Pitt and Sidmouth were never, in Speaker Abbot's judgement, 'upon any footing of cordiality'.[11] The beginning of the end came within a month with the publication of a report by a commission of inquiry on naval affairs set up during Addington's ministry, accusing Melville of connivance as Treasurer of the Navy during Pitt's first administration in corrupt speculation by one of his subordinates. Though Pitt loyally refused to believe in his old friend's guilt he found himself deserted by Sidmouth and Hawkesbury and even, on the backbenches, by Wilberforce. In a motion of censure on 8 April a tied result, 216 to 216, was resolved by the casting vote of the Speaker against Melville. Thus, while Nelson was pursuing the fleets of France and Spain far into the Atlantic, Pitt's opponents, inside his ministry as well as outside, drove on until they had obtained the resignation of the First Lord of the Admiralty. Pitt, in his displeasure, held up any further advancement for Addingtonians and appointed an able if elderly sailor, Lord Barham, to replace Melville. The end of the episode came with Sidmouth's withdrawal from the government early in July, by which time Fox had already improved the shining hour by letting the Doctor know that 'it was a great misrepresentation of his sentiments to say that he had expressed any idea of exclusion against Lord Sidmouth from any broad-bottomed Administration: on the contrary, etc. etc.' To this overture Sidmouth replied with cautious enthusiasm. Not surprisingly Abbot noted: 'Party politics in a very unsettled state.'[12]

With Sidmouth nibbling a Whig bait, doubtless containing new peace proposals, Pitt's ministry was seriously threatened. But before Parliament assembled events took a hand. In October, Nelson met his adversaries at Trafalgar, forestalling any possibility of an invasion attempt on Britain, and, in December, Bonaparte made Allied withdrawal from the war inevitable by defeating the armies of Austria and Russia at Austerlitz. This new setback was too much for a frame weakened by over-reliance on alcohol, and on 23 January 1806 Pitt died, having barely survived the Commons opening at which the opposition outlined their intention to obtain an Address for a change of ministry. Though he might have overcome such an attempt he would scarcely have been able to surmount the weight of public and parliamentary opinion against Melville in impending impeachment proceedings. And if Pitt himself could hardly have resisted the increasingly confident opposition, the remainder of his Cabinet saw little chance of doing so after his death. A majority refused to consider the king's preferred course of appointing Hawkesbury as Pitt's successor; Portland, probably seconded by Hawkesbury himself, advised George to turn to Grenville and the opposition. Grenville's accession to the Whigs had made their opposition once again formidable: the new adherence of Sidmouth made possible their first ministry for twenty-two years.

From the commencement of Grenville's ministry there was no doubt, despite the presence of Sidmouth, that this was to be government in the tradition laid down by Rockingham and Fox. On 31 January, Grenville waited on the new king with a list of the new Cabinet, as had Portland more than two decades before, insisting that the much-criticized Commander-in-Chief, the Duke of York, should henceforth be assisted by a military council. George acquiesced with as little grace as he had ever shown to pressure. The ministry known as 'of all the Talents' was largely opposed to his ideas. A Cabinet of eleven members contained six Foxites including Fox himself as Foreign Secretary and Grey at the Admiralty.[c] In addition, Spencer and Windham rejoined their old friends as Home and War Secretaries respectively. Sidmouth and his friend Ellenborough also sat in the Cabinet and their following added to the ministry's strength in Parliament, but their presence could not disguise from so old a hand as the king that this was no court administration. Ministerial replacements were more complete than at any time since 1783 and were echoed by equally drastic changes at lower levels. But on the credit side, from the monarch's point of view, the presence of Grenville and Sidmouth ensured that reformist principles would be held in check. Abolition of the slave trade would have to be conceded, but parliamentary reform could play no part in ministerial considerations despite growing pressure from the more radical Whigs. Samuel Whitbread, the Radical best-qualified for office, was conspicuously left in the cold; his estrangement from the majority of his colleagues dated from about this time. Moreover, there remained for the king and many others the hope that Grenville might yet tire of his new friends and, perhaps in conjunction with Sidmouth, reconstitute the ministry on Pittite lines. For such reasons royal patronage was not withheld and Grenville obtained a measure of 'confidence' in the form of peerages.[13]

The commencement of the Talents ministry was not inauspicious, especially as its fragile unity was strengthened by agreement on some current issues. The Grenvilles were in full accord with Fox and Grey on the Catholic question and the slave trade, while Sidmouth agreed with his colleagues on the need to try to obtain an honourable peace with Napoleon on the twin bases of Trafalgar and Austerlitz. The relative amity between leaders was reflected in the behaviour of most of their followers, though that of some Addingtonians was influenced by Sidmouth's known reluctance to countenance a slave trade bill and by his fears of some revived schemes for Catholic emancipation. Some of his sixty or so voters in the Commons may have been poor attenders or among the many members reported by Rose as hoping for an early change of administration. The Grenvilles were longer-standing and more loyal allies to the Foxite Whigs, even though many observers would have agreed with Melville's assessment that Grenville had injudiciously 'linked himself too closely in political confederacy with a party adverse to his own opinions and well known principles'. But, unlike Sidmouth, Grenville had no doubts on the slave trade resolutions which went through before the end of the session. Thus the problem of relatively low turnouts in the Commons appeared worrying rather than dangerous, and government majorities continued to be substantial.[14]

While ministerial unity remained unbroken, on the surface at least, the Pittites had yet to find an agreed course of action and a leader. Their internal differences included not only acute personal rivalries but also a basic division between those who had followed Addington from 1801 to 1804 and those who had clung to Pitt out of office. Early in February, Camden, Castlereagh and Hawkesbury agreed 'to keep together in one compact body', to watch the administration but not to oppose unless it adopted measures subversive to those of Pitt. Canning, however, proposed to go on with a vigorous opposition and the others were soon forced into his way of thinking for, as early as February, Speaker Abbot noted a 'strong disposition to make a formidable show of opposition to the new ministry on the part of the discarded and excluded Pitt party'. In March they united in censuring Ellenborough's elevation to the Cabinet, as incompatible with his appointment as Lord Chief Justice, and in opposing Windham's scheme to disband Pitt's popular but expensive volunteer army. From here on, the Pittites rapidly accepted the role and title of 'the opposition' and the concomitant need to hold together so that they might sooner or later force their way into office. In June when Grenville tried to detach Canning by an offer, the latter made it clear that he would not desert his party. Viewing coalition under Grenville as 'less desirable than continued opposition' Canning was by now aware of a scheme for forming a Pittite ministry under Portland, who had already pointed out from Pitt's example in 1784 how much could be done to upset a Commons majority. A month later Portland agreed to become titular head of the party. His emergence as Pitt's successor was formidable from his earlier experience as leader of the Whigs and marked a further stage of the transition of the Pittites to a fully fledged party as ready for the role of opposition as for government.[15]

For the autumn of 1806 the ministry's problems were vastly increased by the death of Fox. His heart condition no longer relieved by digitalis, the well-loved leader succumbed on 13 September. Grenville dissolved Parliament with a view to improving his Commons majority, and made good the loss of Fox in the government by a reshuffle which brought Grey to the Foreign Office and Tom Grenville to the Admiralty. At the same time Holland was brought into the Cabinet to maintain the majority of Foxite members. George III's agreement to a general election nearly three years before one became due was not wholehearted. He was advised by Hawkesbury or other Pittites that 'the party which constituted your Majesty's last administration' had gained strength and unity in the Commons since its fall, and could be expected only to suffer from the effect of Treasury patronage in an election. The king compromised by withholding his usual contribution to the government's election fund, but the results of the election were a vindication of Grenville's judgement. A net gain of about 25 followers in the Commons, bringing the government's theoretical strength up to almost 460 against the opposition's maximum possible of about 200, promised safe majorities, even allowing for the customary poor attendance of many members. The loss of about seventeen followers by Sidmouth could also be regarded as satisfactory, rendering his assistance cheaper and less of a stigma in the eyes of the many who regarded his inclusion in the ministry as unworthy of Whig principles.[16]

When the new Parliament met in December the Pittites were accordingly depressed and diminished, while the government's supporters exuded confidence. A challenge from the Radical Whitbread, censuring the failure of Fox's and Grey's attempts of the summer to negotiate peace, was easily brushed aside. Lord Howick, as Grey had recently become by courtesy of his father's elevation to the peerage, gave in the Commons his opinion that 'until the government of France changed its principles and character, there was no hope of peace for this country, but that we must persist in the contest till we prevailed or perished'. But the party leaders' acceptance of a foreign policy hardly distinguishable from that of the opposition did not alter the Whig and Grenvillite determination to obtain some moderate reforms. Strongly supported still by both Howick and Grenville the bill to outlaw the slave trade was carried in February and March 1807. And in the matter of Catholic relief Grenville decided, fatally for his government, that the time was ripe for some concessions which were being demanded urgently in Ireland. The fears of many Whigs that any such move would be unpopular in the country as well as at court were overridden, in the interest of ministerial solidarity, by their colleagues in the Cabinet.[17]

Thus the last scene of the Talents ministry, like that of Pitt's first ministry, turned upon the claims of Roman Catholics in Ireland. The modest means by which the Cabinet sought to appease Irish opinion was an extension of the range of commissions granted to Catholics in the armed forces. At first the king agreed, albeit reluctantly, but within a month he changed his mind. A fateful Cabinet meeting on 5 March would probably have decided for immediate resignation, on the precedent of Pitt's action, but for the absence of Spencer and Fitzwilliam through illness; in the event, a majority opted to withdraw the proposal but to restate their support for some other Catholic concessions. When George went on to demand that they would never again raise the question, the ministry resigned on the 18th. Sidmouth, however, assured king and opposition of his determination to oppose Catholic relief. His resignation preceded that of his colleagues and pointed the way for his eventual return to the Tory fold. But, for the moment, it was the party under Portland who were both ready and able to take office.[18]

The ministry over which Portland presided, in what he himself realized was a caretaker capacity, contained most of the leading Pittites. No fewer than eight senior ministers had sat in the Cabinet of 1804–6 and Canning, as Foreign Secretary, at last had a post suited to his abilities. With Hawkesbury at the Home Office, Perceval as Chancellor of the Exchequer and Castlereagh as Secretary of War there was a strong team with which government could face a Europe under Bonaparte. Only Sidmouth and his remaining supporters remained outside, estranged from the new government by participation in the Talents ministry but disabled from unequivocal opposition by their recent estrangement from the Whigs over the Catholic proposals. On 9 April, with Sidmouth's followers and the Prince of Wales's coterie voting with government, an opposition motion to censure the pledge on the Catholic issue required of Grenville by the king was rejected by 258 votes to 226 in the fullest House of Commons since 1804. In the Lords on the 13th a similar motion was lost by a more resounding 171 to 90.[19]

Nevertheless, the new ministers were not satisfied and Parliament was dissolved at the end of April. The election was a well-calculated step. Catholic relief, as the Whigs had themselves recognized, was unpopular in England and Scotland, and the fall of the late ministry over this issue was greeted with some enthusiasm. In the depressed words of young Holland 'the general result of the struggles in populous places proved, that if the Court had not gained, the Whigs had lost the people'. Only in some Irish constituencies were government candidates defeated for opposing Catholic relief. Elsewhere it was the Whigs who conceded defeat. Even Howick felt the need to retreat from his seat in Northumberland and get himself returned for a close borough.[20] The Whigs' failure during their time in office to bring any major measure of domestic reform had angered many of their constituency supporters, and several constituencies favoured radical reformers even where these competed against Whigs. At Westminster the Radicals, Burdett and Lord Cochrane, defeated no less a metropolitan celebrity than Sheridan. As well as giving government a substantial majority the election returned a small but determined radical element whose chief spokesman was Whitbread and whose aims often went far beyond those of the more conservative Whigs. In the Commons which assembled after the 1807 election there were about 160 Whigs and 12 Grenvilles in regular opposition, with spasmodic assistance from the prince's 'family'. The prince himself, opposed to Catholic relief and discontented at the failure of the Talents to allow him to rid himself of Princess Caroline on the ground of sexual misconduct, declared that he intended to take no further part in politics. Over the next few years he kept on good terms with the government side.

The new ministry was secure for the moment in its control of the Commons and free to concentrate its attention upon the pressing problems of war. The heaviest burden was upon Castlereagh and Canning, and to them also fell the task of defending in the Commons in January 1808 the more vigorous war strategy they envisaged. They had an easy passage in defending the seizure of neutral Denmark's fleet, to deny it to the French, and even the bombardment of Copenhagen.[21] Emboldened, they continued upon a course which led to the opening of a new theatre of war in the Iberian peninsula. Already Castlereagh had established a substantial force at Gibraltar. Thus when Bonaparte rationalized his ambitions by placing his brother on the Spanish throne Britain was ready to reinforce nationalist reaction to the French measures. This policy was marred by failure to make early or good use of the best commander, Arthur Wellesley, thus providing Canning with a series of grievances against his Cabinet rival. But despite ministerial quarrels British troops were poised for their most important Continental campaign since Marlborough's war a century earlier.

If the Peninsular campaign was mismanaged in its early stages the Whigs were at first in no position to exploit this situation. Within their own party they faced the vociferous, if numerically small, radical element pressing for peace and reform. To the right the Grenvilles continued to resist reformist measures, except Catholic relief, and both Whigs and Grenvilles were now adamant that the Radicals' vision of peace with Bonaparte at this stage was a chimera. Added to divergencies on matters of principle were personal differences which bit deeply. Sheridan, closely associated with the Prince of Wales, had few admirers and was barely on terms of civility with Grenville. Tierney ruffled many feelings and made few close friends by his unpredictability. Grenville remained embittered against his former associate Windham. The prince nurtured his grievance against all those who had thwarted his campaign against his wife, particularly Howick who scarcely bothered to try to conciliate him. The latter was Fox's successor as party leader in the eyes of most Whigs, even the radical camp through his brother-in-law Whitbread, but Howick's chance of rallying the party into a coherent opposition in the Commons came to an end in November 1807 when he took his seat in the Lords as Earl Grey in succession to his father.

The choice of a Commons leader to take Grey's place was canvassed long and anxiously throughout the parliamentary party. Windham, Sheridan and Tierney were all ruled out by current unpopularity, and Tom Grenville by his own choice. Whitbread's reformist views made him unacceptable to the Grenvilles and many others. Finally Grey, in consultation with a circle of close friends including Fitzwilliam and the Cavendishes, adopted George Ponsonby, an unobtrusive Irish member who had been closely associated with the Whigs since well before the parliamentary Union of 1801. Most of the party accepted Ponsonby, though somewhat hesitantly. Bedford more forthrightly commented on the appointment: 'God grant it may not lead to much anarchy and confusion among our friends, but I confess I foresee many difficulties.' He was perceptive, and many others soon came to regret the choice, for Ponsonby remained a shadowy and far from forceful personality commanding little respect from either government or opposition benches.[22] At first, indeed, he provided a focus for most of the party in calling for relief for Catholic Ireland, as well as in attacking the management of the war. Nevertheless, the radicals continued and increased their calls for measures of purification and in doing so often outshone Ponsonby's more timid criticisms of government. Whitbread's stronger personal attraction and idealism won much Whig support. His bill to reform the Poor Law fell, but another for compulsory education passed in the Commons, only to fail in the Upper House. By 1809 the vigour of the reformers' attack brought a triumph when they succeeded in forcing the Duke of York's resignation for the alleged sale of army commissions by his mistress. Next a bill preventing the sale of parliamentary seats was carried by the rich North Country member, John Curwen. Significantly, Curwen received assistance not only from the Whig party but also from the friends of Canning, from Speaker Abbot and even from Hawkesbury, now second Earl of Liverpool; the rising calls outside Parliament for reform affected government as well as the Whigs. The radical initiatives gave a new stimulus to all sympathizers, but further lowered Ponsonby's status as party leader and created a strong rival pole of attraction centred upon Whitbread and other leading reformers.[23]

As an outcome of the Radicals' increasingly successful activities both opposition and government suffered mounting internal tension. Grey and Grenville disapproved of the violent attack on York, and Grenville confessed that he 'disliked the course of harassing opposition' by 'young and ardent minds'. Whitbread, for his part, became so incensed at Ponsonby's timidity that at one point he declared his withdrawal from the party. But the Whigs' divisions were exceeded by those of the ministry, for by the spring of 1809 a new crisis was threatening to tear the Cabinet apart. A successor would soon have to be found for Portland, whose health was finally giving way. Canning was ambitious for the post and seriously concerned over the ministry's parliamentary setbacks and declining popularity in the country. His fears had been inflamed in 1808 when French forces in the Peninsula were given an undeserved chance by the Convention of Cintra to retire and regroup, giving the whole opposition a genuine cause for belabouring the hard-pressed ministers. Canning predictably, if unfairly, held Castlereagh responsible for the convention and began to threaten resignation if his rival were not removed from office.[24] The Radicals' campaign completed the ministry's disunity and confusion. Portland's resignation in September 1809 was followed swiftly by Canning's bid for the premiership, Castlereagh's belated discovery that his rival was pressing for his dismissal, and a challenge from Castlereagh which left Canning wounded and both men excluded from office by their intemperate behaviour. The Cabinet decided upon the existing Commons leader, Spencer Perceval, as Portland's successor, a choice with which the king concurred. But ministers also realized that their own deficiency in talent was a dangerous weakness. On the 18th the Cabinet resolved to advise a coalition overture to Grey and Grenville, describing to the king 'the strength of their opponents in the House of Lords (not less than 110 or 112), and the still greater difficulties which they had to encounter in the House of Commons; where they had scarcely been able to struggle through the last session'. George, though 'extremely adverse' finally consented to the proposal.[25]

Fortunately for the king's preference, Perceval's approach to the opposition leaders 'for the purpose of forming an extended and combined administration' was rejected out of hand by Grey and, after learning of Grey's attitude, no less decisively by Grenville. Grey's view was that 'nothing but a complete change of system can afford the country a chance of safety'. The king, for his part, expressed his dislike of 'an application to the other side' and the consoling thought that since it had failed 'it might be right to have made it'. In Canning's view the ministers had strengthened themselves by the overture: 'if their object was only to get a refusal, Lord Grenville has played their game for them to their heart's content'. Canning's dream of the reconstruction of the Pittites under Grenville, with himself in some leading role, was finally ended; he remained in the wilderness while the two parties rebounded from each other and began to look for ways to heal their wounds.[26]

In the event, Perceval's ministry proved to be less weak than had been feared. Liverpool's administrative talents were transferred to the secretaryship of war, to make good the loss of Castlereagh, while the foreign secretaryship was filled by Wellesley who, though a newcomer to British government, had considerable governmental experience in India. Old Melville's son, Robert Saunders Dundas, came into the Cabinet as President of the Board of Control, a move which shrewdly secured for Perceval the considerable Dundas interest in Scotland. Pitt's one-time faithful associate, Rose, unexpectedly adhered to the government, partially offsetting the loss of William Huskisson who preferred to go out with Canning. Sidmouth's following was now small enough for his exclusion to be continued, for the moment, rather than risk an explosion from his many enemies. Lower down the ranks places were found for such talented young men as Palmerston, Robert Peel and John Wilson Croker. Possessing no charisma, Perceval was a competent leader of the Commons and knew how to choose able and useful colleagues.[27]

The Whigs' attempts to prepare themselves for the meeting of Parliament in January 1810 still found them disunited. Ponsonby delayed his return from Ireland as long as he dared and reacted angrily to criticisms. A serious movement for removing him was afoot; at this stage Grey would have preferred Lansdowne's son, Lord Henry Petty, bluntly remarking that 'under similar circumstances I certainly should at once relinquish this lead'. But Ponsonby clung to his post and the effort of removing him seemed too great. The obstinate Irishman beat off the challenge of 'the young men of the party', and Grey was soon hoping that he would be 'supported as he ought to be'. But with Petty, Tierney and Whitbread dissatisfied the new session was less successful than the last in eroding the government's position.[28] An amendment to the Address failed, by 263 votes to 167, to condemn the Peninsular campaign, though succeeding divisions on the mismanaged Walcheren expedition of the previous summer gave the opposition a small majority for a committee of inquiry in the Commons. Sidmouth's following supported both the Address and the inquiry, continuing their erratic course. Also opposing on the inquiry were Canning's twelve or so followers, similarly unpredictable. But with the resignation of Chatham from the Ordnance, in expiation of his responsibility for the Walcheren failure, the government's majority was restored and the House belatedly exculpated the principle of the expedition. Nor were the Whigs' attempts at reform any more successful, and the Radical Thomas Brand's motion for a committee on the reform of Parliament rallied only 115 votes against the ministers' 234. Much of the session from April onwards was taken up by Burdett, whose arrest for widely publicizing his opposition to the exclusion of strangers from the public gallery during the Walcheren debates led to rioting in London. But though Burdett became the hero of Radical opinion outdoors, the inevitable reaction at Westminster led to a strengthening of the government ranks, while renewed tension between Whitbread and Grenville over the same issue threatened further Whig disunity. Grenville's own prescription for reform, Catholic relief, was kept in the background by Grey's common-sense assessment that there was little point in pursuing it when 'both the King and the People' were against it.[29]

Nevertheless, there were no grounds for government complacency and the summer of 1810 saw attempts to strengthen the ministry either by the readmission of Canning and Castlereagh or by bringing in Sidmouth. The move came to nothing over the continuing animosities of the three main participants, and before Parliament could meet again a new factor entered into all calculations. In October the king's final and permanent mental breakdown took place following the death of his daughter Amelia. As it became clear that there would have to be a regency of the Prince of Wales the hopes of the opposition soared. In December, Perceval's proposal to secure a restricted regency was passed in the Commons by a comfortable 269 votes to 157, with opposition objecting to the restrictions. However, limitations on the prince's power of creating peers and granting pensions and reversions were to exist for only one year. Not dissatisfied, Prince George announced his intention of keeping Perceval during the period of restrictions of his regency. He approved of the ministry's policies and possessed much of his father's view of the political role of monarchy. Grey displeased the prince by insisting that, in any Whig ministry, policy should be made only by duly appointed ministers; such long-standing court advisers as Moira and Sheridan would not be welcomed. Finally, the regent feared that both Grey and Grenville were too closely committed to Catholic relief. His alliance with the Whigs had lasted for three decades, despite periods of coolness, but was now almost worn out. In February 1811 the regency began with the Pittites still firmly in office.[30]

Notes: Chapter 11

a   See above, p. 32.
b   The most recent historian of the House of Lords in this period writes that 'Fox conceded Grenville the lead of the upper house without hesitation believing the Commons, where he had the lead, to be of far greater importance' (McCahill, *Order and Equipoise*, p. 121, n. 3).
c   The others were Fitzwilliam, Erskine, Lord Henry Petty and Moira.

CHAPTER TWELVE

Tories and Whigs Again
1811–22

The government headed by Perceval, later by Liverpool, came under the latter to be generally accepted as Tory. As late as 1812, when the regent was thought to be wavering towards the opposition, ministers protested to him that they were themselves 'a Whig administration'; but already pressure for a term to distinguish them from 'the' Whigs was mounting from government backbenchers and from the constituencies, where the Tory name had never entirely lost its currency. Euphemisms like 'the friends of Mr Pitt' had served this purpose well enough for a generation but were wearing thin years after William Pitt's death. At the same time the last impediment to ministerial adoption of the Tory label was fast disappearing. Its connotation of subservience to the crown was threadbare with the steady decline of court and Treasury support in Parliament since the 1780s, increasing ministerial reliance on party opinion. Moreover, the regent's prodigal expenditure, illegal first marriage and acrimonious second made him dependent on the ministry for money and for support against the princess.[a] Parallel with the decline of crown influence went a diminution of country independence. The revival of reformist activity favoured party differences, and though many members of Parliament clung to the honoured title of independent long into the nineteenth century true independence became rare. Divisions of the Commons, especially with the return of peace after 1815, show that most of those members who were not totally committed to one or other of the parties were, nevertheless, party orientated. Tory 'waverers' could sometimes produce unexpected government defeats on particular occasions but clung persistently to their overall alignment. In the postwar years of national agitation and resultant repression the overall loyalty of the government's 'fringe' was to ensure its survival.

It is never wise to underestimate the enemy's difficulties, and government had little at first to fear from the opposition. Bound by their commitment to Catholic emancipation the Whigs had little to offer the regent. Their weak leadership continued, with Grey often in touch only by letter from distant Northumberland and Ponsonby equally lethargic though less popular. Both men, it is true, faced real difficulties. Wartime opposition always incurred the suspicion of disloyalty, and Wellington's increasingly successful campaign in Spain and France further took the edge off criticisms of government strategy. Moreover, while war continued many Whigs remained unwilling to resort even to mild proposals for reform. But one obstacle to a united approach was progressively removed by a drift of the Grenvilles, away from their friends. Final severance was postponed after differences in 1811 but the removal of Grenvillite participation in party counsels soon after the return of peace eased tension between Whig leadership and reformers. Grey's resistance in 1809, and again in 1811, to the coalition policy preferred by Grenville reflected a new sense of purpose. For Whigs, as for Tories, the regency brought greater unity, albeit with considerable remaining differences on policy, along with a subtle transformation of sympathetic independents into a fringe of basically loyal party men.

The parliamentary activities of 1811 produced no surprises. Brand and other Radicals lost their customary motions for reform in the Commons, though the legal reformer, Samuel Romilly, had the satisfaction of seeing his bill to abolish capital punishment for minor offences pass in the Lower House before being quashed in the Lords. On the whole, the Whigs' opposition appeared low key in view of a need to avoid raising the many issues on which, they were beginning to realize, they differed seriously from the regent. Some opposition came from Canning's followers, whose leader had cooperated with the Whigs during the regency debates in the hope of inclusion in a new Grenville ministry. But by the end of the session Canning was advising his friends to absent themselves from the House rather than become any further identified with opposition. This sensitive stormcock was veering to record the prevailing wind from court. Sidmouth, by comparison, had no doubts about his course, and from the Regency Act onwards gave firm support for Perceval's government, preparing to associate himself with them in office as soon as opportunity should arrive. Nor, when the parliamentary recess arrived, was Grey far behind Sidmouth and Canning in his assessment of the regent's intentions.[1]

But the ministry, too, had problems with the prince. In preparation for his assumption of unrestricted regency he insisted upon a full Civil List, payment of his considerable debts at the public expense and a new separate establishment for his incapacitated father. Perceval's decorous and thrifty instincts were against such expensive concessions but he faced opposition from Wellesley, who strove for a generous settlement in a bid to replace his chief. With most of the prince's voracious brothers backing the challenger, in the hope of further tapping the founts of public money, Wellesley's claims looked feasible. Fortunately for Perceval his own position was strengthened in January 1812, a month before the lapse of the regency restrictions and a likely change of leadership, by Wellesley himself who chose this moment to make a stand in favour of Catholic relief for which Irish Catholics were again pressing strongly. Disoriented and trapped by indecision the regent turned to his old friends and on 12 February offered a share of office to Grey and Grenville. Their reply, in Abbot's succinct paraphrase, was 'in substance that they must have all or none'. As in the case of the similar offer three years earlier their firm stand resulted in the continuance of the ministry.[2]

In the Commons these events resulted in determined opposition activity. On Bankes's latest bill for the permanent abolition of reversions no Whig vote was cast in the majority which narrowly secured rejection; and three months later, when the same 'Saint'[b] brought a bill to prevent sinecure offices from being filled after the current holders, Whigs of all shades helped to secure its passing. When Brand brought in unsuccessful measures for enfranchising copyholders and enlarging the electorate in some borough seats he was supported not only by Whitbread but also by Ponsonby. But the government found an increased strength. With the erratic Wellesley's bid for power averted there was no question of bringing in his friend Canning and the way was therefore open for Castlereagh as Foreign Secretary. Further, new negotiations with Sidmouth resulted in the regent's objection to him being set aside. The Doctor became Lord President, with other Cabinet places for Buckinghamshire and Bragge-Bathurst as well as offices for other followers, bringing this small but useful group back into the Pittite camp at last. By early May the government seemed stabilized, with only Canning and Wellesley out in the cold. On the 11th, however, Perceval was assassinated in the lobby of the House of Commons by the deranged merchant Bellingham.[3]

The new crisis was shortlived. Liverpool's abilities, not least that of being able to get on well with all his difficult party colleagues and rivals, made him the obvious successor though not able to replace Perceval in the lead of the Commons. Wellesley and Canning were approached to join under his banner, but rather than serve with Sidmouth and Castlereagh they advised a coalition with the Whigs. The baffled regent authorized an approach, but Grey objected as usual to sharing power; and, in any case, he was still insistent upon the removal of some of the regent's household advisers as a gesture of confidence. While the leaders closetted and re-closetted, a restive section of the government's backbench supporters led by the Yorkshire member, Stuart Wortley, voted alongside the Whigs on 21 May to carry by four votes an Address for 'a strong and efficient Administration'. The ministry resigned, but with no better alternative available were reappointed under Liverpool after a fortnight. There were few real changes: Sidmouth moved to the Home Office and Nicholas Vansittart became Chancellor of the Exchequer, but eleven of the twelve members had served in Perceval's administration and eight in Pitt's of 1804–6.[4]

More important, however, than the element of Pittite continuity was a change of style from Perceval's narrow, if highminded, conservatism to Liverpool's pragmatism. Stuart Wortley's rebellion pointed to the need for stronger support in the Commons, and the time was auspicious for a new election. Continued successes for Wellington's army in the Peninsula brought popularity. The orders in council which had long caused offence to British traders and to neutral countries like the United States were withdrawn, neatly deflating a vigorous parliamentary campaign led by Henry Brougham, the recently elected luminary of the *Edinburgh Review*. At the same time Catholic emancipation was declared a subject upon which ministers might hold differing opinions. Firm measures by Sidmouth to quell Luddite disturbances also added to the government's credibility with middle-class electors. Even so, the elections resulted in smaller gains than Liverpool expected and he bewailed the decline of government patronage which offset the gain in popularity.[c] In these circumstances, ministers bethought themselves of the other traditional way of strengthening their parliamentary majority and made overtures to the last major Pittite outside the fold. Canning had enjoyed a successful election for the prestigious city of Liverpool where, with the sponsorship of the staunchly Tory merchant, John Gladstone, and under the curious eye of 3-year-old William Ewart, he defeated both Brougham and Creevey of the Whig left. The Tory Achilles was given hope of office (though when it came this took the form of an embassy to distant Lisbon), and even Sidmouth offered a personal reconciliation. Canning was thereby induced to sever his link with Wellesley, break up his 'party' and accept the promise of terms.[5]

The years from 1813 to 1815 provided a good start for Liverpool's leadership and a setback for Grey's. Despite some temporary exclusion of prominent Whigs in the election, the party's principal difficulty still centred upon internal strains and the unpopularity of opposition to an increasingly successful war. In the new Parliament Whitbread seized the initiative from Ponsonby by an amendment to the Address, calling for peace overtures, but received no support from his colleagues. The prospect of replacing Ponsonby in the Commons lead by either Whitbread or Grenville's nominee, Canning, was displeasing to Grey, who determined not to come to the opening of Parliament. Unburdening himself to Holland he wrote: 'I do not believe that it would be possible to get our friends to unite under either Canning or Whitbread, or if it were, that either of them could be brought to act according to our principles and views in party politics.'[6] Grey's stubborn simplicity, endearing to the majority of disoriented Whigs, ensured Ponsonby's continuance. In any case, the possibility of alliance with Canning was past and Whitbread's pretensions were not aided by a lack of progress in recent reconciliation between Whigs and Radicals in the respectable Hampden Club movement. Outside Parliament the pressure of unrest, whether by machine-breaking, calls for immediate peace, or popular support for the charismatic Burdett, alienated most moderate Whigs. At the same time a rift was becoming more visible between Whigs and Grenvillites. In the regency debates Grenville had deviated from the party by supporting limitation on the regent's power to create peers during the probationary period, a matter to which he felt committed by his similar stand as Pitt's subordinate in the crisis of the king's illness in 1788. Moreover, Grenville's insistence on including Canning in any plans for a ministry was seen by many Whigs merely as an attempt to strengthen his own position against themselves. While reform remained impossible for the majority of Whigs in wartime, Grenville's place in party counsels was still secure, but incompatibilities were becoming ever more visible.[7]

While events in continental Europe moved on through Wellington's invasion of France, the defeat of Napoleon at Leipsig and his imprisonment at Elba, British party politics reached near-stagnation. Whitbread added advocacy of Princess Caroline's cause to his parliamentary brief, but received little support at this point from the Whigs. On the other hand, Henry Grattan's attempts to obtain Catholic relief found initial support from most Whigs, and also from Canning and many 'Catholic' Tories; but second thoughts from the government benches about giving Catholics the right to enter Parliament virtually killed the bill before the end of the 1813 session. Falling wheat prices in 1814 stimulated the fears of landowners and in the following March, while the emperor made good his escape from Elba, the Commons voted by 207 to 77 to prohibit the importation of wheat until the price reached eight shillings a quarter. This decision was taken to the accompaniment of 'tumultuous proceedings' outside the walls of Westminster and attacks on the homes of those members, including Whigs like Ponsonby, who had supported the measure.[8] By the time Waterloo had been fought and Parliament prorogued in the summer of 1815, the Liverpool ministry's initial popularity was near its end and the first effects of postwar economic disruption and public distress were already being felt. Canning was nearing the end of his stay in Lisbon but was assured of a Cabinet place at the first opportunity, none too soon to assure government of his much-needed if wayward talents. Whitbread was recently dead by his own hand, shortly to be replaced by such reformers as Henry Brougham, Lord John Russell and Grey's son-in-law, 'Radical Jack' Lambton. A new era was at hand.

The years of nation-wide agitation and repression from Waterloo to Peterloo and the Six Acts in 1819 were the most difficult of Liverpool's ministry. Both parties displayed a new cohesion and sense of purpose on libertarian and reformist issues. Outside Parliament the pressures doubled and redoubled, ranging from Cobbett's polemic in the *Political Register* and Orator Hunt's platform rhetoric to the lunacy of Thistlewood and the Cato Street Conspiracy. Revived calls for universal suffrage from Hunt, Cobbett and Cartwright swept aside even Burdett's long-standing advocacy of a wider tax-paying franchise. The desire for 'a land fit for heroes' was widespread, even if the phrase itself did not come until the end of another great war.[9]

The first postwar session of Parliament met in February 1816 with some confusion on the opposition side. On the return of Napoleon from Elba the Whigs had again been on strained terms with Grenville, who preferred the full reinstatement of the Bourbons to his colleagues' advocacy of less stringent terms. Until the last moment it was not clear whether the Grenvilles would be sitting in the position on the opposition benches which they had occupied for over a decade. But differences were smoothed over, almost for the last time, and agreement was reached to make a series of attacks on government taxation proposals. This campaign was assisted by a deluge of some 400 petitions against the renewal of the property tax. Too great to have been unspontaneous, the surge of public opinion nevertheless owed something of its fury and its timing to the Whigs' activities in the press, with the *Morning Chronicle* and *Edinburgh Review* leading a vigorous campaign. As a preliminary to the property tax Vansittart brought in his army estimates, but was met by a concerted filibuster to gain time while petitions were still pouring in. For several nights the roof of the Commons rang to assertions of the danger of peacetime armies. The call did not go unheeded, for backbench members were, as ever, responsive to possible militarism and encroachment upon their pockets. The culminating vote on 8 March showed an ominous 135 absentees from among the usual government supporters, many of whom were clearly abstaining deliberately. Nevertheless, the defeat of the property tax ten days later by 238 votes to 201, with about 80 government supporters crossing the floor of the Commons to vote with the Whigs, caught the ministry by surprise.[d] As *The Times* reflected with satisfaction, the House had 'felt with the feelings of the country' and Liverpool had misjudged the mood of the hour.[10]

To win a battle is not necessarily to win the war. As so often when government was defeated on an issue of taxation, or some other emotive cause, a rally of its supporters ensued. Two days after the tax had been defeated the Whigs failed to follow up their success, losing by twenty-nine votes a motion attacking an increase of pay for the two secretaries of the Admiralty. The subject was not well chosen, involving as it did the popular senior service and a trivial economy; and Brougham put the final touch to mismanagement by choosing to launch a vitriolic attack on the prince regent in the course of the debate. The Tories rallied to defend government and demonstrated that their opponents could not regularly shake a sound majority. For the remainder of the session an attack on the navy estimates was easily parried by Croker, as Secretary to the Admiralty, and a repetition of the property tax débâcle was avoided by the ministry's decision to give up the wartime tax on malt. Before the end of the session the Tories in the Commons were addressed and rallied by Liverpool, Canning's admission to the Cabinet was at last effected at the Board of Control for India, and the impetus of Whig successes early in the session was largely lost.[11] As one Whig reflected sadly, 'tho' the Government are hated, we are not loved', national economy, it seemed, was not in itself the recipe for opposition success.

Government extravagance was now joined by government repression as the object of opposition attacks. The recess in the summer and autumn of 1816 was marked by new evidence of unemployment and, with potato-crop failure and high wheat prices following the new corn law, by agricultural distress. Luddite riots took place in many counties and violent giant meetings at Spa Fields were addressed by Orator Hunt, culminating in a mass march on the City which was dispersed by force. In the New Year, Parliament was met by a deluge of petitions for relief and parliamentary reform. Canning lost no time in demonstrating his value to his new colleagues by a brilliant speech against parliamentary reform on the opposition's amendment to the Address which was lost by 204 votes to 112. But while Burdett, Cochrane and other Radicals brought armfuls of petitions to the Commons the government and some of the more conservative Whigs were taking alarm at an apparent disintegration of law and order. When the government speakers went on in February to propose the suspension of the Habeas Corpus Act they found support from Grenville and Fitzwilliam in the Lords, William Lamb[e] and other Whigs in the Commons. In such circumstances, the main body of Whigs could achieve only 103 votes against 265 in the Lower House. A belated attempt to revive the campaign for economy likewise fell flat after Castlereagh took the sting out of opposition by proposing a committee on public income, soon known to Whigs as 'the humbug committee', and the Cabinet voluntarily gave up some surviving sinecure offices. In the prevailing atmosphere of alarm among the landed and middle classes, the corruption of the electoral system offered no more lever for opposition than did government overspending and assault on British liberties; in May, Burdett's motion for a select committee on the state of parliamentary representation achieved only 77 votes against a ministerial majority of 205. Only on the election of a new Speaker, with Abbot's retirement after fifteen difficult years, did a Whig vote of 150 achieve the party's full potential, but Manners Sutton carried the day for government with a handsome 312 votes.[12]

By the end of 1817 Grenville's alienation from the Whigs was complete, though the majority of the former's followers chose to remain with their colleagues and only some half-a-dozen 'Stowe' Grenvilles went with their patron. With this group's 'general, five men and a drummer' removed to a separate bench when Parliament met in 1818, and with Ponsonby dead after his exertions in the last year, the chance of closer understanding between Whigs and Radicals emerged. Brougham, who had become marginally less extremist since his return to the Commons in 1815, was seriously discussed as a possible leader, though it was Tierney's quiet assumption of the task which was eventually to carry the day. Unlike Ponsonby's candidature a decade earlier, Tierney's was apparently not sponsored by the great aristocratic families of the party but emerged as a consensus of party opinion in the Commons and was confirmed by Brougham's graceful acknowledgement of the *fait accompli* to a meeting of MPs at Brooks's Club after the end of the session.[13]

To the opposition's leadership problem were added others which made 1818 one of their least successful years in the postwar period. The Cabinet did not attempt to renew the suspension of habeas corpus, thus removing one libertarian grievance. A new one became available when the ministry introduced a bill to indemnify magistrates for their recent activities, especially in protecting government informers. But, on this, the ministerialists found themselves supported, as in the previous session, by uncommitted members and even by the same conservative Whigs who had supported the suspension. The highest vote achieved by the Whigs was sixty-five and, despite Grey's advice 'to debate and *to divide* constantly', the opposition in the Commons failed to register even half their nominal strength before Easter. By this time, too, the ministry's intention of taking advantage of a slight upswing in the economy by holding a general election was known, and members were off to their constituencies making preparations accordingly. Even so, the last weeks of the session saw a heartening of the opposition when Liverpool made the mistake of asking Parliament for marriage grants for some unpopular royal dukes. The mood of the nation, always better reflected on the eve of an election, was not in favour of generosity to George III's profligate, middle-aged sons at a time when national economy was in the air. Cumberland's proposed grant was refused, Clarence's was halved and only those of Cambridge and Kent were allowed to pass. Independents and waverers, whether Whig or Tory, thus signalled a backlash of opinion which gave the opposition a much-needed and unexpected boost. When the country went to the polls in June it was with an immediate memory of the ministry's new extravagance and incautious abandonment of a hardwon, still fragile reputation for independence from royal influence.[14]

For once the premature dissolution of Parliament worked to the disadvantage of government. Ministerial candidates were driven out not only in urban seats like the City of London and Southwark but also in rural Devonshire and Leicestershire. With greater than usual interest in the outcome evidenced throughout the country, Tierney's initial calculation of about thirty gains compared with the last Parliament proved to be about correct. The Whigs were able to rely on some 170 to 180 'decided' votes even without wavering members. The Tory Whip, Charles Arbuthnot, at first admitted to a loss of only about ten seats but the general tenor of ministerial comment, as well as later results in Parliament, proved this to be an underestimate. Huskisson thought that the county voters: 'despise the Whigs; but they are no longer what they were ten years ago in their attachment to the old Tory interests and principles which are prevalent in the nobility and gentry', and he later added 'be assured that the feeling is strong in the country that we have not done enough'. In such sentiments lay the seeds of later attempts, not least by Huskisson himself, to meet public demand by a new 'Liberal Toryism'.[15]

First, however, new trials faced the embarrassed and weakened government. Despite the admission to the Cabinet early in 1819 of the war hero Wellington, as Master-General of the Ordnance, their recent proposals in regard to the royal dukes continued to handicap them in the new Parliament. Opposition speakers criticized the inexpediency of maintaining two courts at high public expense, and the death of Queen Charlotte in the autumn of 1818 determined the Cabinet to offer considerable cuts in the vast establishment of the mad and secluded old king at Windsor. Economy, however, was not enough to restore confidence, and demoralized ministerial voters absented themselves on many occasions. Whig attendance, on the other hand, was good under the strenuous leadership of Tierney. Several early divisions were promising and, in March, Mackintosh carried by nineteen votes a motion for a committee on capital offences, whose large number and often trivial nature excited much criticism in government as well as opposition circles. However, government waverers' inevitable return to allegiance came on 18 May when Tierney moved for a committee on the State of the Nation and achieved only a bare vote of 178 against a triumphant majority of 357. Arbuthnot had made clear that the ministry regarded the matter as one of confidence, and few members other than those committed to opposition wished for a change of government, Catholic relief and perhaps other measures of reform at a time when public discontent was again mounting.[16]

Within a month of the prorogation of Parliament the yeomanry rode into a crowd which had come to hear Hunt at St Peter's Fields in Manchester, killing several spectators and providing a cause upon which all shades of Whigs could agree in condemning government. Widespread condemnation appeared in the press, public meetings were arranged in many counties, and the ministry decided upon the now unusual step of an autumn session to justify itself and restore order. Sidmouth at the Home Office redoubled his efforts to stiffen local authorities by advising the further use of the military wherever danger seemed to threaten from an indignant working class and its Radical leaders. The two parties prepared to confront each other, each confident of a new sense of purpose. Canning, recently the object of fresh suspicions by his colleagues, stood shoulder to shoulder with Sidmouth and Castlereagh: Fitzwilliam rejoined his friends and called a county protest meeting in York to condemn the Peterloo Massacre. When Parliament assembled in November the Whigs had a clear agreed plan of action, for though not all could agree to oppose the entirety of the ministry's proposed restrictive legislation they could concert on which measures were acceptable defences of order and which were to be condemned as destructive of British liberty. No opposition was given to the bill forbidding drilling and other military exercise, while that which empowered magistrates to search for arms was criticized only in respect of the right of night search. But the full force of opposition was unleashed on proposals for restricting the press and rights of public meeting. A long series of divisions secured some modifications and illustrated to observers outside Parliament the Whig party's claim to be more sensitive than its rival to the needs of the people. Even on parliamentary reform, ceaselessly debated in press and nation for the last five years, the Whigs at last gave ground for hope; at the height of the debates Lord John Russell offered a resolution for disenfranchisement of the notorious borough of Grampound, though the effect was somewhat dampened when Castlereagh rose to agree to the proposal in principle. When Parliament dispersed for Christmas the Tories had enhanced their claim to be the defenders of order, but the Whigs had established a reputation with the voteless masses as the castigators of Peterloo and of the Six Acts. The reputation hardly reflected the Whigs' cautious realism; they had in no way impeded the restoration of order, and even youthful Russell's ardour for parliamentary reform was not shared for a further decade by some of his friends. But the party was to derive much benefit in the long run, in terms of unity and popularity, from its modest stand.[17]

The spectacle of public unrest and its harsh repression in 1819 proved to be the last on a large scale for a decade, less on account of government action than because of an upturn in the national economy which became visible in the next two years. Aptly the culmination of a dismal postwar era was accompanied by the end of George III's unhappy decade of mental incapacity and confinement, for on 29 January 1820 he died. His death left the prospect of a lesser monarch and the legal necessity for yet another new Parliament.

The first major political issue of the new reign concerned relations between George IV and his unwanted queen. For six years Caroline had resided abroad and the ministry had been able to avert George's desire for divorce. They were fearful, though he himself seemed oblivious, of an all-too-certain and damaging political scandal if Caroline's alleged infidelities were dragged through Parliament. With Brougham and other Radicals as Caroline's legal advisers, George's own personal life from his illegal first marriage onwards would be the subject of counter-accusations or arguments of extenuation. On such grounds the Cabinet refused as early as July 1816 a request by the prince for proceedings against his wife. His accession to the throne brought matters to a head, not least because Caroline herself was determined not to be deprived of her right to be queen. In such circumstances, governmental prevarication could not long continue and, despite the personal distaste many Whigs felt for Caroline, opposition support for a popular crusade against king and Tories could hardly be avoided. The first skirmish in the royal marital contest came immediately. George demanded the omission of his spouse's name from the Church of England litany and, despite the initial reluctance of Canning and others, the Cabinet agreed. To proceed from this negative gesture to the positive action of divorce, however, was not a step to be lightly taken. After anxious debates the ministers decided to inform the king that his greatest desire was not politically possible. Liverpool, who had the task of communicating this unwelcome news to his monarch, met the full force of George's displeasure; relations between the two men were never the same again, and George began to toy pettishly with the idea of replacing the Tory government.*f* Reason asserted itself, however, and the ministers survived both this crisis and a plot for their assassination by Arthur Thistlewood and other conspirators captured assembling for their proposed crime at a house in Cato Street. But a bad start with both court and extremist agitators heralded two years of shaky government in which the Whigs could hope to fish for advantage.[18]

The first hazard to be met by the Tory party was a general election. The Cabinet decided, wisely as it proved, on an immediate dissolution; six months later they were in the midst of a far worse crisis concerning the royal couple. Initial Whig calculations of gains of up to 15 and a voting strength of just over 200 'thick and thin' men proved roughly correct. Popular rage at Peterloo and the Six Acts was reflected insufficiently, however, by a restricted electorate. When the new Parliament opened in April 1820 Grey did not feel sufficiently encouraged to come to London but offered his followers the sage advice to 'observe the good old opposition maxim of *proposing* nothing. Wait for the measures of the ministers, confine yourselves to general principles and statements favourable to liberty and to retrenchment . . .'. Though the ministers did not oblige by offering many contentious measures the Whigs on one occasion, concerning a proposed appointment to a sinecure office, came within twelve votes of success. But the opposition's best opportunity arose from Queen Caroline, who arrived unexpectedly in England on 5 June to claim her inheritance and so precipitated the crisis which ministers had long feared.[19]

At first, indeed, party reactions were not clear-cut. The ministry, under renewed and desperate urging from the king and on evidence of Caroline's infidelity obtained by his private sources, produced a

Bill of Pains and Penalties in the House of Lords to annul the royal marriage and deprive the queen of her title. This action found the Whigs divided, half-impressed by report of the evidence. On the Tory side Canning was barely persuaded to avoid weakening the government by immediate resignation, and Liverpool himself could not share the enthusiasm of Castlereagh and Wellington for a course of action so likely to deprive government of its vestiges of support outside Parliament. Liverpool's manifest hesitation again caused George to sound out the Whigs, but though Grey and his followers were initially shaken by his case they were not disposed to risk popularity even for the coveted and long-denied chance of office. As the cumbrous procedure got under way through the summer and autumn attitudes hardened on the opposition side, and Canning and many Tories remained doubtful of the wisdom or justice of proceeding against Caroline by legislation. For the first time in many years national attention was focused on the House of peers, where government chose to try out the bill first. Grey's voice was heard among those of other Whigs, and on the second reading they were joined by no fewer than 40 Tories to make a total of 95 peers against 123 for the government. Nor was the ministry allowed an easy withdrawal, for when Liverpool attempted to drop the divorce clause during the committee stage he was defeated by an unscrupulous tactical vote of the Whigs alongside the Tory hardliners for its retention. The bill thus went on to its fate, and on the third reading on 9 November some Tory peers who had voted for it on the previous reading either abstained or voted against, with the result that it was carried by only nine votes. In view of the even greater opposition expected in the Commons the dispirited ministry gave way and the measure was dropped.[20]

The first results of the bill's abandonment were ministerial disarray and royal fury. Canning at last resigned, protesting that Caroline had been exonerated and her name should now be included in the Liturgy. George – raving like an inhabitant of Bedlam according to one unsympathetic source – again approached the opposition, through the Radical Earl of Donoughmore with whom he was on good terms, only to find that, even for the pleasure of punishing his ministers, their price was too great including repeal of some or all of the Six Acts, concessions for the Catholics and greater measures of economy. But, in fact, the Whigs had reached their high-water mark with the defeat of the bill against Caroline. The king might fulminate against Liverpool for abandoning the case, but this grievance was no match for the deep-seated royal fear of a Whig government. In the country the Whigs had made further gains in popularity with a brisk campaign of county meetings to

accompany the trial, but this resulted in no further advance in
Parliament. In their desire to maintain the momentum of Caroline's
cause they endeavoured early in 1821 to revive the issue, but
thereby aroused the inevitable ostentatious return of Tory
dissidents to the ranks now that the main issue was decided. Though
a motion in the Commons condemning the removal of the queen's
name from the Liturgy achieved 209 votes in a full turnout, the
government made the vote one of confidence and rallied 310,
revealing that further pursuit of this hare was hopeless. Caroline's
death a few months later was little heeded, for her political importance was over by the time of her acquittal.[21]

With the eclipse of the queen's cause came a fresh turn to Whig
thinking, together with new spokesmen. Tierney's uncertainty as to
Caroline's guilt made him a spiritless leader during the period of her
trial, often in conflict with the Radical 'Mountain'. The rifts lay
deep, Tierney was exhausted and, in January 1821, he gave up his
leadership. He was not officially replaced. Brougham, the most
obvious candidate, refused to consider the succession, believing
correctly that he was not widely acceptable to the party even after
his brilliant defence of the queen. Though a principal architect of
many of their successes, from the withdrawal of the orders in
council in 1812 to the popular surge of support which swept them
into power eighteen years later, he was too erratic and too deficient
in aristocratic qualifications to charm the Whigs as he charmed the
people. As the Radical Ricardo wrote in 1818 from close observation: 'Sometimes he wishes to conciliate the Whigs, and then the
violent reformers receive no mercy at his hands; at other times one
would conclude that he went so far in the cause of reform as even
Burdett himself.' But even without a recognized leader there were,
in addition to Brougham, several talented young men, headed by
Russell, his associate Althorp, and Lambton, who were becoming
more committed to parliamentary reform. Moreover, the party
now enjoyed the organizational services as party Whip of Lord
Duncannon, who proved himself the most efficient party adminis-
trator since William Adam.[22] By common consent the lead in
the Commons passed to an enthusiastic group.

The pursuit of parliamentary reform to which the new men were
turning was encouraged by the Whigs' repeated failure to exploit
popular support in electoral terms. Though the general elections of
1818 and 1820 resulted in minor gains these proved useless for
shaking the solid Tory majority on all but a few occasions. Grey
himself had made up his mind that parliamentary reform must not
be a half measure but encompass the removal of at least a hundred
seats from that element of private rotten boroughs which was the

government's strongest asset at election time.[g] But Grey's magisterial patience, scorning any 'nibbling at reform' and waiting for the summons to greater things, was not acceptable to his younger colleagues who wanted something sooner. Russell brought his bill to disfranchise Grampound and give its two seats to Leeds, though he had to accept Lord Liverpool's amendment awarding them to Yorkshire as the price of passage in the Upper House. In April, Lambton moved for a committee of the whole to consider the state of representation, arguing for household suffrage and equal electoral districts. This radical programme went too far for the majority of his party, and achieved only forty-three votes in a denuded house. But a month later Russell obtained 124 votes against the ministry's 155 for a Select Committee to consider how and where to enfranchise boroughs whose population appeared to entitle them to representation. The opposition's turnout was, in this case, more encouraging and was followed up by a well-organized series of motions on retrenchment of which one, from Curwen demanding the removal of the horse tax, was successful by 141 votes to 113.[23]

The evidence that the Whigs could make headway even without Queen Caroline was plain for the ministry to see, and before the second session of this Parliament strenuous efforts were made to mend the breached dykes. The problem of an intransigent king solved itself with the death of Caroline, her place having already been taken by Lady Conyngham. The Lords were not likely to revolt again, and had done so only in a legal rather than a political judgement. The Commons party, however, had to be strengthened and, more importantly, there needed to be a change towards policies less provocative to public opinion. Canning's assistance, much needed, was blocked by the king's petulance, though Liverpool's murmur of resignation brought the prospect of concession before long; in the meantime, the Grenvilles, led by Buckingham, were showing unmistakable signs of being tired of trying to be a tiny third party. In December, at the price of a dukedom for Buckingham himself and a Cabinet place for Wynn, they rejoined the Tories after their long period of self-exile, bringing a useful dozen votes of their own or of those who often voted with them. Their continued obstinate adherence to Catholic reform had been demonstrated as recently as the last session, but this concerned Liverpool little in his new shift towards a more flexible approach.[h] In any case, the continuance of a strong 'anti-Catholic' element in the Cabinet was guaranteed early in 1822 when Peel was brought into the Home Office to replace Sidmouth, while the latter continued in his Cabinet place. The restive Huskisson was persuaded to retain his office and Canning was squared with the offer of governor-generalship in India which secured his good behaviour for a further session.[24]

Though Peel's appointment implied a new appeal to public opinion by allowing legal reform, if only to 'dish the Whigs' in this field, further moves towards a conservatively reformist stance were delayed for the moment. But a further vigorous campaign by the Whigs in the Commons demonstrated that by no means enough had been done to reassert the ministry's control. Their majority sank to four at the end of February 1822 on an opposition proposal to lower taxation by reducing the sinking fund, and on 1 March resistance temporarily collapsed when a mass defection from the government side led to a vote of 182 to 128 to cut the naval estimates and reduce the number of Lords of the Admiralty. On 25 April, Russell obtained 164 votes for a resolution condemning the state of representation, the highest vote for parliamentary reform since Pitt's attempt in 1785, and a week later the Whigs carried by 216 votes to 201 a motion to address the king to reduce the joint postmaster-generalship to a single post. Pressure from the Tories' own back-benches was clearly in favour of many aspects of economy and reform, and only the ministry's hint of its impending collapse, announced to supporters at a meeting soon after this defeat, ensured that further opposition motions were beaten off. But the respite was likely to be brief unless some further change were made in the ministry's base.[25]

The opportunity for such a change came in August with the suicide of Castlereagh after showing many signs of strain in combining the role of Foreign Secretary with that of ministerial leader in an increasingly turbulent Commons. There was now no further reason for continuing to exclude Canning, who had not yet departed for India and whose talents had never been more required. If overlooked again, as the king, Eldon and Sidmouth urged, he might cease his benevolent support, leave India to its fate and draw supporters like Huskisson and Robinson out of the government. But such things were unthinkable. Liverpool wanted him, and threatened to resign without him. Wellington lent his weight, performing his usual indispensable function of instructing George in political realities. Peel suppressed his anti-Catholic feelings and was willing to serve with Canning if the ministry could not go on without him. Canning accordingly achieved the coveted Foreign Office at a time when fresh British leadership in Europe and the New World was badly needed, and at the same time took over the government lead of the Commons. Sidmouth's men, sick Bragge-Bathurst and inefficient Vansittart, relinquished their offices and the Exchequer went to Robinson, who had been strenuous in Canning's support. Huskisson replaced Robinson at the Board of Trade, extracting the promise of a Cabinet place within a year. With the liberal Canningites in place fully supported by pragmatic Liverpool, with Sidmouth weakened and Castlereagh gone, and with even Peel convinced of the need for an administration more in tune with the wishes of the people, the Tories changed course in a way rarely hitherto achieved by long-serving administrations.[26]

Notes: Chapter 12

a   For the regent's loss of authority see pp. 25–6 above.

b   The term often applied to William Wilberforce's evangelical friends.

c   On 25 September Liverpool wrote to a supporter 'you will, perhaps, be surprised when I tell you that the Treasury have only one seat free of expense . . . I have two more which personal friends have put at my disposal: and this is the sum total of my powers free of expense. Mr Curwen's bill has put an end to all money transactions . . .' (Yonge, *Liverpool*, Vol. 1, p. 444).

d   In Dr Mitchell's words the usual opposition voters were supported on this occasion by 'half the waverers and a third of the government fringe members'. There were also again many abstentions on the government side (Mitchell, *Whigs in Opposition*, p. 96).

e   Later the Liberal Prime Minister as the second Viscount Melbourne.

f   John Wilson Croker, on hearing of a royal 'plan of a new Government' urged upon one of the king's friends 'that the Whigs, with the sincerest intentions, must fail; that their own followers would desert them; and that I know of no question but this one upon which a Tory Opposition would be formidable', Croker, *Papers*, Vol. 1, p. 147

g   See the progressively strong and detailed statements by Grey in letters to Holland from December 1819 to December 1820 in Trevelyan, *Lord Grey of the Reform Bill*, app. A.

h   Moreover, the slight preponderance which Wynn's admission gave to 'Catholics' in the Cabinet was not without precedent: Castlereagh pointed out that the same situation had existed at the outset of Liverpool's ministry (Yonge, *Liverpool*, Vol. 3, p. 161).

CHAPTER THIRTEEN

The Parties and Reform
1822–32

> Do you not think that the tone of England . . . is more liberal
> – to use an odious but intelligible phrase – than the policy of
> the Government?
>
> Can we resist – I mean, not next session or the session after
> that – but can we resist for seven years Reform in Parliament?
> (Peel to Croker, 23 March, 1820)

Robert Peel was pragmatic enough to recognize that the Tory party
was out of tune with public opinion, and he was ready to take the
lead in producing lesser measures of reform. In 1822 he began as
Home Secretary the overdue task of consolidating criminal statutes,
removing over a hundred capital offences often for very minor
crimes, and making the law more enforceable and useful. His friend
John Wilson Croker would have gone further by dabbling in constituency reform, transferring the seats of a few notoriously venal
boroughs such as Penryn and East Retford to Manchester and other
large unrepresented cities. Neither Peel nor Croker, nor even the
more 'liberal' associates of Canning, contemplated the major
parliamentary readjustment currently under consideration by the
Whigs. But distaste for such reform was combined with recognition
of its popular appeal, and many shared Peel's well-founded fears.
Canning's speech on Russell's bill of 1822, a measure which would
have taken a seat from each of 100 small boroughs and redistributed
them to counties and large towns, has been described as 'the speech
of a man who knows in his heart that he is fighting for a lost cause'.[1]

Liverpool likewise had no relish for parliamentary reform, but he
was one of the first of his Cabinet to concede the need for
adjustment elsewhere. In 1820 he came out strongly in favour of
free trade, giving hope to industry but sounding an ominous note for
any supporter of protection. In the same year government resisted
the demands of landowners for revision of the corn laws in favour of
British agriculture; the ministry had no desire for a repetition of the
scenes at the passing of the 1815 bill. In greater or lesser measure

the men who filled the revised government front bench in the Commons from 1822 were committed to changes already adumbrated by the Prime Minister. Free trade budgets from 1823 to 1825 were made possible by increasing national prosperity, permitting taxation to be lowered while at the same time enabling Robinson and Huskisson to lower a wide range of duties, initiate reciprocity treaties favourable to Britain, and lay the foundations for an era of industrial prosperity." The repeal of Pitt's Combination Acts, introduced by the Radical Joseph Hume but condoned by the ministry in 1824, was intended to improve industrial relations and remove a major constituent of governmental unpopularity. But hurried subsequent legislation to illegalize violence which accompanied strikes following this repeal demonstrated the limits of government's new direction. The liberalism of the last phase of Liverpool's administration was a new and fragile growth grafted on to deep-rooted conservatism. Tory backbenchers looked to Eldon, Sidmouth and Peel to resist Catholic emancipation, parliamentary reform and Canning's liberal foreign policy. Liverpool's main task was not to further liberal policies but to hold the balance between conservative and liberal colleagues.[2]

Canning's outlook on foreign affairs had its first parliamentary airing over a French invasion of Spain to destroy the constitution which King Ferdinand had recently conceded. The new Foreign Secretary's attempts to warn off French intervention brought him popularity with the Whigs but resulted in considerable differences in the Cabinet. On this matter he did not carry his colleagues, but his subsequent attempts to promote Greek independence of the Ottomans and to protect the new nations of South America from Spain and Portugal gradually won Liverpool's support. This was much needed, for Canning had to face opposition not only from his fellow ministers but also from the king, whose 'cottage coterie' of foreign advisers at Windsor influenced the monarch in support of the reactionary rulers of the Holy Alliance. The determination with which the Foreign Secretary kept his policies before Parliament and thus finally overbore both court and Cabinet have often been described. He had the support of the Whigs, the more influential parts of the press and sufficient of his own party to make a substantial contribution to the advancement of European and even American constitutional democracy. But he incurred on the way yet more suspicion from the section of the Tory party which was already beginning to be called 'Ultra'.[3]

An even more important area of dissension within the government ranks was the Catholic question. Here, too, the Liberal Tories were close to the opposition, and a meeting in July 1822 to discuss a bill for Catholic relief included not only leading Whigs but also Canning and Wynn. If Canning's subsequent accession to office suggested any inclination to play down his Catholic sympathies a taunt of desertion from Brougham brought forth, as was intended, the Foreign Secretary's indignant denial in the House. The appointment of the 'Catholics' Wellesley and W. C. Plunkett as Lord-Lieutenant and Attorney-General for Ireland in the remodelled ministry, like that of Fitzwilliam in 1795, stirred up Irish aspirations. Rather than satisfying Catholic opinion, as was hoped, the appointments initiated a period of strong agitation. Aided by failure of the potato crop Daniel O'Connell's Catholic Association was founded in 1823 and quickly replaced other, less effective organizations. Irish unrest, soon to be pronounced by Wellington as likely to lead to civil war, evoked little governmental concession; even a bill to give the franchise to docile English Catholics, though supported by Liverpool and Peel, was rejected in the House of Lords with Wellington, Eldon and the royal Dukes of York and Cumberland against it. Throughout 1823 and the following session differences between High and Liberal Tories continued with the Prime Minister often, and Peel occasionally, veering towards the latter. The conflict included not only foreign policy and Catholic claims but also a range of lesser religious and social issues, and was marked by the ominous development of royal dukes frequently voting on the Ultra side. From mid-1824 fears for Liverpool's state of health and the possibility of his retirement, which in any case could not be postponed indefinitely, kept the Tories in periodic ferment. Canning was the most obvious successor, but if he were passed over a juncture between Canningites and Whigs looked increasingly possible. Either his leadership or his secession spelled danger to the party. Fortunately Liverpool had no intention of retiring yet, and Tory fragmentation was postponed.[4]

Liverpool's last two years saw him more openly supportive of Canning in the desire to keep the ministry together and the Whigs out. By November 1824 the Prime Minister had made up his mind. Sidmouth was under criticism from Canning for poor attendance and was not dissuaded from leaving the Cabinet at his own request, professing disgust at the inadequate provision made for the Addingtonians ejected in 1822. In a very long and reasoned memorandum the Prime Minister argued the pressing case for recognition of independence in the South American republics as a major area of British trade, convincing Wellington enough to keep him from resigning and sweeping aside the king's last resistance. Both Liverpool and Canning felt impelled to use the threat of their own resignation if their advice were not taken. The showdown cleared the sultry air in a number of ways. Sidmouth's disappearance signalled the removal of some of the small remaining royal influence in the Cabinet. At the same time, Canning's triumph in foreign policy meant the downfall of 'cottage' influence on the king and left the way open for the Foreign Secretary to further his plans for assisting Greece. Defeated, George gave way with better grace than usual and became increasingly reconciled with that minister, a development which augured well for Liverpool's belief that Canning should be his successor.[5]

Divisions among the Tories gave ample opportunity for exploitation by the opposition. Whig orators lost no opportunity to insert a lever between High and Liberal Tories by supporting the latter, praising them ostentatiously and reminding them of their need for continued Whig support. The young Radical, John Cam Hobhouse, told Canning across the House that, except on parliamentary reform, many reformers 'looked to him [as Creevey reported] with *gratitude* and *affection* for his conduct since he came into office, which would amount to VENERATION if he would but give way on this vital question'.[6] But such tactics, though embarrassing to the recipient, took the opposition little further. Before the entry of Canningites into the shaken Cabinet the Whigs were on the brink of adopting substantial measures of parliamentary reform.[b] The moment passed and reform of Parliament temporarily lost impetus at a time when the improvement in the British economy was reducing pressure from outside Westminster. A campaign of county meetings early in 1823 stirred little interest, and this medium of public opinion remained quiescent. Russell obtained marginally less support than in the previous year for his proposed reforms.[7] Plagued by ingrained tendencies to inertia, and torn between supporters and opposers of Canning, the Whigs lost interest and their activity steadily declined, a trend marked by a steady decrease in the number of party divisions in the Commons from eighty-eight in 1822 to fifty-six in 1824. By the beginning of 1825, with the major issues of foreign policy settled, the opposition could think only of accelerating the Catholic question.[8]

Accordingly as soon as Lord Liverpool emerged from the South American crisis he found himself in the midst of another. In February 1825 Burdett brought a Catholic Emancipation Bill together with complementary measures designed to make state provision for the Catholic clergy and to raise the county franchise in Ireland from 40s to £10. Thus armed to anticipate reasonable objections he carried his main bill triumphantly in the Commons in April by 268 votes to 241 on its second reading, with only Peel offering strong opposition from the government front bench. In the Lords, however, Liverpool was equally vehement and more effective, obtaining the bill's rejection with a similarly high turnout of 178 votes to 130. Peel had threatened to resign if the measure passed the upper chamber, and Liverpool stated that he could not consider carrying on without his principal Protestant spokesman in the Commons. With the measure's defeat it was the turn of Canning to ponder taking himself and his associates out of the government. But time was on his side, for few believed that the ministry could survive another such traumatic internal debate. The Foreign Secretary, in the knowledge of Liverpool's failing health, insisted upon the freedom of action to revive the Catholic question at an early date.[9] Wellington and other Protestants responded by calling for an appeal to the electorate, where Protestant feeling in England and Scotland could be expected to support their cause. But Canning still carried Liverpool's support as the indispensable member of the government, and dissolution was deferred. In September the two men agreed to play down the divisive Catholic question in the next session, prior to a general election in 1826. But Liverpool was now privately convinced that the tide could not be held back long, and that 'whenever the *crisis does come*, the *Protestants* must go to the wall'.[10]

The session of 1826 was both short and relatively quiet, with the Tories observing their leaders' truce. Much time was taken up with the economy. The repudiation of debts in South America, combined with the overprinting of paper money by country banks, caused widespread bank crashes in December 1825. Wheat prices were up to high levels again, and manufacturers pressed for relief from enhanced labour costs caused by the price of bread. With the help of the main body of the Whigs the worst features of the banking system were swept away, but stubborn resistance from the Tory backbenches prevented any but temporary remedial measures on the provision of corn. The election, when it came in June, presented confused issues to the electorate; the rising level of social disturbances was as yet too subdued, after the quietude of recent years, to encourage the Whigs to exploit parliamentary reform. Instead they relied upon their recent campaigns for lesser reforms, cheaper corn and Catholic relief. The Catholic question dominated in many constituencies and prominent Whigs suffered setbacks, Russell losing in Huntingdonshire and Grey's son, Howick, in Northumberland. In Ireland the Catholic Association swung two constituencies, but this was not enough to offset Protestant gains elsewhere. Many areas saw the ominous new development of Whig voters supporting Liberal Tory candidates against Tory rivals, and in Cambridge the Canningite Palmerston was narrowly returned against Tory opponents. Contemporary assessments of results agreed that if the Whigs suffered setbacks these were to some extent offset by Liberal Tory gains and by the closer links being established between Canningites and the opposition. In December, looking at the new Parliament, Liverpool saw little hope for his government's survival. 'The Catholic question . . .', he informed Robinson gloomily, 'will, I have little doubt, lead to its dissolution in the course of this session.' His forecast proved correct sooner than he expected. Parliament met on 8 February 1827, and just over a week later the Prime Minister suffered a stroke which put an end to his mediating role within the Tory party and opened the way for the overt schism which he had held off for several years.[11]

The removal of Liverpool ushered in three years of stress for both parties, causing a temporary Whig split iin 1827–8 and detaching Canning's friends from the Tories to join the Whigs by 1830. A more dramatic division occurred on the Tory side in 1829 between Ultras and moderates, though this was largely submerged by 1831 in common opposition to the Reform Bill. But it would be misleading to suppose that these events marked anything but a temporary breakdown in the usual Tory–Whig rivalry. The only potentially dangerous internal schism of the years 1827–30, that between moderate and Ultra Tories, lingered after 1830 only in personal distastes of a type common enough in the history of party.

Before a new ministry emerged in April 1827 there were two months of negotiation, for no Tory minister was prepared to form a ministry without Canning's support and Canning would serve under no command but his own. With Whig support, this minister carried a Corn Bill permitting duty-free importation when the domestic price topped seventy shillings. Much now depended upon Peel, who true to his partially liberal principles supported the Corn Bill. But though Canning offered the Foreign Office, Peel refused to join a 'Catholic' leader, suggesting instead that they should both serve under Wellington. The king saw Canning on 28 March, and received confirmation that he required 'the substantive power of First Minister'. By this time the Foreign Secretary had received assurances of continued support from powerful elements of the Whig party including Lansdowne, Brougham and Duncannon, though the quid pro quo remained to be worked out. In the outcome, Canning's dependence on the Whigs proved greater than he may have anticipated, for early in April, with the king's permission to form a government, he was immediately faced with the resignation of seven members of the Cabinet including Peel, Wellington and Eldon. For good measure the duke also resigned his post of Commander-in-Chief. Within three days about forty officeholders had given up their posts in protest against a pro-Catholic Prime Minister, confuting the expectations of both the king and Canning.[12]

In the new Cabinet, Robinson chose to go to the Lords as Viscount Goderich, and Canning himself took on the post of Chancellor of the Exchequer as well as that of First Lord. His friends Dudley and Sturges-Bourne became Foreign and Home Secretaries, while Huskisson remained at the Board of Trade and Palmerston was at last brought into the Cabinet. With a ministry heavily dependent on Canningite talents the entry of some Whigs became a necessity, if only for the support they would command in the Commons. A meeting at Brooks's was swung in favour of Whig participation by Brougham, whose reasoning was 'anything to lock the door for ever on Eldon and Co.'. Led by Lansdowne,[c] Tierney and Carlisle joined the Cabinet and for the moment around half the Whigs in the Commons were satisfied enough to transfer to the government benches, though they maintained a semi-independent status by insisting on supporting the ministry only through Duncannon, their own Whip.[13]

'Canning has dissected both Whigs and Tories', wrote one Whig; but the split on the Whig side was by no means so serious as the other. Grey, Bedford and other dyed-in-the-wool Whigs spoke and voted against what they considered the gullibility of their fellows temporarily in Canning's camp, but there was little personal animus and the later process of healing was neither difficult nor protracted. On the Tory side, however, this split was mortal and unforgiving, for the Canningites knew that they had little to hope for in their future relationship with their former associates. 'The violence of the Tories upon the junction of the Whigs and C[annin]g', commented another observer, 'shows how completely they look upon it as their death blow'. The session widened the breach. In the House of Lords the Corn Bill was wrecked, to Canning's great rage, on an amendment by Wellington. Canning himself opposed a motion by Russell to disfranchise Penryn, but it was passed with the support of other Liberal Tory ministers and he acquired no credit from the High Tories. By the end of the session even Peel, who agreed with the Prime Minister on so much, was planning a regular opposition with Arbuthnot. When Parliament rose early in July, Canning was tired and disheartened. In addition to his official posts he had been carrying Dudley's responsibilities at the Foreign Office and his health had weakened progressively since taking office. He died on 8 August, the event hastened by overwork.[14]

Though speculation named Wellington, Lansdowne, Wellesley or even Grey as possible successors, the king's only thought was to avoid a further period of uncertainty so soon after the protracted process which had taken place on Liverpool's removal. George was angered at what he considered to be High Tory desertion after Canning's appointment, and he now turned to Goderich to maintain the existing arrangement. But this succession, derided from all sides, was doomed from the start. Under pressure from Protestant Tories to appoint Peel and from the Whigs to resist anti-Catholics the new Prime Minister had to find a Chancellor of the Exchequer to replace Canning. After Sturges-Bourne refused the proffered office Goderich's choice fell upon the king's nominee, J. C. Herries, an experienced financial secretary of the Treasury, rather than upon Palmerston whom he would probably have preferred. Palmerston's own mild view of Herries was 'that the Catholic question is not the only subject on which he agrees with the illiberals'. Wellington consented to become Commander-in-Chief again, now that Canning was gone. The Whigs at once took alarm and Carlisle urged that they should withdraw immediately at these signs of royal and High Tory influence. Lansdowne saw 'indications of a general system of interference in matters which constitutionally should be left to his responsible ministers'. Others, however, believed that a Goderich administration must be tried for the same reason that Canning's had been, to keep Wellington and Peel out. Despite the contempt of hardliners like Bedford at 'keeping out one set of Tories to support another set' it was this view which prevailed with Lansdowne. He allowed himself to be persuaded by an appeal from Huskisson, by Whig appointments to some minor offices and by the vague prospect of a future Cabinet place for Holland. On this basis the ministry struggled on for a few months, but was not destined to face the final test of meeting Parliament.[15] Before the end of 1827 the Canningite ministry, bereft of the omniscient power of its dead leader, was staggering. With Herries threatening resignation at the Whigs' nomination of Althorp as Chairman of the Commons' Finance Committee Goderich himself resigned. On 9 January 1828 the king asked Wellington to form a government.[16]

The collapse of the Goderich experiment put an end to the possibility of continued Canningite government. Such, however, were the tensions likely to be placed upon any ministry by the Catholic question that responsible Tory politicians were agreed with the king that the best hope lay in a return to the type of balance established by Liverpool. Much to the disgust of High Tories, who urged 'a sound, plain-dealing *Protestant Administration*', Wellington now professed himself willing to lead such an attempt, citing the argument of Peel that 'those who are for forming an exclusive

Ministry, expect that I am to go into the House of Commons with *half a party*, to fight *a party and a half*'. Peel, the indispensable man for the Commons leadership, specified against a Protestant or Ultra-Tory ministry and professed to be unable to manage the Commons without Huskisson. Peel's long-standing belief that he had no significant differences with his former Liberal Tory colleagues except on parliamentary reform and the Catholic question made him welcome the retention of most of the leading Canningites. Huskisson and his friends professed themselves satisfied, by Dudley's continuance at the Foreign Office, that Canning's liberal ideas would continue to rule in overseas affairs. Wellington, for his part, suppressed considerable private misgivings about the Canningites' liberal and Catholic views. In Ireland he decided to appoint the Marquis of Anglesey, a veteran of the Peninsula and Waterloo, as his brother's successor. Peel replaced Lansdowne at the Home Office and the latter's coalition Whig colleagues, Carlisle and Tierney, promptly resigned. In the Cabinet the 'Catholics', including four Canningites, retained eight of the fourteen places. Wellington himself was persuaded by Peel and others that he must now again relinquish the commandership-in-chief as a further guarantee of his government's moderate complexion.[17]

Good intentions proved abortive. In February a Whig motion for the repeal of the Test and Corporation Acts found the Tories unprepared, and Peel's insistence that this should be rejected by a united government vote failed to prevent its adoption by 237 votes to 193. Overdue by a century the repeal of the obsolescent measures excluding Protestant Nonconformists from national and local offices aroused little objection in the country, the Cabinet or even the House of Lords. But when the Lords killed a proposal to transfer corrupt Penryn's seats to Manchester neither Huskisson nor Palmerston felt themselves bound to government, and their resignations were accepted by Wellington with alacrity.[18] Subsequent ministerial changes included the unfortunate appointment, through no fault of the holder's, of William Vesey Fitzgerald to the Board of Trade. Vesey Fitzgerald was an Irishman and had to stand for re-election in County Clare where he was opposed and defeated by Daniel O'Connell, thus precipitating the final phase of the struggle for Catholic relief. For O'Connell, as a Roman Catholic, was not entitled to sit at Westminster yet no Protestant could win the seat. The result of Pitt's enfranchisement of Irish freeholders in 1793 was at last becoming apparent.[19]

For the Whigs the break-up of Goderich's ministry was a landmark in the journey towards party reunion after the tensions set up by the Canning–Lansdowne coalition. Grey, still condemning the original and 'fatal mistake' of those who had joined the Canning-ites, only gradually came to accept the need for reconciliation with the schismatics. Younger members such as Russell, however, were anxious to get on with the business of harassing government with a united opposition. His initiation of the repeal of legislation against the Protestant Dissenters was a tactical one, nicely calcu-lated to provide a highly successful cause and to encourage the whole party. Catholic relief, though more greatly desired, seemed further away; Burdett's bill for relief passed the Commons by six votes in the course of the 1828 session but was duly rejected in the Lords. The successful repeal of the tests, however, gave a fillip and also pointed the way to further religious reform. As Russell wrote: 'It is really a gratifying thing to force the enemy to give up his first line, that none but churchmen are worthy to serve the state, and I trust we shall soon make him give up the second, that none but protestants are.' Good prospects much furthered the determination of those who wished to bind up party wounds and return the party to the position, in Althorp's words, 'in which it was before the insur-rection at Brooks's and Lord Lansdowne's weakness did the great injury of destroying party in the country'. Nevertheless, the very bitterness of Althorp's tone indicated that the return would not be without difficulties. At the end of the session there was still no generally recognized Whig leader in the Commons, though the need was greater than ever as a result of the disagreements of the previous year. Moreover, Lansdowne had lost his authority in the Upper House by his lack of success, but Grey still refused to stand forth and resume the leadership. Though the repeal of the Test and Corporation Acts helped the situation, it was Catholic emancipa-tion which provided the final incentive for reconciliation.[20]

By the autumn of 1828 the election of the leader of the Catholic Association for County Clare was the main subject of concern to government and of hope to the opposition. As early as August, Peel had informed Wellington that concession of Catholic relief was now inevitable, though he thought himself not the fittest man to carry it in the Commons. He rejected as inadequate the Prime Minister's suggestion of annual suspension of the laws excluding Catholics from Parliament. Ireland was alight with the flame lit by O'Connell. Anglesey, struggling to keep rebellion down by counter-force, had to advise concession and was dismissed by the angry Prime Minister, thus redoubling agitation in Ireland. But even Wellington was now forced to see that only thoroughgoing emancipation would meet the case, and with determination that the Whigs should not be allowed to carry it he brushed aside Peel's desire for retirement and prepared the retreat. The Cabinet were convinced, and the former anti-Catholics were dispatched to Windsor to remonstrate with the king. Before Parliament met in February 1829 government was united and the king partially convinced of the necessity for reform, though he had to be brought into line again by a threat of resignation from Wellington and Peel before the measure passed.[21]

The secret of the Cabinet's decision was not revealed until almost the eve of Parliament's meeting, when at Brooks's Club Charles Greville found 'all the Whigs very merry at the Catholic news'. Lansdowne had urged in December that they should 'fight the Catholic question resolutely as a party', advice from which none dissented. But when it was learned that government had decided to adopt emancipation themselves the Whigs could find no scope for opposition without endangering the measure. Little other legislation was passed, apart from the uncontroversial establishment of a Metropolitan Police Force, the culmination of Peel's reforms to establish law and order on a more efficient basis. Althorp drew a little ahead of his possible rivals as opposition leader, except in his own estimation, though a final incentive for decisive leadership was still lacking.

But if the session did little to further Whig aspirations it did much to destroy Tory dominance. From the outset High Tory opposition was assured so that Peel had to rely on Whig votes, as he had himself forced Canning to do, to carry his measure. His punctilious resignation and recontest of his seat for Oxford University was followed by his defeat at the hands of a High Tory opponent and he had to take refuge in a pocket borough. In introducing the substantive measure of relief the ministry carefully prefaced the bill by another suppressing the Catholic Association, and accompanied it with yet another bill raising the franchise in Irish county elections from the 40s freehold to £10 household, in order to reduce the influence of the Catholic lower-income voters. But such concessions and qualifications failed to win the Ultra Tories. Despite heavy government pressure on officeholders, and even on members of the royal household, the main bill was opposed by 173 Tories on the second reading in the Commons and later by 109 Tory peers. They were too many to discipline, though Sir Charles Wetherell was dismissed for vehemently opposing the bill from his position as Attorney-General. By the end of the session all the bills were law, and the Tory party was divided hopelessly.[22]

The recess of summer and autumn did little to alleviate either the weakness of government or the disorientation of the Whigs resulting from the events of the foregoing session. Wellington appeared oblivious of Ultra plots to replace him with the king's assistance, which Palmerston believed showed 'how much the Duke deceives himself if he really fancies that he is getting back the Tory party'. But the Prime Minister now enjoyed, unwontedly, considerable sympathy from a section of the Whigs. He responded to this to the extent of filling Wetherell's place by the Whig lawyer, James Scarlett, but there the matter rested. Grey maintained a cautious stand, being unwilling to enter into any opposition move which might favour the Ultras.[23] When Parliament assembled in February 1830 the Address was opposed by amendments from the Ultra Tory Sir Edward Knatchbull, supported by the Canningites and most Whigs. Outside Parliament there was renewed recession and the foundation of political unions for obtaining parliamentary reform. Handweavers in Manchester, Spitalfields, Norwich and other areas hit by depression formed an articulate spearhead to artisan agitation. Wellington, who ignored even his supporters' plea for minor reform concessions, was soon confronted with the astonishing spectacle of proposals for parliamentary reform from the Ultra Tory Blandford, who had assisted Knatchbull on the Address. Blandford argued that Catholic emancipation, carried against the wishes of English and most Scottish voters, had demonstrated the inadequacy of the existing parliamentary system. On 18 February he produced a mishmash of old and new proposals ranging from the abolition of rotten borough franchises to the exclusion of ministers from Parliament and the abolition of the Septennial Act. That he achieved even fifty-seven votes was the measure of his group's discontent. On parliamentary reform, however, the Ultras' stance was revealed as obstructive rather than genuinely reformist when they nearly all abstained on Russell's motion to enfranchise Manchester, Leeds and Birmingham, a proposal which was lost by only 188 votes to 140.[24]

The religious reforms of the last two sessions, it soon became clear, had opened a Pandora's box of proposed changes in society and constitution from conservative country gentry, wealthy middle classes and unpropertied Radicals. The defection of forty to fifty Ultras could put the government in a minority if pressed from all quarters at once. Reviving pressure for reform, and the scent of victory, brought from Grey the guarded comment that there appeared to be 'a stronger feeling in favour of that measure than has for some time, or perhaps ever, existed'. In April he found the possibilities sufficient to leave Northumberland for Westminster and take up the initiative abandoned by Lansdowne. Some weeks earlier in the Commons a group of Whigs had asked Althorp to lead them, and after consulting Russell, Brougham and Graham he accepted the charge. The group increased for the remainder of the session until Althorp was accepted by virtually all the party, so that for the first time in a decade the party had both an active head in Grey and a generally acceptable leader in the Lower House.[25]

On 26 June occurred the death of George IV and the accession of the Duke of Clarence as William IV. Wellington determined upon an early dissolution and, in the last few days of Parliament, Grey and Althorp joined with Goderich and Huskisson in the two Houses in outlining opposition to government in anticipation of the general election. Although these leaders were cautious, their guarded criticisms were enough to align them with reform in the minds of the electorate; and if this were not enough then the enthusiastic campaigning of Brougham in Yorkshire, where he was the cynosure of the national press, made the reform platform specific for all who had eyes to see. Although estimates of the results varied from a government gain of twenty-five seats to a loss of fifty it was the ministry's calculations which were unrealistically optimistic.[d] Fifteen of seventeen new members for English counties who later took part in the division which brought down the government voted with the opposition. Croker lost his seat for supporting Catholic emancipation and the backlash of High Tory disapproval added further ministerial defeats to those brought about by Whigs or Canningites. In the three months which followed the election the new members had ample opportunity to reflect upon what the electorate wanted of them, and reformist agitation was further stimulated by the events of the July Revolution in France as it quickly spread to Belgium and beyond. Brougham continued to lead the press, with articles in the *Edinburgh Review*, and did more than most not only to turn any waverers but also to determine that the Whigs should have no last-minute doubts about the cry for reform. At a party meeting at the beginning of November, Althorp, who with Russell was still thinking in terms of the moderate proposals in the last Parliament, 'gave notice that J. Russell meant in the present month to give notice of the renewal of his motion for giving representatives to the three great towns, but the feeling of all present was so strongly expressed that such a motion as not going far enough ought not to be made that he engaged to write to J.R. to induce him to give it up'. As so often in the party's history the backbenchers swayed the leadership. Grey was confirmed in his belief that a more sweeping reform, on the lines of the 1822 proposals, was now possible.[26]

Before the new Parliament assembled the Whigs had come to terms with the Canningites, an outcome already half decided before the death in September of Huskisson after being struck by Stephenson's *Rocket* at the opening of the Liverpool and Manchester railway. Palmerston, on behalf of his fifteen or so colleagues, virtually turned down an offer from Wellington by demanding a complete reconstruction of the ministry, and the way was open for juncture with the Whigs on the basis of agreement on wide-ranging parliamentary reform. The Prime Minister decided to put a good face on his situation. If the Canningites were lost he could still hope for co-operation, if not forgiveness, from the Ultras. Perhaps to this end he decided upon the strong tone of the royal speech at the opening of Parliament on 2 November. Extolling the excellence of the existing system of representation the speech made clear that Wellington would 'never propose' and 'ever resist' reform. Grey and Althorp in their respective Houses called for reform of Parliament, and Althorp expressed his party's readiness to take over government. Brougham gave notice of a reform resolution to be brought on the 16th, and middle-class agitators organized their followers to refuse payment of taxes if satisfaction were not obtained. But on the night of the 15th Peel was beaten by 233 votes to 204 on a Whig proposal to set up a committee to consider the Civil List. Of English county members forty-seven voted with the Whigs and only fifteen with the ministry. Wellington resigned the next day rather than face a repetition, and the king sent for Grey to form a government and by implication to carry reform.[27]

Grey's thirteen-member Cabinet included four former Canningites of whom three, Palmerston, Melbourne and Goderich, occupied the secretaryships for foreign, home and colonial affairs respectively. But despite the inclusion of this element the ministry was overwhelmingly Whig and became more so with the rapid assimilation of the Canningites, a process simplified by the close connection which already existed through Melbourne as a former Whig. The Exchequer and the lead in the Commons were taken by Althorp whose first task was to persuade Brougham to go to the Upper House as Lord Chancellor. The balance in the Commons was narrow, and the continued presence of this brilliant but abrasive reformer would have alarmed the Whigs' new allies and any Ultras who might support the ministry. One Ultra peer, Richmond, joined the Cabinet and a further slightly unexpected inclusion was Sir James Graham, a conservative Whig who had only recently come to the fore as a Commons spokesman. Durham was the only Radical, his relationship with Grey giving him a privileged if constrained position. Further down the ministerial ranks the Prime Minister made a clean sweep; the thirst of the Whigs for office would brook no half measures. Fortunately for this thirst, Grey's politic offer of places to the Ultra Tories, Sir Richard Vyvian and Knatchbull, was refused. With the king's agreement, members of his and the queen's households who were MPs were informed that their offices were continued subject to their support for the government. In the case of the queen's household there was no precedent for this stand, but it was later enforced by the dismissal of her Chamberlain, Lord Howe. The claims of Rockingham and Fox on a prime ministerial right to control appointments were rigidly applied and even extended by Grey.[28]

The key problem to be tackled was reform. Even moderate Tories were now convinced that some move must be made beyond the grudging concession on East Retford. Croker had no objection in January 1831 when he heard that the Cabinet planned to give seats to 'half a dozen great towns'. Such men may be forgiven for thinking that any plan produced by the Whigs after their recent timorous record and union with the Canningites would be of a restrained nature. But Tory assumptions overlooked Grey's long track record and his deepest convictions. He greatly feared revolution, as did all aristocrats of the era of European revolutions, and his responses to earlier bursts of unrest in 1790 and 1819 had been to urge a substantial measure of borough reform. The year of European revolutions and British unrest in 1830 revived and enhanced this reaction. Setting up a small committee to devise reform, Grey ensured that its proposals would be sweeping by appointing Durham as its chairman along with Russell as its key member. Of the other two members, Duncannon and Graham, only the latter proved less innovative than the others and his objections were not insuperable. The committee's instructions from the Cabinet were to produce: 'the outline of a measure . . . large enough to satisfy public opinion and to afford sure ground of resistance to further innovation, yet so based on property, and on existing franchises and territorial divisions, as to run no risk of overthrowing the [existing] form of government'. And, despite the emphasis on preservation (possibly overstressed by Graham who recorded the instructions), the brief for a major measure was clear. Russell, plucking up the courage of his former convictions after his rather mild recent proposals, produced a scheme which, despite substantial changes in detail over the next year and a half, was to form the framework of the Whig Reform Act. As amended by the committee the plan was to redistribute both seats from sixty-one nomination boroughs and one from a further forty-seven, the majority to be allocated to English counties and unrepresented cities.[e] A uniform borough franchise was to be based on households rated at £20 a year. The Cabinet reduced this to £10 and rejected a linked proposal for secret ballot, included in the committee's report at Durham's insistence; the middle class thus enfranchised, more orthodox Whigs argued, would be less corrupt and the ballot would therefore be less needed than in many existing boroughs. For England the overall number of seats was to be reduced but Scotland and Ireland were to have more, though the £10 franchise brought in fewer householders for these poorer countries. Neither at this stage nor later was Pitt's plan in his 1785 Reform Bill for compensation of borough owners revived. Both the large number of proprietors to be dispossessed and the neglect to mollify them may be attributed mainly to the fact that Tory-controlled boroughs exceeded Whig ones by a proportion of three to one, about 203 seats to 73 by Croker's computation in 1827. In any case, those proprietors who lost their control by reason of an enlarged electorate rather than by the abolition of seats could hardly have qualified for compensation, and the measure's popularity might have been threatened by any such generosity to those who had so long enjoyed patronal power.[29]

While the committee's work was being carried on in strict secrecy during the winter months of 1830/1 Parliament remained in a state of subdued expectancy. At the Home Office, Melbourne took a stern line with agitators, urging sentences of transportation to make up for Peel's reduction of capital offences. Thus although Palmerston carried on Canning's liberal tradition in foreign policy, by recognizing Belgian independence of Holland, the administration had little to offer for the relief of distress at home. Pinning their hopes on parliamentary changes the ministers had no desire for further 'economical' reforms now that offices were in great demand by their supporters. Althorp's budget attempt to remove some unpopular taxes proved ill-considered and had to be so greatly trimmed that by mid-February Arbuthnot could ask hopefully, 'Is it possible they can go on?' But opposition could find little else to seize upon, and Peel was too busy attempting to distance himself from both the duke and the Ultras to obtain an effective Tory rally in the Commons. The end of this phase came on 1 March when Russell introduced the Reform Bill with staggeringly long lists in both Schedule A, boroughs losing both members, and Schedule B, those losing one.[30]

The production of the ministry's bombshell completed the fresh polarization of Parliament into two parties, except for a small vestigial body of independents, forcing the former Canningites to commit themselves unequivocally to the Whigs while all but a few Ultras rejoined the Tories, in voting if not in social intercourse.[f] Once again the two sides were ranged against each other on a clear and overriding issue. On the day Russell unveiled the bill to members who had found seats between the piled hundreds of reform petitions there was astonishment, jubilation and trepidation on the government benches, stupefaction and outrage on the opposition side of the House. In a matter so momentous there was little memorable debate while members took stock. Orator Hunt, recently returned for Preston, sounded an ominous note for future years by complaining that the bill did not satisfy working-class aspirations, but he was little heeded. In view of the state of national opinion the opposition had agreed beforehand not to resist the bill at its first introduction, but at the second reading at 3 a.m. on the 23rd over 600 members were present for the contest. The Tories included 46 of the 58 Ultras identified by Planta after the last election, and it was Vyvian who moved for the reading's deferment for six months. The motion was lost by 302 to 301 amid a scene of unparalleled tension. In all 97 more members voted against the bill than had voted for Wellington on the division which brought about his resignation. The ministry's majority of a single vote was too minute for optimism. At Grey's insistence the king dismissed household officers who had voted with the Ayes; but with the stick came the carrot and at the committee stage, on 18 April, Russell offered the concessions of five boroughs moved from Schedule A to Schedule B and a further seven Schedule B boroughs reprieved entirely. Such measures were not enough, and Peel saw his opportunity in the still substantial diminution of the total of English members. A carefully chosen motion from General Gascoyne that the number of seats for England should not be reduced struck a chauvinistic note which caused the Whigs to be defeated by 299 votes to 291.[g] At once the Cabinet decided to seek dissolution and the king reluctantly granted it.[31]

If the election of the previous year had shown support for reform candidates, where identifiable, that of 1831 saw what one historian calls 'the Reform hurricane' thrown solidly behind a Whig party now irrevocably committed to the bill. The Tories, Greville reported, were 'dead beat everywhere'. With the list of voters for Gascoyne's amendment given wide publicity, Gascoyne himself and many of those who voted with him were mown down. In thirty-five of the forty English counties the Whigs took both seats. Seven Ultra county members lost their seats and only one survived. In the boroughs the fabled 'Lowther interest' of Cumberland led a distinguished list of proprietors who lost long-established control. Nevertheless, it was still the closed and rotten boroughs which formed the backbone of surviving Tory voting strength. Of some 187 English Tory members returned over 90 per cent represented boroughs destined for disfranchisement. 'In the last analysis', writes Professor Cannon, 'the living part of the representative system confronted the dead part'.[32]

In view of the nation's decision the last 'unreformed' Parliament saw much of the interest shifted to the final bastion of vested interests, the House of Lords. Russell's new bill, presented in the Commons in June, showed little difference from its predecessors and passed on the second reading by 367 votes to 231. In committee, despite extended and minute scrutiny, little was conceded other than the important amendment moved by a Tory, Chandos, to allow tenants with properties of £50 per annum to vote in county elections. On this occasion, ministers could not withstand a back-lash from Whig proprietors who had been remarkably loyal to the party in allowing the abolition of much of their borough patronage. With many Whigs joining the Tories in support of Chandos even Althorp could not prevent the motion's passing by a decisive 232 votes against 148. But the Tories' fullest hopes, based on superior forecasts of their voting strength in the Lords, lay with the House where the prevailing spirit of reform was still resisted despite the creation of twenty-five new Whig peers since the ministry came in. With Wellington leading the opposition the debate lasted a week and the bill was rejected easily by forty-one votes.[33]

Ministers had long expected this defeat, though not the size of the majority, and had discussed plans for a further major increase in the number of Whig peers. But this prospect was not much more pleasing to Whig aristocrats than to their opponents and lesser measures were tried first. Tory 'waverers', including the bishops and a group of lay peers whose spokesman was the former Canningite, Lord Wharncliffe, were threatened by a mass creation of members and cajoled by the offer of further amelioration of the proposed measure. Riots and disturbances throughout the country, notably at Bristol, furthered the Whig argument that reform was the only alternative to revolution. At the price of deferring resolutions on slavery in the colonies, a project much desired by Althorp and many other Whigs, yet another Reform Bill was introduced in the Commons in December with sufficient concessions to influence Tory waverers in both Houses. The number of English seats was now to be retained closer to the existing level by once more reducing the Schedule B list, thus moderating what many Tories saw as an undesirable expansion in the number of single-member constituencies and, at the same time, reducing objections to the fall in overall English membership which had brought success to Gascoyne's motion in April. Croker's immediate reaction that the revised measure was 'a great triumph for me and for our party' had some colour as regards his own part in former debates, for he had been active in pointing out many previous anomalies now removed from the bill. But the claim that the revision constituted a triumph for the

Tory party is an indication of the degree to which some Tories had reluctantly come to accept wide-ranging reform as inevitable. The relatively low voting of 162 against the ministry's 324 on the second reading was a response to marginal concessions, but also resulted from the belief that the bill could be halted, if at all, only in the Upper House.[34]

Thus while the measure continued through the Commons in the first three months of 1832 all eyes were already turned to the House of Lords, to the court and, above all, to the Prime Minister. Grey's first task was to counter the king's reluctance to create more peers by stressing the possibility of revolution if the bill did not pass on the next occasion; but, at the same time, the wavering Tory peers had to be convinced that an enormous increase in the Whig peerage was inevitable if the House again refused reform. It was a skilled balancing feat and Grey was aided by an honest conviction that reform would avert revolution, as well as by an unquestioned respectability and social conservatism which carried conviction. At first the waverers were brought to agree to the bill and, on 26 March, Wharncliffe and the Bishop of London announced their co-operation. But though the bill passed its second reading by nine votes in April rejoicing was premature. When the committee stage opened on 7 May an unexpected motion by Lyndhurst on behalf of the Tory leadership to postpone consideration of the disfranchisement clauses rallied blind party support. The motion was not intended to provoke the ministry's fall, and when Lyndhurst obtained 151 votes against 116 another Tory was hurriedly put up to explain that there was no objection to the bill's most prominent feature, the complete abolition of representation for boroughs in Schedule A. But the explanation was too late and otherwise unacceptable, and the next day saw the ministers offer their resignations to the king, adding that 'the alternative of creating peers presented itself'. Any minority Tory government would now have to carry a reform measure, for dissolution of Parliament was impracticable when a successor to the existing House of Commons was likely to show an even greater Whig majority. In fact William's efforts to form a Tory ministry were not very prolonged. Peel, true to his advice to Croker twelve years earlier, saw reform as inevitable and did not intend to incur the odium of passing it. With Peel's closest Commons associates of the same mind, Wellington's willingness to undertake the leadership was seen to be hopeless. On the 18th the king gave Grey the task of continuing his ministry, with the necessary promise of sufficient new peers to carry the bill.[35] The threat was enough, and in June the measure became law without recourse to this expedient.

During the course of the reform crisis the two parties had taken strongly marked and mutually exclusive positions. Some differences of opinion were not, of course, lacking within the parties. There were Whigs who were well satisfied with the reform achieved, and Radicals who thought it had not gone far enough; there were Tories who continued to deplore all reforms of the past ten years, and their more pragmatic colleagues who had come to accept the need for these measures. But, in the new era, party struggle could continue the mainly two-sided aspect which was its normal tendency, though with increasing use of the terms Conservative and Liberal which denoted that the parties had passed into a phase of greater response to the enlarged electorate and an even more politically aware nation.

Notes: Chapter 13

a   The results of the Liberal Tories' trade policies were not necessarily in accordance with their intentions which were perhaps less 'progressive' than is sometimes claimed – see Boyd Hilton, *Corn, Cash, Commerce* (Oxford, 1977).

b   Encouraged by research which brought out the Tory preponderance in small and Scottish boroughs. At this point many of the grandees and most of the party rank and file were actively favourable to reform – see Mitchell, *Whigs in Opposition*, pp. 167–8.

c   Third Marquis and formerly, as Lord Henry Petty, Chancellor of the Exchequer in the Talents ministry of 1806–7. From 1824 Grey largely left leadership initiatives to Lansdowne, whose hope of coalition with Canning was echoed by many Whigs.

d   The often-noted discrepancy between the government's calculations, particularly those of Joseph Planta, the Secretary to the Treasury, and its actual strength when Parliament met, may perhaps be partly explained by the observation of one experienced observer who wrote on 26 August: 'Those candidates who stood on the support of Government found no advantage from it, but on the contrary were invariably obliged to abandon such ground for the ground of reform and economy, and are committed in almost every instance to conditional engagement on these points' (Buckingham, *William IV and Victoria*, Vol. 1, p. 45).

e   As finally passed in the Reform Act these figures were reduced to fifty-six boroughs losing both seats and thirty losing one. The protracted passage and amendment of the reform proposals can be touched upon only in bare outline here. Good modern analyses exist in Cannon's *Parliamentary Reform*, esp. chs 10 and 11, and Brock's *Great Reform Act*.

f   In February 1832 Croker could describe a few of the Ultras, especially Wetherell and Inglis, as 'very cordial' while others, including Vyvian, 'though they vote with us, are evidently a different party' who 'will never, I think, be reconciled to Peel . . .', Croker, *Papers*, Vol. 1, p. 541.

g   The fifteen 'moderates, the men of the parliamentary centre', who voted for the second reading on 23 March, but for Gascoyne's motion, were perhaps effectively all that remained of a once-formidable body of members independent of party – for their identity see Mark O'Neill and Ged Martin, 'A backbencher on parliamentary reform, 1831–1832', *HJ*, vol. 23 (1980), pp. 539–63.

Conclusion

Since Butterfield first questioned Namier's interpretations of eighteenth-century politics these interpretations have often been the subject of specialist criticism. But general histories lag behind monographic literature, and many continue to present a Namierite picture. It is hoped, therefore, the present volume will make clear that the court, country and 'connexion' hypothesis offered by Namier is an inadequate explanation of the development of political life throughout the period and even for the early 1760s, the years in which he specialized. In particular, the chapters above have pointed out that Namier's two key contentions, a Tory 'disintegration' after about 1761 and a refusal by the leading Whigs to go into opposition after their loss of office in 1762, had little basis in fact. Over three-quarters of the Tories joined in support of Bute and succeeding ministers favoured by King George III, while, at the same time, the Old Corps of Whigs under Newcastle and Rockingham went into determined opposition. Before the 1830s reversals of party fortunes were neither as abrupt nor so frequent as they later became, but the change which occurred in the first two years of George III's reign was as decisive as any between the Revolution of 1688 and the first Reform Act.

The survival of Toryism as an effective force down to 1742 has been described in my earlier book on party history, and the story is extended to the 1750s by the work of Colley and others. In 1748 the Tory party adapted itself to continued exclusion from office by allying with Prince Frederick, who promised the leading Tories a share in appointments when he should succeed his father. The prince's early death in 1751 proved only a temporary setback for the Tories and by 1755 they were in close understanding with his son, Prince George. The party joined the younger prince's court in support of William Pitt when he took office in 1756 but adhered to the heir and Bute when they fell out with Pitt after about two years. By 1760 Newcastle and other Old Corps Whigs in Pitt's Coalition ministry were becoming increasingly worried by the possibility of a Tory revival, justifiably so given Prince George's intention to carry out the policies of the late Prince Frederick. In the 1761 general election 113 identifiable Tories, over a fifth of the Commons, were returned.

Such a body of Tories was in itself no threat to the hegemony of the Old Corps Whigs. But George III's determination when he came to the throne in 1760 to 'put an end to those unhappy distinctions of party called Whigs and Tories' led to his increasingly confident, stage-by-stage elevation of Bute; and by 1762 the work of removing the despised Pitt, Newcastle and the 'Whig oligarchy' was complete. The king's successive ministers from Bute onwards managed the Commons with the support of compliant Whigs, many of them from families converted from Toryism only in the last generation, and the great majority of the Tory party. This combination was usually described indiscriminately by the opposition as Tory. On certain predictable issues, especially those connected with Wilkes's various campaigns for 'Liberty', some Old Tories occasionally withdrew their support from the court, but these issues became few and far between after 1770. From 1762 there is a discernible continuance of two-sided strife between King's Friends and Tories, on the one hand, and the principal Whig party led by Newcastle and later by Rockingham on the other. Of smaller Whig groups in existence in the early part of George III's reign the Bedfords and Grenvilles were usually on the court side, while the Pittites (later called Chathamites) were usually in uneasy alliance with the main Whig party. It was this 'Rockingham' party which gradually brought about a Whig revival in opposition. With the publication of Burke's *Present Discontents* and other similar manifestos around 1770 there was no room to doubt that Rockingham had established his party as the chief opponent of royal influence, an opposition in which other Whigs might join on party terms.

Chatham's small but vociferous band of associates never accepted these terms though they remained in *ad hoc* alliance with the Rockingham Whigs until the effective end of the American War in 1782. Soon after this, Chatham's son and political heir, the younger William Pitt, joined the court, though with his father's reservations as to the political role of the crown. Pitt was a parliamentary reformer in youth and remained a reformer in respect of crown influence throughout his short life. Foiled by an unusual combination of court and Whigs in his early attempts at borough abolition he began instead a long campaign of administrative reform which went far beyond anything Rockingham had contemplated in cutting away the 'influence of the Crown'. Obtaining a degree of control which by the later 1790s was becoming unacceptable to the king, Pitt resigned over royal opposition to Catholic emancipation in 1801 along with his major Cabinet colleagues, rather than preside over a government whose policy was thus jeopardized. Three years later he gave up an attempt at neutrality, overthrew and replaced the weak ministry of Addington. By this time, too, Pitt's virtual abolition of government patronage by administrative means ensured that in future the Tories would be as dependent on party resources as the Whigs themselves. But the Foxites, too, were moving with the times. Their unpopularity at the polls after the American War encouraged them to improve their parliamentary organization and means of appeal to the public; and while Fox's approval of the French Revolution lost him the more conservative section of the party to Pitt in 1794, it ensured that the Whig opposition was more reformist and united than it had ever been. Though small in numbers it was poised to grow stronger from 1801 onwards.

The more ideological basis upon which events in France placed both Foxite and Pittite parties ushered in the Whig–Tory conflict over reform in the early nineteenth century. Within a few years of Pitt's death in 1806, Lord Liverpool's ministry healed the party splits of 1801 and stood united in suppressing disorder while the Whigs drew new strength from the country's postwar demand for reform. The opposition leaders' gradual move towards the greatest reform of all, that of Parliament, was partly the result of a growing conviction that during their long exclusion from office the closed boroughs had become overwhelmingly Tory in complexion. Tory reforms in the 1820s, often adopted to 'dish the Whigs' though not extended to parliamentary reform, split the Tory party temporarily into moderates and Ultras and also induced an ephemeral division among the Whigs between those who assisted Canning's ministry in 1827 and those who held back in the hope of an early Whig government. By 1830, however, the Whig division was forgotten and the Tory one largely healed. A relatively small transfer of Canningites to the Whig side in the same year ended a three-year partial breakdown of the usual party alignment, and the passing of the Reform Bill was disputed between clearly arrayed Whig government and Tory opposition.

Much confusion has arisen from two features of the late-eighteenth-century political scene. One was the artificial situation whereby one side managed for several decades without a generally acceptable name, a state of affairs which came about mainly because King George III's preferred ministers were unwilling to accept the implication of support for arbitrary monarchy connoted by the term 'Tory'. However, such denominations as 'court', 'government', or 'Pittite' party did much in practice to fill the terminological gap. The second feature was the absence of a rapid alternation of the major parties such as existed after 1832, though such an alternation had prevailed from 1689 until 1714. Essentially, there was only one change in the party balance between 1714 and 1830, that which broke the Whig domination in 1760–2 with the result of that party's (in Byron's phrase) '*not* getting into place', except for four very short intervals, in the next sixty-eight years. The great length of each party's period of superiority, Whig from 1714 to 1762 and court/Pittite/Tory from 1762 until 1830, certainly delayed the promise of the decades before 1714. But though the parties existed under difficult conditions, when the existence of nomination boroughs in large numbers could prolong party domination for many decades, the Tories and Whigs of the eighteenth century laid the foundations of the later fully fledged party system. The survival in 1832 of both parties under their original names after a century and a half, in spite of numerous attempts to extirpate or ignore them, indicates that they served a need too important to be denied. Their continuance was neither an accident nor an illusion.

APPENDIX: Later Allegiance of 113 Tories Elected in the 1761 General Election[a]

The careers of the following members of Parliament are described by various historians in *History of Parliament, 1754–1790* and, in some cases, also in *History of Parliament, 1715–1754*.

1 The forty-four Tories who became government supporters after 1762:

Sir John Astley	John Jolliffe
William Bagot	Sir Charles Kemys Tynte
Sir Richard Bampfylde	Robert Lane
Thomas Best	Robert Lee
William Blackstone	Edward Lewis
Sir Robert Burdett	Herbert Lloyd
Sir Lynch Salusbury Cotton	Herbert Mackworth
Assheton Curzon	Sir Charles Mordaunt
Sir James Dashwood	John Morton
William Drake	William Northey
Nicholas Fazakerley	Armstead Parker
Benet Garrard	Sir John Philipps
Sir Richard Glyn	George Pitt
Sir John Glynne	Henry Pye
Charles Gray	Coningsby Sibthorp
Robert Harley	Edward Southwell
Thomas Harley	Sir Thomas Stapleton
Sir Henry Harpur	Simeon Stuart
Eliab Harvey	Arthur Vansittart
Francis Herne	John Ward
Jacob Houblon	James Wigley
Sir Edmund Isham	Sir Armine Wodehouse

2 The eight Tories who remained independent at first but joined in support of North's government in the 1770s:

Sir Walter Blackett	Humphrey Mackworth Praed
Edward Dering	Sir Roger Newdigate
Thomas Grosvenor	Clement Tudway
Rowland Holt	John Rolle Walter

3 The two Tories who joined the Duke of Bedford:

Marshe Dickinson	Robert Henley-Ongley

4 The two Tories who joined George Grenville:
   Edward Kynaston   Richard Lowndes

5 The twelve Tories who joined in opposition, often with Rockingham or
   Pitt:[b]
   Charles Barrow   Thomas Foley
   William Beckford (Pittite)   Peter Legh
   Peregrine Bertie   Richard Milles
   Thomas Cholmondeley   John Parker
   Sir William Codrington   Edward Popham
   George Cooke (Pittite)   Denys Rolle

6 The four Tories who remained independent at first but joined in opposi-
   tion in the 1770s:
   Henry Dawkins   Chase Price
   The Hon. Thomas Howard   Humphrey Sturt

7 The eight Tories whose allegiance was erratic after 1762:
   Edward Bouverie   John Pugh Pryse
   Samuel Egerton   Sir John St Aubyn
   Thomas Knight   Thomas Staunton
   Sir William Meredith   Richard Wilbraham Bootle

8 Thirty-three Tories either died or left Parliament too soon for their
   affinities after 1762 to appear clearly. They were:
   Benjamin Bathurst   Sir John Morgan
   Julines Beckford   Sir Gerard Napier
   Norbonne Berkeley   Peregrine Palmer
   James Buller   Sir Thomas Palmer
   William Cartwright   Richard Price
   Thomas Chester   Thomas Prowse
   Francis Child   Jonathan Rashleigh
   Velters Cornewall   James Shuttleworth
   Henry R. Courteney   Edward Smith
   Sir William Courteney   Jarrit Smith
   William Craven   Edmund Starkie
   Richard Glover   John Symons
   William Harvey   John Tempest
   Thomas Lister   John Tuckfield
   Sir Robert Long   Randle Wilbraham
   Richard Lyster   George Wrighte
   John Michell

Notes: Appendix

a   Of the 113 Tories listed here, 112 correspond with the list of 113 included by Sir
    Lewis Namier in *England in the Age of the American Revolution* (Appendix A) as
    'Tories returned to Parliament at the General Election of 1761'. Namier omits the

name of Sir William Blackstone (of the *Commentaries on the Laws of England*), included here, but includes William Dowdeswell, omitted here because Dowdeswell's supposed Toryism is highly questionable (see above, pp. 45–6).

b   Those members in this section who were definitely supporters of Pitt are indicated in brackets, but several had overlapping loyalties, connected with both Newcastle/Rockingham and Pitt, or held to a general opposition stance.

NOTES

Chapter 1

1   Herbert Butterfield, *The Whig Interpretation of History* (1931).
2   Namier, 'Monarchy and the party system', in *Crossroads*, p. 231.
3   Butterfield, *George III and the Historians*, pp. 182–9; C. W. Alvord, *The Mississippi Valley in British Politics* (1917), Vol. 1, ch. 1; P. B. M. Blaas, *Continuity and Anachronism . . . the Anti-Whig Reaction between 1890 and 1930* (The Hague, 1978).
4   W. R. Fryer, 'King George III: his political character and conduct, 1760–1784. A new Whig interpretation', *Renaissance and Modern Studies*, vol. 6 (1962), pp. 68–101. See also Brewer, *Party Ideology*, and O'Gorman, *Rise of Party*.
5   Robert Walcott, *English Politics in the Early Eighteenth Century* (Oxford, 1956). For critiques see p. 240, n. 36.
6   Hill, *Growth of Parliamentary Parties*; Colley, *In Defiance of Oligarchy*; Clark, *Dynamics of Change*; O'Gorman, *Rise of Party* and *Whig Party and the French Revolution*; Brewer, *Party Ideology*; Cannon, *Fox–North Coalition*, p. 240.
7   Browning, *Newcastle*, p. x.
8   *Crossroads*, pp. 229–30.
9   Brewer, *Party Ideology*, p. 40.
10 Steven Watson, 'Parliamentary proceedings as a key . . .', *Burke Newsletter* (1962), p. 108; *History of Parliament, 1715–1754*, Vol. 1, pp. ix, 19–114, 162–87; *History of Parliament, 1754–1790*, Vol. 1, p. 198; Namier, *England*, p. 418.
11 Namier, *Crossroads*, p. 214.
12 Namier, *England*, app. A. pp. 419–21.
13 W. R. Laprade (ed.), *The Parliamentary Papers of John Robinson, 1774–1784* (1922), and 'Public opinion and the election of 1784', *EHR*, vol. 31 (1916), pp. 224–37.
14 Browning, *Newcastle*, p. 137.
15 Phillips, *Electoral Behaviour*, p. 68, fig. 2.1.
16 Mrs E. George, 'Fox's Martyrs: the general election of 1784', *TRHS*, 4th ser., vol. 21 (1939), pp. 133–68.
17 *Walpole Corr.*, Vol. 1, p. 154.
18 *Gentleman's Magazine* (1742), pp. 29–30, 96–7, 159–60, 216.
19 L. S. Sutherland, 'The City of London and the Devonshire–Pitt administration, 1756–7', *Proc. Royal Academy*, vol. 46 (1960), p. 157.
20 Walpole, *Memoirs of George II*, Vol. 1, p. 344.
21 Sutherland, loc. cit, at n. 19; cf. Brewer, *Party Ideology*, esp. ch. 6 for Pitt's popular position in the 1760s.
22 Peters, *Pitt and Popularity*, pp. 1–2.
23 *History of Parliament, 1754–1790*, Vol. 1, p. 86; O'Gorman, *Emergence of the British Two-Party System*, p. 47.
24 *Crossroads*, p. 220.

25   The 'Worsley List', in *History of Parliament, 1715–1754*, Vol. 1, pp. 162–87; W. A. Speck, *Tory and Whig: the Struggle in the Constituencies, 1701–1715* (1970), app. D.

26   Namier, *England*, p. 228; Christie, *End of North's Ministry*, p. 188.

27   Stewart, *Foundation of the Conservative Party*, p. 16.

28   *English Historical Documents*, Vol. 11, p. 278.

29   Brock, *Lord Liverpool*, pp. 91–3, 98.

30   Pares, *George III*, p. 14.

31   Derek Jarrett, 'The myth of "patriotism" in eighteenth-century English politics', in J. S. Bromley and E. H. Kossmann (eds), *Britain and the Netherlands* (The Hague, 1975), Vol. 5, pp. 122, 137–8.

32   Cannon, *Fox–North Coalition*, p. 236.

33   Namier, *England*, pp. 208–15.

34   Owen, *Rise of the Pelhams*, p. 84.

35   ibid., pp. 80–1; Wiggin, *Faction of Cousins*, p. 303.

36   J. H. Plumb, *The Growth of Political Stability in England, 1675–1725* (1967); Geoffrey Holmes, *British Politics in the Age of Anne* (1967); Speck, op. cit. at n. 25; Hill, *Growth of Parliamentary Parties*.

37   Pares, *George III*, p. 71.

38   Wiggin, *Faction of Cousins*, p. 303; Pares, *George III*, p. 37.

39   Namier, *England*, p. 212.

40   Brooke, *Chatham Administration*, pp. 238–47.

41   James J. Sack, 'The House of Lords and parliamentary patronage . . . 1802–1832', *HJ*, vol. 23 (1980), pp. 913–37. Wiggin, op. cit. at n. 38.

Chapter 2

1   Gilbert Burnet, *History of my Own Time* (1833 edn.), Vol. 4, p. 287n.

2   Greville, *Memoirs*, Vol. 1, p. 177.

3   Sedgwick, *Letters*, p. 50; Brooke, *King George III*, p. 90.

4   *George III Corr.*, Vol. 3, p. 256.

5   Pares, *George III*, p. 67.

6   Add. MS 41,691, f. 4.

7   A. N. Newman, 'Leicester House politics, 1748–1751', *EHR*, vol. 76 (1961), pp. 577–89.

8   Namier, *England*, p. 113; Pares, *George III*, pp. 182–3; W. R. Fryer, 'King George III: his political character and conduct, 1760–1784. A new Whig Interpretation', *Renaissance and Modern Studies*, vol. 6 (1962), pp. 68–101.

9   Piers Mackesy, *The War for America 1775–1783* (1964), p. 263.

10   *George III Corr.*, Vol. 5, p. 395; Foord, *Opposition*, p. 363.

11   Buckingham, *George III*, Vol. 1, p. 192.

12   Cannon, *Fox–North Coalition*, p. 4.

13   Brooke, *King George III*, p. 255.

14   Malmesbury, *Diaries and Correspondence*, Vol. 4, p. 2.

15   Colchester, *Diary*, Vol. 2, p. 401.

16   ibid., Vol. 3, p. 501.

17   Hill, *Growth of Parliamentary Parties*, p. 83.

18   J. H. Plumb, 'The organization of the Cabinet in the reign of Queen Anne', *TRHS*, 5th ser., vol. 7 (1957), pp. 137–57.

19   Hill, *Growth of Parliamentary Parties, passim*; J. M. Beattie, *The English Court in the Reign of George I* (Cambridge, 1967), pp. 234–9.

20   Add. MS 34,521, f. 20.

21   Add. MS 35,337, ff. 4–5.

22 Coxe, *Pelham*, Vol. 1, p. 166.
23 M. A. Thomson, *A Constitutional History of England* (1938), p. 368; Foord, *Opposition*, p. 259, n. 4.
24 Add. MS 51,379, f. 93.
25 *Chatham Corr.*, Vol. 1, pp. 90–4.
26 Peters, *Pitt and Popularity*, p. 202.
27 *George III Corr.*, Vol. 4, pp. 210, 213, 216–17.
28 Russell, *Memorials*, Vol. 2, p. 38.
29 Barnes, *George III*, pp. 441–2.
30 P. Kelly, 'British politics, 1783–4: the emergence and triumph of the Younger Pitt's administration', *BIHR*, vol. 54 (1981), pp. 62–78.
31 Mrs E. George, 'Fox's Martyrs; the general election of 1784,' *TRHS*, 4th ser., vol. 21 (1939), pp. 133–68.
32 'Third party circular', in Namier, *Crossroads*, p. 229.
33 Paul Langford, *The Eighteenth Century, 1688–1815* (1976), pp. 189–90.
34 George III, 30 September 1794, Portland (Nottingham) MSS, PwF 4068.
35 Rose, *Life of Pitt*, pt 2, pp. 445–6.
36 Malmesbury, *Diaries and Correspondence*, Vol. 4, p. 4.
37 'Memorandum on Pitt's retirement', printed by R. Willis, 'William Pitt's resignation in 1801', *BIHR*, vol. 44 (1971), p. 255.
38 Pitt, 15 April 1803, PRO 30/58/4, no. 95.
39 Barnes, *George III*, p. 443.
40 Colchester, *Diary*, Vol. 1, p. 506.
41 Arbuthnot, *Correspondence*, p. 31.
42 Brock, *Lord Liverpool*, p. 68.
43 M. McCahill, 'Peerage creations . . . 1750–1830', *EHR*, vol. 96 (1981), p. 282.

Chapter 3

1 Hill, *Growth of Parliamentary Parties*; Colley, *In Defiance of Oligarchy*; J. C. D. Clark, 'The decline of party 1740–1760', *EHR*, vol. 93 (1978), p. 505, and *Dynamics of Change*.
2 *Spectator*, vol. 163 (1939), p. 261.
3 Harvey, *Britain*, pp. 203–4.
4 Foord, *Opposition*, p. 444.
5 ibid., p. 470 and *passim*.
6 Phillips, *Electoral Behaviour*, p. 308.
7 O'Gorman, *Emergence of the British Two-Party System*, p. 75.
8 Mitchell, *Whigs in Opposition*, p. 66.
9 Namier, *Crossroads*, p. 34; cf. *England*, p. 182.
10 Namier, *Crossroads*, p. 37; Linda Colley, 'The Loyal Brotherhood . . . the London Organization of the Tory Party, 1727–1760', *HJ*, vol. 20 (1977), pp. 77–95, and *In Defiance of Oligarchy, passim*.
11 Forrester, *Northamptonshire County Elections and Electioneering*, p. 151.
12 Colley, 'The Loyal Brotherhood', loc. cit. at n. 10 above pp. 78–9, and *In Defiance of Oligarchy*, p. 234.
13 Linda Colley, 'The Mitchell election division, 24 March 1755', *BIHR*, vol. 49 (1976), p. 82, n. 2.
14 Colley, *In Defiance of Oligarchy, passim*, and 'Eighteenth-century English radicalism before Wilkes', *TRHS*, 5th ser., vol. 31 (1981), pp. 1–19.
15 Namier, *Crossroads*, p. 42; *History of Parliament, 1754–1790, sub* Holt, Newdigate and Wodehouse.
16 Cobbett, *Parliamentary History*, Vol. 16, p. 919.

17 *Corr. of Burke*, Vol. 2, p. 126.
18 Hill, *Growth of Parliamentary Parties*, pp. 160–1.
19 P. W. J. Riley, *The English Ministers and Scotland 1707–1727* (1964), p. 104, n. 1, and p. 106, n. 2.
20 Brewer, *Party Ideology*, p. 86 and n. 55.
21 *Grenville Papers*, Vol. 3, pp. 81–4.
22 Langford, *Rockingham Administration*, p. 268.
23 Namier, *England*, p. 53; cf. Brooke, *Chatham Administration*, p. 219.
24 *History of Parliament, 1745–1790, sub* Pelham, Thomas (1728–1805), Pelham, Thomas (1756–1826) and Pelham, Henry (1759–1797).
25 Foord, *Opposition*, p. 337.
26 ibid., p. 337; *History of Parliament, 1754–1790, sub* Hill, Noel, and Grosvenor, Thomas.
27 Feiling, *Second Tory Party*, pp. 248–9; Foord, *Opposition*, pp. 435–8.
28 Croker, *Papers*, Vol. 1, p. 126.
29 O'Gorman, *Rise of Party in England*, pp. 53–4 and n. 26; see also ch. 6 below, p. 99 and p. 245, n. 15.
30 Namier, *England*, p. 53.
31 *History of Parliament, 1715–1754, sub* Dowdeswell, William (1682–1728) and Dowdeswell, William (1721–75), and *History of Parliament, 1754–1790, sub* Dowdeswell and Meredith.
32 Brooke, *History of Parliament, 1754–1790*, Vol. 1, p. 188.
33 Namier, *England*, p. 219.
34 O'Gorman, *Rise of Party in England*, pp. 320–1.
35 Add. MS 38,206, f. 308.
36 Norris, *Shelburne*, p. 20.
37 Olsen, *The Radical Duke*, p. 142.
38 Wentworth Woodhouse (Sheffield) MSS, R1–842.
39 Portland (Nottingham) MSS, PwF 9023.
40 Cobbett, *Parliamentary History*, Vol. 20, p. 1124.
41 *Corr. of Burke*, Vol. 2, p. 121.
42 *London Courant*, 26 February, 1782.
43 Brewer, *Party Ideology*, pp. 94–5.
44 *History of Parliament, 1754–1790, sub* Coke.

Chapter 4

1 Harley Diary, Vol. 2, f. 42; Ryder Diary, *History of Parliament, 1715–1754*, Vol. 1, pp. 51–3; Hill, *Growth of Parliamentary Parties*, pp. 224–5.
2 Hill, *Growth of Parliamentary Parties*, p. 192; Owen, *Rise of the Pelhams*, pp. 97–8; Add. MS 9200, f. 80; Add. MS 47,089, p. 1.
3 Harley Diary, Vol. 2, pp. 52–3; *Walpole Corr.*, Vol. 1, pp. 158, 178; Add. MS 6043, f. 110.
4 HMC, *Egmont Diary*, Vol. 3, p. 256; Harley Diary, Vol. 2, p. 47; *Walpole Corr.*, Vol. 1, p. 146; Add. MS 6043, f. 113.
5 Hervey *Memoirs of George II*, Vol. 3, pp. 942–59; *Walpole Corr.*, Vol. 1, pp. 187–8.
6 Add. MS 9,213, f. 18; Add. MS 32,199, f. 412; PRO 30/29/1/11, f. 3.
7 Add. MS 35,363, f. 15; Add. MS 51,437, ff. 20–1; HMC, *Egmont Diary*, Vol. 3, pp. 267–8; *History of Parliament, 1715–1754*, Vol. 1, pp. 53, 72 and 104.
8 Coxe, *Pelham*, Vol. 1, p. 35.
9 Add. MS 9200, f. 80.

10 Coxe, *Pelham*, Vol. 7, pp. 91–6, 109, 103–5; Add. MS 51,437, f. 53; Ilchester, *Fox*, Vol. 1, p. 99.

11 Add. MSS 35407, f. 295; Foord, *Opposition*, p. 248.

12 Add. MSS 35,337, ff. 4–5; Williams, *Pitt*, Vol. 1, p. 114; *History of Parliament, 1715–1754*, Vol. 1, pp. 55 and 104; Foord, *Opposition*, p. 241; Linda Colley, 'The Loyal Brotherhood . . . the London organization of the Tory Party, 1727–1760', *HJ*, vol. 20 (1977), p. 78.

13 *Walpole Corr.*, Vol. 1, pp. 333–5; Harley Diary, Vol. 2, p. 86; Owen, *Rise of the Pelhams*, pp. 230–8.

14 Williams, *Pitt*, Vol. 1, p. 122; Coxe, *Pelham*, Vol. 1, p. 168.

15 *Walpole Corr.*, Vol. 1, pp. 334, 341; Yorke, *Hardwicke,* Vol. 1, pp. 374–5 (cf. BL Stowe MS 254, f. 1); Owen, *Rise of the Pelhams*, pp. 249. 260–1; Colley, 'The Loyal Brotherhood, loc. cit. at n. 12, p. 86.

16 Harley Diary, Vol. 2, pp. 92–4; Add. MS 35,602, f. 46; *Private Corr.*, pp. 40–1; *Walpole Corr.*, Vol. 1., pp. 346–7; PRO 30/29/1/11, f. 11; Add. MS 32,704, ff. 145, 158, and 32,993 f. 289; Colley, *In Defiance of Oligarchy*, pp. 248–9.

17 Owen, *Rise of the Pelhams*, pp. 277, 281–2; Cruickshanks, *Political Untouchables*, p. 86.

18 Newcastle (Nottingham) MSS, NeC 388; Add. MSS 32,705, f. 187 and 47,097–8 (Egmont's Diary); Williams, *Pitt*, Vol. 1, pp. 141–5; Owen, *Rise of the Pelhams*, p. 295.

19 *Walpole Corr.*, Vol. 2, p. 8; Coxe, *Pelham*, Vol. 1, pp. 291–2; *Private Corr.*, pp. 108–12, 113–19; Ilchester, *Fox*, Vol. 1, pp. 118, 122–3, 126; Owen, *Rise of the Pelhams*, pp. 289–96.

20 Owen, *Rise of the Pelhams*, pp. 298–301.

21 Ryder Diary, *History of Parliament, 1715–1754*, Vol. 1, pp. 56–7; HMC, *Egmont Diary*, Vol. 3, p. 315; Foord, *Opposition*, p. 266; Owen, *Rise of the Pelhams*, p. 312.

22 *History of Parliament, 1715–1754*, Vol. 1, p. 57; *Lyttelton Memoirs*, Vol. 1, p. 257; Nicholas Rogers, 'Resistance to oligarchy', in John Stevenson (ed.), *London in the Age of Reform* (Oxford, 1977), pp. 20–2.

23 Owen, *Rise of the Pelhams*, pp. 312–14; Foord, *Opposition*, p. 264; Harley Diary, Vol. 2, p. 122.

Chapter 5

1 Add. MS. 35,337, ff. 112–13; Wyndham, *Chronicles of the Eighteenth Century*, Vol. 1, p. 203.

2 Yorke, *Hardwicke*, Vol. 2, p. 117; Coxe, *Pelham*, Vol. 2, p. 398; Samuel Squire, *An Historical Essay upon the Balance of Civil Power in England* (1748), pp. xxix–xxx.

3 *History of Parliament, 1715–1754*, Vol. 1, pp. 57 and 107; A. N. Newman, 'The political patronage of Frederick Lewis, Prince of Wales', *HJ*, Vol. 1 (1958), p. 74; Foord, *Opposition*, p. 267.

4 Walpole, *Memoirs of George II*, Vol. 1, p. 47; A. N. Newman, 'Leicester House politics, 1748–1751', *EHR*, Vol. 76 (1961), p. 580.

5 Add. MS 47,012 (formerly 47097/98); *Walpole Corr.*, Vol. 2, pp. 134, 145 and 153–4; Dodington, *Journal*, p. 25.

6 Dodington, *Journal*, pp. 25, 101 and 45; *History of Parliament, 1715–1754*, Vol. 1, p. 76; A. N. Newman, Egmont MSS in 'Leicester House politics, 1750–1760', *Camden Miscellany*, vol. 23 (Royal Historical Society, Camden 4th ser. vol. 7), pp. 143, 115–17, 119.

7 Newman, 'Leicester House politics, 1750–60', pp. 174–5; Sedgwick, Introduction to Harvey, *Memoirs of George II*, Vol. 1, pp. xxxiv–xxxv.

8 Walpole, *Memoirs of George II*, Vol. 1, pp. 12–13; Coxe, *Pelham*, Vol. 2, p. 165; Newman, 'Leicester House politics, 1750–60', loc. cit. at n. 6, p. 213.

9 Newman, loc. cit. at n. 6, p. 209; Coxe, *Pelham*, Vol. 2, p. 366.

10 Ilchester, *Fox*, Vol. 1, pp. 169, 179, and Vol. 2, p. 145; *Walpole Corr.*, Vol. 2, pp. 272 and 277–8.

11 Ilchester, *Fox*, Vol. 1, pp. 361–2 and Vol. 2, p. 183; *Bedford Corr.*, Vol. 2, p. 125; *History of Parliament, 1715–1754, sub* Murray, citing Chesterfield, 6 April 1753.

12 *Walpole Corr.*, Vol. 2, pp. 373, 379; Yorke, *Hardwicke*, Vol. 2, p. 206; *History of Parliament, 1715–1754, sub* Fox; *History of Parliament, 1754–1790, sub* Murray; *Lyttelton Memoirs*, Vol. 2, p. 457; Add. MSS 32,736, f. 389 and 51,351, ff. 7–8.

13 *The Balance, or the Merits of Whig and Tory exactly weighed and Fairly Determined* (1753), p. 8; *History of Parliament, 1715–1754, sub* Aldworth, R. N.

14 R. J. Robson, *The Oxfordshire Election of 1754* (Oxford, 1949), pp. 139 *et sqq.*; *History of Parliament, 1754–1790*, Vol. 1, p. 62

15 Walpole, *Memoirs of George II*, Vol. 1, pp. 407–20.

16 Walpole, *Memoirs of George II*, Vol. 2, pp. 10–14; Add. MS 41,355, f. 28; *Bedford Corr.*, Vol. 2, p. 157; Linda Colley, 'The Mitchell election division, 24 March 1755', *BIHR*, vol. 49 (1976), pp. 80–107; J. C. D. Clark, 'The decline of party, 1740–1760', *EHR*, vol. 93 (1978), p. 506.

17 Yorke, *Hardwicke*, Vol. 2, pp. 229, 236–49; Sedgwick, *Letters*, pp. xlvi *et sqq.*; Sedgwick, 'Letters from William Pitt to Lord Bute: 1755–1758', in Richard Pares and A. J. P. Taylor (eds), *Essays Presented to Sir Lewis Namier* (1956), pp. 109–12.

18 *Walpole Corr.*, Vol. 2, pp. 483, 487; *Grenville Papers*, Vol. 1, p. 435; Add. MSS 32,860, f. 471; Williams, *Pitt*, Vol. 1, pp. 267–70.

19 Walpole, *Memoirs of George II*, Vol. 2, pp. 191, 201–2; *Lyttelton Memoirs*, Vol. 2, p. 507; Sedgwick, *Letters*, p. 7; Add. MS 6832, ff. 177–8.

20 Add. MSS 6832, f. 128; *Bedford Corr.*, Vol. 2, p. 207.

21 Ilchester, *Fox*, Vol. 2, p. 19; BL Stowe MS 263, f. 12; Wyndham, *Chronicles of the Eighteenth Century*, Vol. 2, p. 228; Add. MSS 32,869, ff. 253, 266, 33,353, f. 204, and 6834, f. 9; *Lyttelton Memoirs*, Vol. 2, p. 584.

22 PRO 30/8/53, pt 1, f. 92; Peters *Pitt and Popularity*, pp. 67, 71; *Bedford Corr.*, Vol. 2, p. 223; *Walpole Corr.*, Vol. 3, p. 62; Linda Colley, 'The Loyal Brotherhood . . . the London organization of the Tory Party, 1727–1760', *HJ*, vol. 20 (1977), p. 90.

23 Ilchester, *Fox*, Vol. 2, pp. 20, 31–2 and *Letters to Fox*, p. 120; *Walpole Corr.*, Vol. 3, p. 70; Wiggin *Faction of Cousins*, pp. 193, 196.

24 Paul Langford, 'William Pitt and public opinion, 1757', *EHR*, vol. 88 (1973), pp. 54–80, Colley, *In Defiance of Oligarchy*, p. 280.

25 Add. MS 32,870, f. 399; Yorke, *Hardwicke*, Vol. 2, pp. 392 and 394; Waldegrave, *Memoirs*, pp. 129–30.

26 *Walpole Corr.*, Vol. 3, p. 81; cf. Walpole, *Memoirs of George II*, Vol. 3, pp. 25–8.

27 Peters, pp. 104, 109; Walpole, *Memoirs of George II*, Vol. 3, p. 156; Clark, *Dynamics of Change*, p. 444.

28 Peters, *Pitt and Popularity*, pp. 138–42, 158–9; Foord, *Opposition*, p. 296; Add. MS 35,374, f. 144.

29 Walpole, *Memoirs of George II*, Vol. 3, p. 279; Williams, *Pitt*, Vol. 2, pp. 61–2; Add. MS 35,419, f. 260.

30 Add. MS 35,419, f. 257; Yorke, *Hardwicke*, Vol. 3, p. 110.
31 Sedgwick, *Letters*, pp. lvii and 18 *et sqq.*; Ilchester, *Fox,* Vol. 2, pp. 109–10.

Chapter 6

1 Brooke, *King George III*, pp. 56, 58, 90; Namier, *England*, p. 91.
2 Dodington, *Journal*, p. 407; Williams, *Pitt*, Vol. 2, p. 70; Peters, *Pitt and Popularity*, p. 180.
3 Add. MSS 35,491, f. 257 and 32,915, f. 333; Wentworth Woodhouse (Sheffield) MSS R1–172, 2 December 1760.
4 Add. MSS 32,916, ff. 208, 210.
5 Dodington, *Journal*, pp. 412, 414; Peters, *Pitt and Popularity*, p. 193; Williams, *Pitt*, Vol. 2, pp. 65–73; Add. MSS 6832, f. 234 and 32,921, f. 60; O'Gorman, *Rise of Party*, pp. 32–3; Browning, *Newcastle*, p. 275.
6 Peters, *Pitt and Popularity*, pp. 191–3; Namier, *England*, p. 197 *et sqq.*; Feiling, *Second Tory Party*, pp. 72–3.
7 Sedgwick, *Letters*, pp. 63–4; Add. MS 6834. ff. 31, 33; Dodington, *Journal*, p. 426; Peters, *Pitt and Popularity*, pp. 212–13, 230; *Devonshire Diary*, pp. 110, 118–40.
8 Namier, *England*, pp. 298–9; Yorke, *Hardwicke*, Vol. 3, p. 430.
9 Add. MSS 32,926, f. 351, 32,927, ff. 70–1 and 32,929, ff. 258, 332; Yorke, *Hardwicke*, Vol. 3, pp. 328, 331; *Grenville Papers*, Vol. 1, pp. 395–7, 402–3; Newcastle, 4 May 1762, Wentworth Woodhouse (Sheffield) MSS R1–238.
10 *Grenville Papers*, Vol. 1, pp. 450–2; Add. MSS 36,797, ff. 6, 17, 32,939, ff. 264, and 32,941, f. 371; Namier, *England*, p. 337; Ilchester, *Letters to Fox*, p. 160.
11 Add. MS 32,944, f. 190; Bodleian, North MS d. 23, f. 156; PRO 30/8/61, f. 80.
12 *A Consolatory Epistle to Members of the Old Faction* (1762); Add, MS 32,945, ff. 82–3; *History of Parliament, 1754–90, sub* Mordaunt; Peters, *Pitt and Popularity*, p. 254.
13 *Bedford Corr.*, Vol. 3, pp. 161–2, 208–10, 218–19; Add. MSS 32,945, f. 239 and 6834, f. 41.
14 O'Gorman, *Rise of Party*, pp. 54–5; *Rockingham Memoirs*, Vol. 1, p. 155; HMC, *Townshend*, p. 398; *History of Parliament, 1754–1790, sub* Newdigate, Eliab Harvey, Sir Charles Mordaunt, etc.
15 Foord, *Opposition*, p. 314, n. 1; D. Watson, 'The rise of opposition at Wildman's Club', *BIHR*, vol. 44 (1971), pp. 55–77; O'Gorman, *Rise of Party*, pp. 53–7; Brewer, *Party Ideology*, pp. 77–8.
16 Add. MS 32,947, f. 182; Feiling, *Second Tory Party*, p. 78; *Grenville Papers*, Vol. 2, p. 191.
17 Add. MS 32,946, ff. 257 and 267; O'Gorman, *Rise of Party*, p. 115.
18 Add. MSS 32,947, ff. 21 and 182; *Bedford Corr.*, Vol. 3, pp. 208–9, 219; *History of Parliament, 1754–1790, sub* Philips.
19 *History of the Late Minority* (1765), pp. 91–2; O'Gorman, *Rise of Party*, pp. 59–61; *History of Parliament, 1754–1790, sub* Philips.
20 *Rockingham Memoirs*, Vol. 1, p. 169; Add. MSS 32,949, f. 191 and 36,797, f. 37; Sedgwick, *Letters*, p. 204; Brooke, *King George III*, pp. 102–3.
21 O'Gorman, *Rise of Party*, pp. 96 and 520, n. 5; cf. Derek Jarrett, 'The regency crisis of 1765', *EHR*, vol. 85 (1970), p. 296; Add. MS 32,948, f. 291; *History of Parliament, 1754–1790, sub* Perceval, John and Jenkinson, Charles; Sedgwick, *Letters*, p. 210; *Jenkinson Papers*, p. 155 and *passim*; *Grenville Papers*, Vol. 2, p. 199.
22 *Grenville Papers*, Vol. 2, pp. 83–8, and 195–203; Fitzmaurice, *Life of Shelburne*, Vol. 2, pp. 284–5; Ilchester, *Letters to Fox*, pp. 179–82.

23 Devonshire, 30 August, Wentworth Woodhouse (Sheffield) MSS, R1–382; Add. MSS 32,950, f. 323 and 32,951; *Grenville Papers*, Vol. 2, p. 118.
24 Namier, *England*, pp. 201–2.
25 Add. MS. 32,958, f. 309, 32,964, f. 95, and 32,965, f. 318; Browning, *Newcastle*, 299–300; Sir George Yonge, 17 October 1764, Portland (Nottingham) MSS PwF 7448; Williams, *Pitt*, Vol. 2, p. 168.
26 Grafton, *Autobiography*, pp. 42–3; Lord Frederick Cavendish, 21 May 1765, Wentworth Woodhouse (Sheffield) MSS, R1–449; Add. MS 34,713, f. 239 and *Grenville Papers*, Vol. 3, p. 41.
27 Newcastle to Albemarle, 3 July 1765, Wentworth Woodhouse (Sheffield), MSS, R–455 and R1–458; Bateson, *Narrative*, pp. 28–31; *Rockingham Memoirs*, Vol. 1, pp. 218–20; Brewer, *Party Ideology*, p. 78; O'Gorman, *Rise of Party*, pp. 103–6 and 108–9.
28 *History of the Late Minority* (1765), p. 76.

Chapter 7

1   *George III Corr.*, Vol. 1, p. 173; Add. MS 32,969, ff. 392–3; *Jenkinson Papers*, p. 380; *Grenville Papers*, Vol. 3, pp. 81–2.
2   O'Gorman, *Rise of Party*, pp. 127–8; Thomas, *Lord North*, pp. 15–17.
3   O'Gorman, *Rise of Party*, p. 220; 'Measures, Claremont, July 6th 1765', Wentworth Woodhouse (Sheffield) MSS, R1–456. See also Chapter 6, note 27.
4   Wentworth Woodhouse (Sheffield) MSS, R1–456–1; *History of Parliament, 1754–1790*, sub Cooke, George; Add. MSS 32,969, ff. 392–3, 32,972, f. 60 and 32,973, f. 12; Wentworth Woodhouse (Sheffield), MSS, R1–551.
5   Add. MSS 32,973, ff. 194–6 and 237–40.
6   Sedgwick, *Letters*, pp. 242 and 245; Langford, *Rockingham Administration*, pp. 135, 143–4; Wentworth Woodhouse (Sheffield) MSS, Burke 1–44.
7   Langford, *Rockingham Administration*, p. 156; Add. MS 32,973, f. 321; O'Gorman, *Rise of Party*, pp. 148–51; *Bedford Corr.*, Vol. 3, pp. 326–9.
8   Add. MS 32,974, ff. 167, 169; Feiling, *Second Tory Party*, pp. 89–90; Namier, *Crossroads*, p. 43; O'Gorman, *Rise of Party*, pp. 158, 163–4; Bateson, *Narrative*, p. 50.
9   O'Gorman, *Rise of Party*, pp. 169–70; Grafton, *Autobiography*, pp. 71–4; Wentworth Woodhouse (Sheffield) MSS, R–600.
10 *George III Corr.*, Vol. 1, pp. 305–6; Sedgwick, *Letters*, p. 248.
11 *George III Corr.*, Vol. 1, pp. 354–5; Langford, *Rockingham Administration*, pp. 256–7; Rockingham 9 July, Portland (Nottingham) MSS, PwF 8983.
12 *George III Corr.*, Vol. 1, p. 175, misdated 1765; Edmund Burke, *Thoughts on the Cause of the Present Discontents* (1770).
13 Add. MSS 32,976, ff. 253–4 and 32,978, f. 2; *Rockingham Memoirs*, Vol. 2, pp. 12–13; Portland (Nottingham) MSS, PwF 8984; Langford, *Rockingham Administration*, p. 264; Wentworth Woodhouse (Sheffield) MSS, R1–708 and R1–715; *Corr. of Burke*, Vol. 1, p. 281, n. 1.
14 Add. MS 32,978, ff. 229, 418; *Cavendish Debates*, Vol. 1, pp. 581–2; Philip Lawson, 'George Grenville and America', *WMQ*, Vol. 37 (1980), pp. 561–76.
15 Add. MSS 32,980, ff. 139, 248, 250; *Corr. of Burke*, Vol. 1, pp. 296–7; Walpole, *Memoirs of George III*, Vol. 2, p. 298; D. Watson, 'Rockingham Whigs and the Townshend duties', *EHR*, vol. 84 (1969), pp. 561–5; O'Gorman, *Rise of Party*, pp. 197–9.
16 O'Gorman, *Rise of Party*, pp. 206–8; *Bedford Corr.*, Vol. 3, p. 370; *Cavendish Debates*, Vol. 1, p. 584; Christie, *Myth and Reality*, p. 50, n. 1; Add. MSS 32,983, f. 193 and 32,984, f. 8.

17 Wentworth Woodhouse (Sheffield) MSS, R1–885 and 982; Walpole, *Memoirs of George III*, Vol. 3, pp. 112-13; O'Gorman, *Rise of Party*, pp. 215–616; Brooke, *Chatham Administration*, pp. 243–7.
18 Feiling, *Second Tory Party*, p. 97; *History of Parliament, 1754–1790, sub* Oxford University; O'Gorman, *Rise of Party*, pp. 224–7; Newcastle, Portland (Nottingham) MSS, PwF 7595.
19 Wentworth Woodhouse (Sheffield) MS, R1–1058b.
20 Portland (Nottingham) MS, PwF 2662a.
21 Feiling, *Second Tory Party*, pp. 111–12; *Chatham Corr.*, Vol. 3, p. 365; Samuel Johnson, *The False Alarm* (1770); O'Gorman, *Rise of Party*, p. 273; Thomas, *Lord North*, p. 71.
22 Add. MSS 35,375, f. 77 and 35,609, f. 169; Wentworth Woodhouse (Sheffield) MS, R1–1294; PRO 30/8/54, ff. 197, 199, 201, 203, 205, 207 and PRO 30/8/56, f. 98; *Corr. of Burke*, Vol. 2, pp. 126–7; *Rockingham Memoirs*, Vol. 2, p. 194; Wentworth Woodhouse (Sheffield) MS, R1–1327.
23 O'Gorman, *Rise of Party*, pp. 280–5; Wentworth Woodhouse (Sheffield) MS, R–1356; *Chatham Corr.*, Vol. 4, p. 187.
24 Portland (Nottingham) MSS, PwF 9061–2 and 2664; Wentworth Woodhouse (Sheffield) MSS, R1-1397 and 1409 and Burke 1–238.
25 O'Gorman, *Rise of Party*, pp. 298–302; Wentworth Woodhouse (Sheffield) MSS, R1–1042; Portland (Nottingham) MS, PwF 9064; *Chatham Corr.*, Vol. 4, pp. 252, 254.
26 Thomas, *Lord North*, p. 74.

Chapter 8

1 *Corr. of Burke*, Vol. 2, p. 516; Wentworth Woodhouse (Sheffield) MSS, R1–1479; Thomas, *Lord North*, p. 76; O'Gorman, *Rise of Party*, pp. 311–12; Donoughue, *British Politics*, pp. 76–104.
2 Wentworth Woodhouse (Sheffield) MSS, R1–1478.
3 Thomas, *Lord North*, pp. 80–1; Portland (Nottingham) MSS, PwF 9084a; *George III Corr.*, Vol. 3, pp. 152–3; O'Gorman, *Rise of Party*, pp. 320–1.
4 Cobbett, *Parliamentary History*, Vol. 18, pp. 42–6.
5 ibid., Vol. 18, pp. 149–68.
6 Grafton, *Autobiography*, pp. 274–5; Add. MS 35,612, f. 191; Wentworth Woodhouse (Sheffield) MSS, R1–1569 and R1–1601; *Corr. of Burke*, Vol. 3, p. 143; Cobbett, *Parliamentary History*, Vol. 18, pp. 963–92; O'Gorman, *Rise of Party*, pp. 343–7.
7 Portland (Nottingham) MSS, PwF 9115; Wentworth Woodhouse (Sheffield) MSS, R1–1720; *Corr. of Burke*, Vol. 3, p. 294; O'Gorman, *Rise of Party*, pp. 354–5.
8 *George III Corr.*, Vol. 4, pp. 26–31, 33, 54–7, 68–71; *Corr. of Burke*, Vol. 3, pp. 382–3; *Chatham Corr.*, Vol. 4, pp. 490–2; Fitzmaurice, *Life of Shelburne*, Vol. 3, pp. 23–5.
9 O'Gorman, *Rise of Party*, pp. 364–5; Russell, *Memorials*, Vol. 1, p. 168.
10 Wentworth Woodhouse (Sheffield) MSS, R1–1792 and R1–1811; O'Gorman, *Rise of Party*, pp. 384–5; Feiling, *Second Tory Party*, p. 132; Add. MS. 38,306, f. 120; *George III Corr.*, Vol. 4, p. 350.
11 Feiling, *Second Tory Party*, p. 133; BL Egerton MS 2232, f. 17; Add. MS 37,835, f. 46.
12 *George III Corr.*, Vol. 4, p. 522; O'Gorman, *Rise of Party*, pp. 400–1; Wentworth Woodhouse (Sheffield) MSS, R1–1869.
13 Brooke, *King George III*, pp. 220–1; *General Evening Post*, 24 June 1780; Christie, *End of North's Ministry*, pp. 22–3, and *Myth and Reality*, pp. 296–310.

14 Christie, *End of North's Ministry*, pp. 24–30.
15 Add. MS 35,617, f. 9; Portland (Nottingham) MS, PwF 9140a; Christie, *End of North's Ministry*, pp. 34–8, 116, 159–62.
16 O'Gorman, *Rise of Party*, pp. 430–5; Fitzmaurice, *Life of Shelburne*, Vol. 3, pp. 106–7; *Political Memoir*, pp. 35–6.
17 Add. MSS 35,379, ff. 246–9, 313, 322, 338; Christie, *End of North's Ministry*, pp. 237–8, 252–7; O'Gorman, *Rise of Party*, pp. 436–7; Ehrman, *Younger Pitt*, Vol. 1, p. 58.
18 Wentworth Woodhouse (Sheffield) MS, R1–1967; Foord, *Opposition*, p. 344; Add. MSS 38,308, f. 8 and 35,380, f. 132; Christie, *End of North's Ministry*, pp. 272 *et sqq.*
19 O'Gorman, *Rise of Party*, pp. 443–4; *Commons Journal*, vol. 38, pp. 814, 861; Add. MS 35,380, f. 188; Christie, *End of North's Ministry*, pp. 325 *et sqq.*
20 *George III Corr.*, Vol. 5, p. 394; Christie, *End of North's Ministry*, pp. 339 *et sqq.*; Foord, *Opposition*, p. 337.
21 *Rockingham Memoirs*, Vol. 2, pp. 451–3; Debrett, *Parliamentary Register*, vol. 6, pp. 497–8.
22 Fitzmaurice, *Life of Shelburne*, Vol. 3, pp. 130–1; Add. MS 38,364, f. 33.
23 O'Gorman, *Rise of Party*, p. 453; Russell, *Memorials*, Vol. 1, pp. 289–93; *George III Corr.*, Vol. 5, p. 421; Foord, *Opposition*, p. 373, n. 4; Cannon, *Fox–North Coalition*, p. 3, n. 4.

Chapter 9

1 Ehrman, *Younger Pitt*, Vol. 1, pp. 52, 70–1. Russell, *Memorials*, Vol. 1, p. 322.
2 Fitzmaurice, *Life of Shelburne*, Vol. 3, pp. 131, 155–9; Cannon, *Fox–North Coalition*, pp. 4 *et sqq.*; Pares, *George III*, p. 123, n. 1; Russell, *Memorials*, Vol. 1, pp. 292 and 435; Add. MSS 47,561, f. 27, and 47,582, f. 91; O'Gorman, *Rise of Party*, p. 463; Grafton, *Autobiography*, p. 322.
3 BL Egerton MS 2136, f. 95; Russell, *Memorials*, Vol. 1, p. 459; Add. MSS, 33,128, ff. 83–6 and 47,561, f. 41; *Public Advertiser*, 8 July; HMC, *Carlisle*, pp. 632–3; Smith, *Whig Principles*, p. 37.
4 *Public Advertiser*, 10 July; Add. MS 34,418, f. 484.
5 Cannon, *Fox–North Coalition*, pp. 27–9; Add. MS 38,567, f. 101.
6 Cannon, *Fox–North Coalition*, pp. 30–5; Blair-Adam MSS, General Corr. 1780–3, North to Adam, 2 October; BL Egerton MSS 2136, f. 213.
7 Cannon, *Fox–North Coalition*, pp. 38–43; Thomas, *Lord North*, pp. 135–6.
8 Cannon, *Fox–North Coalition*, pp. 45–9; Grafton, *Autobiography*, pp. 354–6; Russell, *Memorials*, Vol. 2, pp. 37–8.
9 Cannon, *Fox–North Coalition*, pp. 51–5.
10 Grafton, *Autobiography*, pp. 370, 377; Cannon, *Fox–North Coalition*, pp. 68–9; Thomas, *Lord North*, pp. 138–9.
11 Cannon, *Fox–North Coalition*, pp. 71–2, 79–80, 83; Russell, *Memorials*, Vol. 2, p. 200; Brooke, *King George III*, p. 240; Pares, *George III*, p. 125; *George III Corr.*, Vol. 6, p. 330.
12 Cannon, *Fox–North Coalition*, pp. 95–8; HMC, *Fortescue*, Vol. 1, pp. 214–19; Buckingham, *George III*, Vol. 1, p. 304; Blair-Adam MSS, General Corr. 1780–3, Adam to Sheridan, 18 June 1783.
13 Ehrman, *Younger Pitt*, Vol. 1, p. 151; Cannon, *Fox–North Coalition*, pp. 117–23, 128–31, and 137–44; *Auckland Corr.*, Vol. 1, pp. 68–9.
14 Buckingham, *George III*, Vol. 1, p. 255; Cannon, *Fox–North Coalition*, pp. 131 and 149–51; Add. MS 33,100, f. 471; Feiling, *Second Tory Party*, p. 158; P. J. Jupp, 'Earl Temple's resignation', *HJ*, vol. 15 (1972), pp. 309–13.

15 Cannon, *Fox–North Coalition*, pp. 155–63; Blair-Adam MSS, General Corr.
    1784–5, Adam to Fox, 11 June 1784.
16 Cannon, *Fox–North Coalition*, pp. 164–71, 176–80, 190–6, 236; Russell, *Memorials*, Vol. 2, pp. 234–41; *Pitt–Rutland Corr.*, p. 7; Add. MS 35,381, f. 270.
17 Cannon, *Fox–North Coalition*, pp. 185–90, 198–204; *Pitt–Rutland Corr.*, p. 10;
    Mrs E. George, 'Fox's Martyrs: the general election of 1784', *TRHS*, 4th ser.,
    vol. 21 (1939), pp. 133–68; D. R. McAdams, 'Addresses to the king . . .', *HLQ*,
    vol. 35 (1972), pp. 381–5.
18 Add. MSS 38,309, f. 89 and 35,381, f. 268.
19 Add. MS 35382, f. 100; O. Browning (ed.), *Political Memoranda of Francis, 5th
    Duke of Leeds* (1884), pp. 101–2.
20 *Pitt–Rutland Corr.*, p. 105; 'Third party circular', in Namier, *Crossroads*, p. 229.
21 Add. MS 35,383, f. 1.
22 O'Gorman, *Whig Party and the French Revolution*, app. 1.
23 Adam to North, 15 January 1784, Blair-Adam MSS, General Corr. 1783–4;
    O'Gorman, *Whig Party and the French Revolution*; Donald E. Ginter, 'The financing of the Whig party organization, 1783–1793', *AHR*, vol. 71 (1966), pp. 421–40.
24 Portland to Fitzwilliam, 20 August 1784, Wentworth Woodhouse (Sheffield)
    MSS F 63/44; B. W. Hill, 'Fox and Burke . . . 1784–1789', *EHR*, vol. 89 (1974),
    pp. 1–24.
25 Add. MS 47,561, ff. 80–2, printed Russell, *Memorials*, Vol. 4, pp. 279–81;
    Corr. of Burke, Vol. 5, pp. 165–6; Debrett, *Parliamentary Register*, vol. 16,
    pp. 278–83, 302–3; Add. MSS 35,382, f. 251 and 35,383, f. 13.
26 *Pitt–Rutland Corr.*, p. 105; *Corr. of Burke*, Vol. 5, pp. 241–4; Debrett, *Parliamentary Register*, vol. 19, pp. 119–26, 137; *Auckland Corr.*, Vol. 1, p. 377.
27 Mitchell, *Charles James Fox*, p. 114; *Bland Burges Letters*, p. 101; *Corr. of
    Burke*, Vol. 5, pp. 395–6; Sichel, *Sheridan*, Vol. 2, p. 404; Debrett, *Parliamentary Register*, vol. 21, pp. 556–61, 565–7; A. S. Turberville, *House of
    Lords in the Eighteenth Century* (1924), vol. 2, p. 201; G. M. Ditchfield,
    'Parliamentary struggle . . . 1782–1790', *EHR*, vol. 89 (1974), pp. 551–77.
28 Debrett, *Parliamentary Register*, vol. 25, pp. 5–29, 125–30, 138–52; Buckingham, *George III*, Vol. 2, pp. 53–4; Add. MSS 41,579, ff. 15, 18 and 47,561,
    f. 93; Sichel, *Sheridan*, Vol. 2, p. 415; for a full account of the constitutional
    debate see Derry, *Regency Crisis*.
29 Minto, *Life and Letters of Elliot*, Vol. 1, p. 248; Ginter, Introduction to *Whig
    Organization . . . 1790*; *Corr. of Burke*, Vol. 5, pp. 470, 472–4; O'Gorman, *Whig
    Party and the French Revolution*, pp. 44–5; Fox to Fitzwilliam, 13 November
    1789, Wentworth Woodhouse (Sheffield) MSS F 115/12.

Chapter 10

1 Ginter, Introduction to *Whig Organization . . . 1790*, pp. xxvii–xliii and *passim*.
2 Smith, *Whig Principles*, pp. 111–12; O'Gorman *Whig Party and the French
   Revolution*, pp. 51, 248–9.
3 Edmund Burke, *Reflections on the Revolution in France* (1790); Richard Price,
   A Discourse upon the Love of Our Country (1790). The literature on Burke is
   voluminous. Two modern assessments of Burke's contribution are Frank
   O'Gorman, *Edmund Burke, His Political Philosophy* (1973) and B. W. Hill,
   Edmund Burke on Government, Politics and Society, Introduction: 'The
   philosopher in action', and pp. 277–8.
4 *Political Memoir*, pp. 154–68; Barnes, *George III*, pp. 229–34.
5 Wentworth Woodhouse (Sheffield) MSS, F 115/54, Portland to Fitzwilliam, 21
   April 1791; *Corr. of Burke*, Vol. 6, p. 161, n. 2.

6   *Corr. of Burke*, Vol. 6, pp. 415–16 and Vol. 9, p. 446; Wentworth Woodhouse (Sheffield) MSS F 115/25, Loughborough to Fitzwilliam, 1 August 1791.
7   PRO 30/8/168, ff. 101 and 103.
8   *English Historical Documents*, Vol. 11, p. 287; *Political Memoir*, p. 182; *Corr. of Burke*, Vol. 7, pp. 206–7.
9   *Corr. of Burke*, Vol. 7, p. 315.
10 O'Gorman, *Whig Party and the French Revolution*, pp. 112–39; Mitchell, *Charles James Fox*, pp. 200–20.
11 Add. MSS 47,569, f. 28 and 33,129, f. 232; O'Gorman, *Whig Party and the French Revolution*, pp. 178–9.
12 Portland (Nottingham) MSS, PwF 3762a, 14 July 1794, and 3763b, 15 June 1794.
13 O'Gorman, *Whig Party and the French Revolution*, app. 3 and 4.
14 Wentworth Woodhouse (Sheffield) MSS, F 31c, F 79, F 81–4; Smith, *Whig Principles*, ch. 7.
15 Add. MS 47,569, f. 54; Russell, *Memorials*, Vol. 3, p. 105.
16 Grey MSS, box 7, file 10, 20 August 1795; Holland, *Memoirs of the Whig Party*, Vol. 1, p. 77; McCahill, *Order and Equipoise*, p. 74.
17 Grey MSS, box 7, file 10, 11 November 1795, 1 January 1796.
18 Colchester, *Diary*, Vol. 1, pp. 8, 14, 32, 57; Feiling, *Second Tory Party*, p. 204.
19 Colchester, *Diary*, Vol. 1, pp. 78, 87, 91, 102, 105; Grey MSS, box 7, file 10, 15 June 1797; *English Historical Documents*, Vol. 11, pp. 306–7; Russell, *Memorials*, Vol. 3, p. 136; Holland, *Memoirs of the Whig Party*, Vol. 1, p. 84; Cannon, *Parliamentary Reform*, p. 131, n. 2.
20 Colchester, *Diary*, Vol. 1, pp. 132, 146, 166–7, 171–2, 192–3; Grey MSS, box 7, file 10, 29 November 1797; Holland, *Memoirs of the Whig Party*, Vol. 1, p. 143; Add. MSS 37,416, f. 43.
21 Holland, *Memoirs of the Whig Party*, Vol. 1, p. 161.
22 *English Historical Documents*, Vol. 11, pp. 176–7.
23 Feiling, *Second Tory Party*, p. 221; Malmesbury, *Diaries and Correspondence*, Vol. 4, p. 2; Colchester, *Diary*, Vol. 1, p. 232.
24 Colchester, *Diary*, Vol. 1, p. 221; Rose, *Life of Pitt*, pt 2, pp. 438. 445–6.
25 Rose, *Diaries*, Vol. 1, pp. 286, 312, 360; Feiling, *Second Tory Party*, pp. 223–4; Rose, *Life of Pitt*, pt 2, p. 448.

Chapter 11

1   *English Historical Documents*, Vol. 11, p. 125.
2   Rose, *Diaries*, Vol. 1, pp. 442–3; P. C. Lipscombe, 'Party politics 1801–1802 . . .', *HJ*, vol. 11 (1969), pp. 451–3.
3   R. E. Willis, 'Fox, Grenville and the recovery of opposition, 1801–1804', *JBS*, vol. 11 (1971–2), p. 27; Holland, *Memoirs of the Whig Party*, Vol. 2, pp. 181–2, 187.
4   Pitt, 22 October, Canning MSS, 30; Add. MSS 35,901, f. 145 and 38,833, f. 54; Tierney, 17 December, Grey MSS, box 55.
5   PRO 30/29/8/2, ff. 196–7, 220–1; Harvey, *Britain*, pp. 127–8.
6   Tierney, postmarked 4 December 1802, Grey MSS, box 55; Colchester, *Diary*, Vol. 1, pp. 411–12; Add. MSS 41,852, ff. 130–1; Harvey, *Britain*, pp. 133–4; Willis, 'Fox, Grenville', loc. cit. at n. 3, pp. 36–7; Malmesbury, *Diaries and Correspondence*, Vol. 4, pp. 183–4; PRO 58/4, no. 95.
7   Pitt to Canning, 6 May 1803, Canning MSS, 30; Add MS 35,702, f. 283.
8   Russell, *Memorials*, Vol. 3, p. 429 (amended from Grey MSS) and pp. 449–50; Grey, 7 January 1804, Grey MSS, box 16, file 2; Add. MS 41,852, f. 194.

9 PRO 30/29/8/3, ff. 300–1; Harvey, *Britain*, p. 144; Buckingham, *George III*, Vol. 3, p. 351; McCahill, *Order and Equipoise*, pp. 85–6.
10 Rose, *Diaries*, Vol. 2, p. 119; Russell, *Memorials*, Vol. 4, p. 98 (cf. modern estimates of parties, not greatly divergent, in Lipscombe, 'Party Politics', loc. cit. at n. 2, p. 445 and Willis, 'Fox, Grenville', loc. cit. at n. 3, p. 41); Grey, 2 February 1804, Grey MSS, box 16, file 2; Colchester, *Diary*, Vol. 2, pp. 481–2.
11 Colchester, *Diary*, Vol. 1, pp. 519–20 and Vol. 2, p. 5; *English Historical Documents*, Vol. 11, pp. 254–5; PRO 30/29/8/3, f. 346.
12 Add. MSS 7569, ff. 236–7, 239; Colchester, *Diary*, Vol. 2, pp. 13–14.
13 HMC, *Dropmore*, Vol. 8, p. 140.
14 *English Historical Documents*, Vol. 11, p. 255; Add. MS 38,737, f. 123; Canning MSS, 21, 1 July.
15 Rose, *Diaries*, Vol. 2, pp. 244–7, 263; Add. MS 35,706, f. 348; Colchester, *Diary*, Vol. 2, p. 38; Foord, *Opposition*, p. 436; Canning, 20 June, Canning MSS, 21; Harvey, *Britain*, p. 181; *English Historical Documents*, Vol. 11, p. 116; Hinde, *Canning*, p. 146.
16 Yonge, *Liverpool*, Vol. 1, p. 218; Holland, *Memoirs of the Whig Party*, Vol. 1, pp. 93–4; Buckingham, *George III*, Vol. 4, p. 155; Harvey, *Britain*, p. 190; Feiling, *Second Tory Party*, p. 251.
17 Colchester, *Diary*, Vol. 2, p. 89; Holland, *Memoirs of the Whig Party*, Vol. 1, pp. 196–8.
18 Harvey, *Britain*, pp. 191–6; Ziegler, *Addington*, p. 266; Add. MS 49,184, f. 93.
19 Howick, 24 April, Grey MSS, box 47, file 11; Colchester, *Diary*, Vol. 2, p. 120.
20 Holland, *Memoirs of the Whig Party*, Vol. 2, pp. 227–30; P. J. Jupp, 'Irish parliamentary elections', *HJ*, vol. 10 (1967), pp. 183–96.
21 Colchester, *Diary*, Vol. 2, pp. 139–40.
22 Holland, received 13 December, Portland (Nottingham) MSS, F 32/61; Holland, *Memoirs of the Whig Party*, Vol. 2, pp. 236–8; Ponsonby, 23 November 1807; Grey MSS, box 47, file 11; Grey, 6 December, Add. MS 51,550, unfol.; Bedford, 2 December, Blair-Adam MSS, General Corr., 1807.
23 Ponsonby, 7 December 1808 [*recte*. 1809], Wentworth Woodhouse (Sheffield) MSS, F 32/63; Colchester, *Diary*, Vol. 2, pp. 187–93, 197–8.
24 Colchester, *Diary*, Vol. 2, pp. 179–81; Canning, 5 May 1809, Canning MSS, 33; PRO 30/29/8/4, ff. 481–4 (Canning to Portland 24 March, sent with same to same of 2 April, Canning MSS, 33).
25 Colchester, *Diary*, Vol. 2, pp. 215–17; Feiling, *Second Tory Party*, pp. 260–1.
26 Perceval, 23 September, Grey and Grenville, 25 September, Wentworth Woodhouse (Sheffield) MSS, F 32/37; Grey, 26 September, F 32/41; Grey, 11 November 1809; Add. MS 51,551, unfol.; Add. MS 38,737, f. 370.
27 Harvey, *Britain*, pp. 261–3.
28 Tierney, 9 and 27 December, 1809, Grey MSS, box 55; Grey, 26 December 1809, Add. MS 51,551, unfol.; Grey, 6 January 1810, Wentworth Woodhouse (Sheffield) MSS, F 32/36, and Grey, 13 January, F 32/69.
29 Colchester, *Diary*, Vol. 2, pp. 230, 243 and 277; Harvey, *Britain*, pp. 268–71; Ziegler, *Addington*, p. 291; Grey, 5 January 1810, Add. MS 51,551, unfol.
30 Ziegler, *Addington*, pp. 292–3; Harvey, *Britain*, pp. 271–9; Rose, *Diaries*, Vol. 2, p. 471.

Chapter 12

1 Add. MSS 38,738, f. 91 and 51,551, unfol., Grey, 4 August 1811; *English Historical Documents*, Vol. 11, p. 258; Mitchell, *Whigs in Opposition, passim*.

2 Harvey, *Britain*, pp. 279–82; Colchester, *Diary*, Vol. 2, pp. 369–70.
3 Roberts, *Whig Party*, pp. 188–9, 195; Colchester, *Diary*, Vol. 2, p. 379.
4 *Wellesley Papers*, Vol. 2, pp. 87 *et sqq.*; Colchester, *Diary*, Vol. 2, pp. 379–401; Yonge, *Liverpool*, Vol. 1, pp. 385–95; Feiling, *Second Tory Party*, pp. 271–2; *English Historical Documents*, Vol. 11, p. 290.
5 Mitchell, *Whigs in Opposition*, p. 81, n. 1; Colchester, *Diary*, p. 410; Hinde, *Canning*, pp. 258–66; Ziegler, *Addington*, pp. 331–2; Buckingham, *Regency*, Vol. 1, pp. 409–10; Yonge, *Liverpool*, Vol. 1, pp. 444–5.
6 Add. MS 51,584, unfol., Tierney, 18 November 1812; Grey MSS, box 35, file 1, Grey, 25 October 1812; Colchester, *Diary*, Vol. 2, p. 412.
7 Rose, *Diaries*, Vol. 2, p. 471; Harvey, *Britain*, p. 275.
8 Colchester, *Diary*, Vol. 2, pp. 420–34, 438–9, 447, 498, 533.
9 J. R. Dinwiddy, 'Sir Francis Burdett and Burdettite radicalism', *History*, vol. 65 (1980), pp. 17–31.
10 Mitchell, *Whigs in Opposition*, pp. 82–8; *Creevey Papers*, Vol. 1, p. 251; Cookson, *Liverpool*, pp. 47–65; Colchester, *Diary*, Vol. 2, p. 570.
11 Mitchell, *Whigs in Opposition*, pp. 97–101; Cookson, *Liverpool*, pp. 72 *et sqq.*; *Creevey Papers*, Vol. 1, p. 257
12 Cookson, *Liverpool*, pp. 125–9; Colchester, *Diary*, Vol. 2, pp. 601, 605, 615, 620; Mitchell, *Whigs in Opposition*, pp. 104–6.
13 Sack, *Grenvilles*, p. 121; Cookson, *Liverpool*, p. 134; Buckingham, *Regency*, Vol. 2, p. 213; Mitchell, *Whigs in Opposition*, pp. 33–4; Olphin, *Tierney*, pp. 185–6; Holland, *Further Memoirs*, p. 265.
14 Mitchell, *Whigs in Opposition*, pp. 112–14; Cookson, *Liverpool*, pp. 137–41.
15 Buckingham, *Regency*, Vol. 2, pp. 267–8; HMC, *Dropmore*, Vol. 10, p. 441; Cookson, *Liverpool*, p. 143.
16 Colchester, *Diary*, Vol. 3, p. 73; Mitchell, *Whigs in Opposition*, pp. 121–4.
17 Mitchell, *Whigs in Opposition*, pp. 134–5.
18 Greville, *Memoirs*, Vol. 1, p. 25; Yonge, *Liverpool*, Vol. 3, pp. 25–45; Croker, *Papers*, Vol. 1, pp. 146–7; Cookson, *Liverpool*, pp. 206–14; Hinde, *Canning*, p. 298.
19 Mitchell, *Whigs in Opposition*, pp. 61 and 140–1.
20 Colchester, *Diary*, Vol. 3, pp. 179–80; Mitchell, *Whigs in Opposition*, pp. 144–8; Feiling, *Second Tory Party*, pp. 307–8.
21 Mrs Arbuthnot, *Journal*, Vol. 1, p. 53; Mitchell, *Whigs in Opposition*, pp. 148–53, 156–7; John Stevenson, 'The Queen Caroline affair', in *London in the Age of Reform* (Oxford, 1977), pp. 130–4.
22 Olphin, *Tierney*, pp. 220–2; New, *Brougham*, p. 183.
23 Yonge, *Liverpool*, Vol. 3, pp. 139–40; Mitchell, *Whigs in Opposition*, pp. 159–61; Prest, *Russell*, p. 31.
24 Croker, *Papers*, Vol. 1, pp. 173–7 and 186–7; Yonge, *Liverpool*, Vol. 3, pp. 142–50, 154–5.
25 Mitchell, *Whigs in Opposition*, pp. 163–7.
26 Croker, *Papers*, Vol. 1, pp. 208–14; Yonge, *Liverpool*, Vol. 3, pp. 193 n. 1, 195–201, 208–17.

Chapter 13

1 Croker, *Papers*, Vol. 1, pp. 125–6, 155–6; Cannon, *Parliamentary Reform*, pp. 183–4.
2 Buckingham, *George IV*, Vol. 1, p. 291; Brock, *Lord Liverpool*, p. 76.
3 Buckingham, *George IV*, Vol. 1, pp. 418–19; Hinde, *Canning, passim.*
4 Buckingham, *George IV*, Vol. 1, pp. 314–15, Vol. 2, pp. 70, 76, 91, 109, 111,

113; *Creevey Papers*, Vol. 2, p. 68; Colchester, *Diary*, Vol. 3, pp. 279, 292–3, 300, 321–2, 324–7, 335, 351; Machin, *The Catholic Question*, pp. 42–3.

5 Colchester, *Diary*, Vol. 3, pp. 351–4; Yonge, *Liverpool*, Vol. 3, pp. 297–305; Brock, *Lord Liverpool*, pp. 253–9, 269.

6 *Creevey Papers*, Vol. 2, p. 99; Twiss, *Eldon*, Vol. 2, p. 467; Smith, *Whig Principles*, p. 371.

7 Mitchell, *Whigs in Opposition*, pp. 180–1.

8 Mitchell, *Holland House*, p. 135; Mitchell, *Whigs in Opposition*, pp. 183–4.

9 Colchester, *Diary*, Vol. 3, pp. 385, 390; Arbuthnot, *Correspondence*, pp. 175–8; Gash, *Secretary Peel*, pp. 417–20; Yonge, *Liverpool*, Vol. 3, pp. 328–42; Buckingham, *George IV*, Vol. 2, p. 260.

10 Buckingham, *George IV*, Vol. 2, p. 263; Colchester, *Diary*, Vol. 3, p. 390; Croker, *Papers*, Vol. 1, pp. 257–8; Brock, *Lord Liverpool*, pp. 269, 271.

11 *Creevey Papers*, Vol. 2, pp. 100–1; Colchester, *Diary*, Vol. 3, pp. 439, 452; Brock, *Lord Liverpool*, p. 273; New, *Brougham*, p. 307; Yonge, *Liverpool*, Vol. 3, pp. 438–9, cf. Arbuthnot, *Correspondence*, p. 86.

12 Colchester, *Diary*, Vol. 3, p. 465; Feiling, *Second Tory Party*, pp. 348–52; Hinde, *Canning*, pp. 437–43; Croker, *Papers*, Vol. 1, pp. 333–43.

13 Le Marchant, *Memoirs*, pp. 215–16; *Creevey Papers*, Vol. 2, p. 114; Hinde, *Canning*, pp. 446–51; Aspinall, *Lord Brougham*, pp. 145–50; Mitchell, *Whigs in Opposition*, pp. 196–201; Mitchell, *Holland House*, pp. 136–7; *Palmerston–Sullivan Letters*, p. 187.

14 A. Aspinall, 'The formation of Canning's ministry', Camden Society, 3rd ser., vol. 59 (1937), p. 218; Colchester, *Diary*, Vol. 3, pp. 514–16; Feiling, *Second Tory Party*, pp. 354–7; Hinde, *Canning*, pp. 451–5, 458–61.

15 *Palmerston–Sullivan Letters*, pp. 191–7, 200; Croker, *Papers*, Vol. 1, pp. 354–62; Arbuthnot, *Correspondence*, p. 90; Aspinall, *Lord Brougham*, p. 153; Mitchell, *Holland House*, p. 144; *Creevey Papers*, Vol. 2, p. 125; Greville, *Memoirs*, Vol. 1, pp. 109, 115; Add. MS 38,349, f. 187.

16 *Palmerston–Sullivan Letters*, p. 204; Le Marchant, *Memoirs*, pp. 210, 225–7; Croker. *Papers*, Vol. 1, p. 370; E. A. Wasson, 'The coalitions of 1827', *HJ*, vol. 20 (1977), pp. 587–606.

17 *Peel Memoirs*, Vol. 1, pp. 13–16; Gash, *Secretary Peel*, pp. 452–3; Twiss, *Eldon*, Vol. 2, pp. 589–90; Colchester, *Diary*, Vol. 3, pp. 537–8, 547; *English Historical Documents*, Vol. 11, p. 134; Greville, *Memoirs*, Vol. 1, pp. 125–6; Croker, *Papers*, Vol. 1, p. 372.

18 Feiling, *Second Tory Party*, pp. 365–7; Croker, *Papers*, Vol. 1, pp. 378–9, 383, 387–8; Colchester, *Diary*, Vol. 3, pp. 555–7; Greville, *Memoirs*, Vol. 1, p. 131; Arbuthnot, *Correspondence*, p. 109.

19 *Palmerston–Sullivan Letters*, pp. 205–6; Colchester, *Diary*, Vol. 3, pp. 567–8; Gash, *Secretary Peel*, pp. 475–6; Buckingham, *George IV*, Vol. 2, p. 380.

20 Russell, *Early Correspondence*, pp. 263, 271–2; G. I. T. Machin, 'Resistance to repeal of the Test and Corporation Acts, 1828', *HJ*, vol. 22 (1979), pp. 115–39; Machin, *The Catholic Question*, p. 115; Wasson, loc. cit. at n. 16, p. 604; Mitchell, *Whigs in Opposition*, pp. 209–12.

21 *Peel Memoirs*, Vol. 1, pp. 178–202, 278–81, 347–9; Gash, *Secretary Peel*, pp. 529–31, 545–7; Croker, *Papers*, Vol. 1, pp. 407–8, 412.

22 Arbuthnot, *Correspondence*, p. 114; Greville, *Memoirs*, Vol. 1, pp. 165, 174; Mitchell, *Whigs in Opposition*, p. 213.

23 *Palmerston–Sullivan Letters*, p. 235; *Creevey Papers*, Vol. 2, pp. 201–2; Russell, *Early Correspondence*, pp. 299–300, 302.

24 Greville, *Memoirs*, Vol. 1, p. 275; Croker, *Papers*, Vol. 1, pp. 448–51; Cannon, *Parliamentary Reform*, pp. 193–5; Feiling, *Second Tory Party*, pp. 374–6.

25 *English Historical Documents*, Vol. 11, pp. 259–60; Croker, *Papers*, Vol. 1, pp. 454–5; Arbuthnot, *Correspondence*, pp. 125–6; Cannon, *Parliamentary Reform*, pp. 193–6; Mitchell, *Whigs in Opposition*, pp. 223–9.
26 Greville, *Memoirs*, Vol. 2, pp. 20, 29; Aspinall, *Brougham*, pp. 175–9; Cannon, *Parliamentary Reform*, pp. 197–9; Mitchell, *Whigs in Opposition*, pp. 231–3, 237, 242–3.
27 Croker, *Papers*, Vol. 1, p. 468; Mitchell, *Whigs in Opposition*, pp. 235, 238–40, 244–5; Cannon, *Parliamentary Reform*, p. 202; Gash, *Secretary Peel*, pp. 640–3.
28 Croker, *Papers*, Vol. 1, p. 473; *English Historical Documents*, Vol. 11, pp. 25, 27; Le Marchant, *Memoirs*, p. 261; Aspinall, *Brougham*, p. 187; Brock, *Great Reform Act*, pp. 131–2; B. T. Bradfield, 'Sir Richard Vyvian and the country gentlemen, 1830–1834', *EHR*, vol. 83 (1968), p. 731; Knatchbull-Hugessen, *Kentish Family*, pp. 200–1.
29 Croker, *Papers*, Vol. 1, pp. 342, 490; Le Marchant, *Memoirs*, p. 292; Cannon, *Parliamentary Reform*, pp. 204–11; Brock, *Great Reform Act*, pp. 36–41.
30 Arbuthnot, *Correspondence*, p. 135; Le Marchant, *Memoirs*, pp. 272–87; Brock, *Great Reform Act*, pp. 135–6.
31 Croker, *Papers*, Vol. 1, pp. 501–2, 506; Greville, *Memoirs*, Vol. 2, pp. 121–2; *Creevey Papers*, Vol. 1, p. 225; Knatchbull-Hugessen, *Kentish Family*, p. 204; Stewart, *Foundation of the Conservative Party*, p. 57; Brock, *Great Reform Act*, pp. 176–83, 185–6; Cannon, *Parliamentary Reform*, pp. 216, 219.
32 Greville, *Memoirs*, Vol. 2, p. 145; Bradfield, loc. cit. at n. 28, p. 733; Knatchbull-Hugessen, *Kentish Family*, pp. 204–5; Cannon, *Parliamentary Reform*, pp. 220–1, Brock, *Great Reform Act*, pp. 194–7.
33 Le Marchant, *Memoirs*, pp. 339–40; Prest, *Russell*, p. 50.
34 Aspinall, *Three Diaries*, pp. 157–9; Greville, *Memoirs*, Vol. 2, pp. 211–14; Croker, *Papers*, Vol. 1, p. 531; Arbuthnot, *Correspondence*, pp. 145, 147; Kriegel, *Holland House Diaries*, pp. 64–5, 91; Buckingham, *William IV*, Vol. 1, pp. 360–1; Mitchell, *Holland House*, pp. 150–1.
35 Kriegel, *Holland House Diaries*, pp. 176–7; Brock, *Great Reform Act*, pp. 290–1; Cannon, *Parliamentary Reform*, pp. 230–8; Croker, *Papers*, Vol. 1, pp. 545–51; Aspinall, *Three Diaries*, pp. 241–2.

Select Bibliography

The following entries are intended only to give the location or title of manuscript and printed sources mentioned in the Notes (on pp. 239–54 and at the end of each chapter) by more abbreviated descriptions. Place of publication is London unless otherwise stated.

Other sources which are traceable directly from the Notes, including all the contemporary tracts and modern articles cited, are not listed here.

1 Manuscript Collections

British Library
  Additional MSS
  Egerton MSS
  Stowe MSS

Public Record Office
  PRO 30

Bodleian Library
  North MSS

Cambridge University Library
  Harley Diary (Edward Harley, third Earl of Oxford)

Durham University Library
  Grey MSS

Nottingham University Library
  Portland MSS
  Newcastle MSS

Leeds City Libraries
  Canning MSS

Sheffield City Library
  Wentworth Woodhouse MSS
    Burke Papers
    Rockingham Papers

Blair-Adam, by Fife
  Adam MSS

2 Printed Sources

Arbuthnot, Charles, *Correspondence of Charles Arbuthnot, 1808–1850*, ed. Arthur Aspinall (Camden Society, 3rd ser., vol. 65, 1941).

Aspinall, Arthur, *Three Early Nineteenth-Century Diaries* (1952).

[*Auckland Corr.*] *Journals & Correspondence of William, Lord Auckland*, ed. Bishop of Bath and Wells, 4 vols (1861–2).

Bateson, Mary, *A Narrative of the Changes in the Ministry 1765–1767* (1898).

[*Bedford Corr.*] *Correspondence of the fourth Duke of Bedford*, ed. Lord John Russell, 3 vols (1842–6).

[*Bland Burges Letters*] *Letters & Life of Sir James Bland Burges Bt.*, ed. J. Hutton (1885).

Buckingham, *Memoirs of the Court and Cabinets of George III*, by the Duke of Buckingham and Chandos, 2nd edn, 2 vols (1853–5).

Buckingham, *Memoirs of the Court during the Regency*, by the Duke of Buckingham and Chandos, 2 vols (1856).

Buckingham, *Memoirs of the Court of George IV*, by the Duke of Buckingham and Chandos, 2 vols (1859).

Buckingham, *Memoirs of the Courts and Cabinets of William IV and Victoria*, by the Duke of Buckingham and Chandos, 2 vols (1861).

[*Cavendish Debates*] *Sir Henry Cavendish's Debates of the House of Commons*, ed. J. Wright, 2 vols (1841).

[*Chatham Corr.*] *The Chatham Correspondence*, ed. W. S. Taylor and J. H. Pringle, 4 vols (1838–40).

Cobbett, William, *Parliamentary History of England*, 36 vols (1806–20).

[*Colchester, Diary*] *The Diary and Correspondence of Charles Abbot, Lord Colchester*, ed. Charles, Lord Colchester, 3 vols (1861).

[*Corr. of Burke*] *The Correspondence of Edmund Burke*, general ed. Thomas W. Copeland, 10 vols (Cambridge and Chicago, 1958–78).

Coxe, William, *Memoirs of . . . Henry Pelham*, 2 vols (1829).

[*Creevey Papers*] Thomas Creevey, *The Creevey Papers*, ed. Sir H. Maxwell, 2 vols (1903).

[*Croker, Papers*] *The Croker Papers*, ed. L. J. Jennings, 3 vols (1884).

Debrett, John, *The Parliamentary Register*, 45 vols (1781–96).

[*Devonshire Diary*] *The Devonshire Diary, William Cavendish, fourth Duke of Devonshire*, ed. Peter D. Brown and Karl W. Schweizer (1982).

[*Dodington, Journal*] *The Political Journal of George Bubb Dodington*, ed. John Carswell and Lewis Arnold Dralle (Oxford, 1965).

[*English Historical Documents*, Vol. 11] *English Historical Documents, 1783–1832*, ed. A. Aspinall and E. Anthony Smith (1959).

Fitzmaurice, Lord, *Life of William, Earl of Shelburne, afterwards first Marquess of Lansdowne*, 3 vols (1875–6).

[*George III Corr.*] *The Correspondence of George III, 1760–83*, ed. Sir John Fortescue, 6 vols (1927–8).

[*Grafton, Autobiography*] *Autobiographical . . . Correspondence of . . . third Duke of Grafton*, ed. Sir William R. Anson (1898).

[*Grenville Papers*] *The Grenville Papers*, ed. W. J. Smith, 4 vols (1852–3).

Greville, Charles C. F., *The Greville Memoirs, A Journal of the Reigns of George IV and William IV*, ed. Henry Reeve, 3 vols (1874–8).

Hervey, John, *Some Material towards Memoirs of . . . George II*, ed. Romney Sedgwick, 3 vols (1931).

Historical Manuscripts Commission (HMC), various *Reports* of the HMC, described by name or title of owner of manuscripts.

Holland, Henry Richard, Lord, *Memoirs of the Whig Party during My Time*, 2 vols (1852–4).

Holland, Henry Richard, Lord, *Further Memoirs of the Whig Party* (1905).

Ilchester, Earl of, *Letters to Henry Fox, Lord Holland* (1915).

[*Jenkinson Papers*] *The Jenkinson Papers 1760–1766*, ed. Ninetta S. Jucker, (1949).

Kriegel, A. D., *Holland House Diaries 1831–1840* (1977).

[*Lyttelton Memoirs*] *Memoirs . . . of George, Lord Lyttelton*, ed. Robert Phillimore, 2 vols (1845).

Malmesbury, *Diaries and Correspondence of James Harris, first Earl of Malmesbury*, ed. by the third Earl of Malmesbury, 4 vols (1844).

[Mrs Arbuthnot, *Journal*] Harriet Arbuthnot, *Journal 1821–32*, ed. S. Bamford and the Duke of Wellington, 2 vols (1950).

Minto, *Life and Letters of Sir Gilbert Elliot, first Earl of Minto*, ed. Countess of Minto, 3 vols (1874).

[*Palmerston–Sullivan Letters*] *Letters of Palmerston . . . 1804–1863*, ed. Kenneth Bourne (1979).

[*Peel Memoirs*] *Memoirs by Sir Robert Peel*, ed. Lord Mahan and Edward Cardwell, 2 vols (1857).

[*Pitt–Rutland Corr.*] *Correspondence between William Pitt and Charles, Duke of Rutland . . . 1781–87* (1890).

[*Political Memoir*] *Political Memoranda of the Duke of Leeds*, ed. O. Browning (1884).

[*Private Corr.*] *Private Correspondence of Chesterfield and Newcastle, 1744–46*, ed. Sir Richard Lodge (1930).

[*Rockingham Memoirs*] *Memoirs of the Marquis of Rockingham*, ed. Earl of Albemarle, 2 vols (1852).

[Rose, *Diaries*] *Diaries & Correspondence of George Rose*, ed. L. V. Harcourt, 2 vols (1860).

Russell, Lord John (ed.), *Memorials and Correspondence of Charles James Fox*, 4 vols (1853–7).

Russell, R., *Early Correspondence of Lord John Russell*, 2 vols (1913).

[Sedgwick, *Letters*] *Letters from George III to Lord Bute 1756–1766*, ed. Romney Sedgwick (1939).

[Waldegrave, *Memoirs*] *Memoirs from 1754 to 1758 by James, Earl Waldegrave* (1821).

[*Walpole Corr.*] *The Letters of Horace Walpole, Earl of Orford*, ed. Peter Cunningham, 9 vols (1861).

Walpole, Horace, *Memoirs of the Reign of King George II*, 3 vols (1846).

Walpole, Horace, *Memoirs of the Reign of King George III*, ed. G. F. Russell Barker, 4 vols (1894)

[*Wellesley Papers*] Marquess of Wellesley, *The Wellesley Papers*, 2 vols (1914).

Wyndham, Maud, *Chronicles of the Eighteenth Century*, 2 vols (1924).

3 Secondary Works

Aspinall, Arthur, *Lord Brougham and the Whig Party* (1927).
Barnes, Donald Grove, *George III and William Pitt, 1783–1806* (reprint, New York, 1965).
Brewer, John, *Party Ideology and Popular Politics of the Accession of George III* (Cambridge, 1976).
Brock, Michael, *The Great Reform Act* (1973).
Brock, W. R., *Lord Liverpool and Liberal Toryism 1820–1824* (Cambridge, 1941).
Brooke, John, *The Chatham Administration, 1766–1768* (1956).
Brooke, John, *King George III* (1972).
Brown, G. S., *The American Secretary . . . Lord George Germaine 1775–78* (Ann Arbor, Mich., 1963).
Browning, Reed, *The Duke of Newcastle* (New Haven, Conn., 1975).
Butterfield, Herbert, *George III and the Historians* (1957).
Cannon, John, *The Fox–North Coalition, Crisis of the Constitution 1782–4* (Cambridge, 1969).
Cannon, John, *Parliamentary Reform 1640–1832* (Cambridge, 1973).
Cannon, John (ed.), *The Whig Ascendancy, Colloquies on Hanoverian England* (1981).
Christie, Ian R., *The End of North's Ministry, 1780–1782* (1958).
Christie, Ian R., *Myth and Reality in Late-Eighteenth-Century British Politics, and Other Papers* (1970).
Clark, J. C. D., *The Dynamics of Change, the Crisis of the 1750's and English Party Systems* (Cambridge, 1982).
Colley, Linda, *In Defiance of Oligarchy, the Tory Party 1714–1760* (Cambridge, 1982).
Cookson, J. E., *Lord Liverpool's Administration, the Crucial Years, 1815–1822* (Edinburgh, 1975).
Cruickshanks, Eveline, *Political Untouchables: The Tories and the '45* (1979).
Derry, John, *Charles James Fox* (1972).
Derry, John, *The Regency Crisis and the Whigs, 1788–9* (Cambridge, 1963).
Dickinson, H. T., *Bolingbroke* (1970).
Dickinson, H. T., *Liberty and Property, Political Ideology in Eighteenth-Century Britain* (1977).
Donoughue, B., *British Politics and the American Revolution, 1773–5* (1964).
Ehrman, John, *The Younger Pitt, the Years of Acclaim* (1969).
Feiling, Keith Graham, *The Second Tory Party, 1714–1832* (1938).
Foord, Archibald, S., *His Majesty's Opposition 1714–1830* (Oxford, 1964).
Forrester, Eric G., *Northamptonshire County Elections and Electioneering, 1695–1832* (Oxford, 1941).
Gash, Norman, *Aristocracy and People, Britain 1815–1865* (1979).
Gash, Norman, *Mr. Secretary Peel: Life of Sir Robert Peel to 1830* (1961).
Ginter, Donald, E., *Whig Organization in the General Election of 1790* (Berkeley, Calif., 1967).

Grey, C., *Some Account of the Life of Charles, second Earl Grey* (1861).

Harvey, A. D., *Britain in the Early Nineteenth Century* (1978).

Hill, B. W., *Edmund Burke on Government, Politics and Society* (Hassocks, Sussex, 1975).

Hill, B. W., *The Growth of Parliamentary Parties, 1689–1742* (1976).

Hinde, Wendy, *George Canning* (1973).

[*History of Parliament, 1715–1754*] *The History of Parliament, the House of Commons 1715–1754*, ed. Romney Sedgwick, 2 vols (1970).

[*History of Parliament, 1754–1790*] *The History of Parliament, the House of Commons 1754–1790*, ed. Sir Lewis Namier and John Brooke, 3 vols (1964).

Ilchester, Earl of, *Henry Fox, first Lord Holland*, 2 vols (1920).

Knatchbull-Hugesson, Sir Hughe, *Kentish Family* (1960).

Langford, Paul, *The First Rockingham Administration, 1765–1766* (Oxford, 1973).

Le Marchant, D., *Memoirs of John Charles, Viscount Althorp, third Earl Spencer* (1876).

Machin, G. I. T., *The Catholic Question in English Politics, 1820–1830* (Oxford, 1964).

McCahill, M. W., *Order and Equipoise, the Peerage and the House of Lords 1783–1806* (1978).

Mitchell, Austin, *The Whigs in Opposition, 1815–1830* (Oxford, 1967).

Mitchell, L. G., *Charles James Fox and the Disintegration of the Whig Party, 1782–1794* (Oxford, 1971).

Mitchell, L. G., *Holland House* (1980).

Namier, Sir Lewis, *Crossroads of Power, Essays on Eighteenth-Century England* (1962).

Namier, Sir Lewis, *England in the Age of the American Revolution* (2nd edn, 1961).

Namier, Sir Lewis, *The Structure of Politics at the Accession of George III* (2nd edn, 1957).

New, Chester, *Life of Henry Brougham to 1830* (Oxford, 1961).

Norris, John, *Shelburne and Reform* (1963).

O'Gorman, Frank, *The Emergence of the British Two-Party System, 1760–1832* (1982).

O'Gorman, Frank, *The Rise of Party in England, the Rockingham Whigs 1760–82* (1975).

O'Gorman, Frank, *The Whig Party and the French Revolution* (1967).

Olphin, H. K., *George Tierney* (1934).

Olsen, Alison Gilbert, *The Radical Duke, Career and Correspondence of Charles Lennox, third Duke of Richmond* (Oxford, 1961).

Owen, John B., *The Rise of the Pelhams* (1957).

Pares, Richard, *King George III and the Politicians* (Oxford, 1953).

Perry, Thomas W., *Public Opinion, Propaganda and Politics, the Jew Bill of 1753* (Cambridge, Mass., 1962).

Peters, Marie, *Pitt and Popularity, The Patriot Minister and London Opinion during the Seven Years War* (Oxford, 1980).

Phillips, John A., *Electoral Behaviour in Unreformed England, Plumpers, Splitters and Straights* (Princeton, NJ, 1982).

Plumb, J. H., *The First Four Georges* (1956).
Plumb, J. H., *Sir Robert Walpole*, 2 vols (1956–60).
Prest, John, *Lord John Russell* (1972).
Roberts, Michael, *The Whig Party, 1807–1812* (2nd edn, 1965).
Rose, J. Holland, *Life of William Pitt* (1923).
Sack, James J., *The Grenvilles 1801–1821: Party Politics and Factionalism* (Urbana, Ill., 1979).
Sichel, W., *Sheridan*, 2 vols (1909).
Smith, E. A., *Whig Principles and Party Politics, Earl Fitzwilliam and the Whig Party 1748–1833* (Manchester, 1975).
Stewart, Robert, *The Foundation of the Conservative Party, 1830–1867* (1978).
Thomas, Peter D. G., *Lord North* (1976).
Trevelyan, G. M., *Lord Grey of the Reform Bill* (reprint 1952).
Twiss, Horace, *Public and Private Life of Eldon*, 3 vols (1844).
Wiggin, Lewis M., *The Faction of Cousins, A Political Account of the Grenvilles, 1733–1763* (New Haven, Conn., 1958).
Wilkes, John W., *A Whig in Power, The Political Career of Henry Pelham* (Evanston, Ill., 1964).
Williams, Basil, *Life of William Pitt, Earl of Chatham*, 2 vols (1966 reprint).
Yonge, C. D., *Life of Robert Banks Jenkinson, second Earl of Liverpool*, 3 vols (1868).
Yorke, Philip, C., *Life and Correspondence of Philip Yorke, Earl of Hardwicke*, 3 vols (Cambridge, 1913).
Ziegler, Philip, *Addington* (1965).

Index

Index

46,610

DATE			
FEB 15 1990			
MAR 0 1 1990			
MAR 1 5 1990			
MAR 3 1 1990			
APR 16 1990			
APR 1 5 2006			
APR 1 0 2006			

© THE BAKER & TAYLOR CO.